A HISTORY OF THE CHICAGO PORTAGE

A HISTORY OF THE CHICAGO PORTAGE

THE CROSSROADS THAT MADE CHICAGO AND HELPED MAKE AMERICA

BENJAMIN SELLS

NORTHWESTERN UNIVERSITY PRESS
EVANSTON, ILLINOIS

Northwestern University Press
www.nupress.northwestern.edu

Printed in the United States of America

10 9 8 7 6 5 4 3 2 1

Library of Congress Cataloging-in-Publication Data

Names: Sells, Benjamin, author.
Title: A history of the Chicago portage : the crossroads that made Chicago and helped make America / Benjamin Sells.
Description: Evanston, Illinois : Northwestern University Press, 2021. | Series: Second to none: chicago stories | Includes bibliographical references and index.
Identifiers: LCCN 2021006558 | ISBN 9780810143906 (paperback) | ISBN 9780810143913 (ebook)
Subjects: LCSH: Portages—Illinois—Chicago—History. | Navigation—Illinois—Chicago—History. | Navigation—Great Lakes (North America)—History. | Chicago (Ill.)—History. | Illinois and Michigan Canal (Ill.)—History. | Chicago Portage National Historic Site (Ill.)—History.
Classification: LCC F548.3 .S54 2021 | DDC 977.311—dc23
LC record available at https://lccn.loc.gov/2021006558

For Jill

CONTENTS

Introduction

Key to the Continent

> We could go with facility to Florida in a bark, and by very easy navigation. It would only be necessary to make a canal, by cutting through but half a league of prairie, to pass from the foot of the lake of the Illinois [Lake Michigan] to the river Saint Louis [Illinois River]. Here is the route that would be followed: the bark would be built on lake Erie, which is near lake Ontario; it would easily pass from lake Erie to lake Huron, whence it would enter lake Illinois. At the end of that lake the canal or excavation of which I have spoken would be made, to gain a passage into the river Saint Louis, which falls into the Mississipi. The bark, when there, would easily sail to the gulf of Mexico.
>
> —Louis Jolliet, August 1, 1674

In 1673, Louis Jolliet, along with Jacques Marquette and a hardy team of French explorers, became the first recorded Europeans to see the Mississippi River. They were ascending the Illinois River on their way back home when members of the Kaskaskia Tribe showed them a shortcut using the Des Plaines River through the Chicago Portage to the Chicago River and then on to Lake Michigan. Even at that early date, Jolliet recognized the significance of the Chicago Portage as the connecting point between the Atlantic Ocean, via the St. Lawrence River and Great Lakes, to the Gulf of Mexico via the Des Plaines, Illinois, and Mississippi Rivers. This portage was used for centuries prior to the arrival of Europeans, who, upon their arrival, soon imposed on this natural crossing the idea of constructing a "canal." Jolliet's vision remained alive throughout Native American, French, and British control of the Chicago Portage in the seventeenth and eighteenth centuries before being realized by the young American nation in the nineteenth and twentieth centuries with the building of the Illinois and Michigan Canal and the Sanitary and Ship Canal.

The Chicago Portage is one of the most important, and neglected, places in the early history of the United States. Its significance began in prehistory as a place of habitation by the earliest Native Americans in the Midwest, and it became part of a major trade route for Native American tribes. It was heavily used during the fur trade, was a focal point for the missionary and imperialistic dreams of the French and British throughout the seventeenth and eighteenth centuries, and was a military concern for the British during the American Revolution. It was a gateway for settler expansion westward, and it served as a template for some of the most significant waterways created in the nineteenth and twentieth centuries. The Chicago Portage gave the city of Chicago its name and was the original impetus for its success. And it is because of the Chicago Portage that Chicago ended up being in Illinois instead of in Wisconsin.

These are big statements to make about a roughly seven-mile stretch of marsh that lay between the Chicago River and the Des Plaines River. But that seven miles connected the two most influential watersheds of North America—the Great Lakes watershed basin flowing to the St. Lawrence River and into the Atlantic Ocean, and the Mississippi River watershed basin flowing into the Gulf of Mexico. The Chicago Portage was one of the "keys to the continent,"[1] and it was through the Chicago Portage that the commercial life of the continent first took hold, to be followed later by a flow of farmers and settlers that would make America's heartland.

The Chicago Portage connected east and west. Heading west from Lake Michigan, travelers would paddle up the Chicago River to the eastern end of Chicago Portage. From there, except in periods of high water, boats would be taken from the river and carried, or "portaged," overland across the St. Lawrence Continental Divide that separated the Mississippi River watershed basin from the Great Lakes watershed basin. The boats would then be launched into Mud Lake, a marshy area that began at the continental divide and extended west to a small stream just east of Harlem Avenue called Portage Creek. That creek in turn flowed into the Des Plaines River that then connected to the Illinois River and onto the Mississippi River, flowing to the Gulf of Mexico. Off the main artery of the Mississippi River were many tributaries that reached like capillaries into the heartland, providing routes for the life-giving trade that fueled the growth of the United States.

In times of high water, such as was present when Jolliet and his team crossed the portage in 1673, the portage was a continuous waterway, and boats could make their way unimpeded between the Chicago and Des Plaines Rivers. It was the ease of that high-water crossing that sparked Jolliet's now-famous insight about how easy it would be to build a canal linking the waterways from the Atlantic Ocean to the Gulf of Mexico.

After Jolliet and Marquette, the Chicago Portage became the main route used by Native American, French, and British traders during the heyday of the fur trade. But this trade only extended a long, preexisting history. The Chicago Portage had been used for centuries by the Native Americans of the region. Archeological finds throughout the Great Lakes and beyond suggest

Fig. 1. *Chicago's Place in the Water Routes of the Native American World, 1600–1830* (detail). From Helen Hornbeck Tanner and Michael P. Conzen, *Encyclopedia of Chicago* (Chicago: University of Chicago Press, 2004), 139. Copyright © 2004 The Newberry Library.

a vibrant trade network among the Indigenous tribes of North America, and the Chicago Portage was an integral part of their system of transportation and commerce. Prior to the introduction of horses, there were only two ways to get anywhere—on foot or by canoe—and the waterways of the continent were the primary highways (fig. 1).

There were four main portage routes from Lake Michigan to the Mississippi River: (1) by Green Bay, Lake Winnebago, and the Fox River to the Wisconsin River and then to the Mississippi (this was the route taken by Jolliet and his team); (2) by the Chicago Portage route; (3) by the St. Joseph River, at the southeast corner of Lake Michigan, to the Kankakee River and on to the Illinois River (this was René-Robert Cavelier de La Salle's preferred route); and (4) by the St. Joseph River to the Wabash River to the Ohio River and on to the Mississippi River.[2] Of these routes, two became the subject for a long-standing disagreement over which was the best route to connect Lake Michigan to the Mississippi River—the Chicago Portage route favored by Jolliet, or the St. Joseph route favored by La Salle. This debate was still alive in the landmark case of *Economy Light & Power Company v. United*

States of America in the early twentieth century, a case in which the Chicago Portage played a decisive role.

The Chicago Portage became the focal point for the French fur trade and for the diverging political strands of New France that pitted the imperialistic vision of men like La Salle against the missionary zeal of the Jesuits. The French and the British struggled to control the portage as the hub of the fur trade before the British finally won out in 1763. The British worried about the Chicago Portage as a military concern throughout the American Revolution, and even after the Americans' victory in 1783, the Chicago Portage remained a source of conflict between the British and the Americans for decades. The United States built Fort Dearborn in 1804 to protect and control the Chicago Portage, and the Chicago Portage remained a point of contention until the War of 1812. Just as the Chicago Portage saw the beginning and expansion of the fur trade, the portage also witnessed the decline and demise of the trade, ending with the forced exodus of the Native Americans from the Chicago region in the first third of the nineteenth century.

The Chicago Portage was heavily used from the mid-eighteenth to early nineteenth centuries. For many years it was primarily a place of transit, although various military and religious outposts were built there in the early years after European contact. This was the time of the *voyageurs* (travelers), the French Canadians who transported the merchandise of the fur trade overland and by canoe and other boats. The *voyageurs* were part of the legal fur trade and were later joined by their outlaw cousins, the *coureurs de bois* (runners of the woods). Although the first boats to go through the Chicago Portage were dugout canoes, later came birchbark canoes and other vessels, some of which were capable of carrying several tons.[3] Stories of the passages through the portage reveal that they were not for the faint of heart.

The *voyageurs* and *coureurs de bois* were incredibly resilient and resourceful men who were the backbone of the actual transportation of goods during the fur trade years, but there would have been no trade to transport without the critical influence of Native American women. European traders would never have been able to barter European goods for furs without access to the tribal kinship networks. Marrying Native American women provided that essential access, and Native American women became active and important players in the trade itself. The intermarriage of French traders and Native Americans gave rise to the significant and influential "middle ground" of Métis culture.

The Chicago Portage became a place of transition in the late eighteenth century when some entrepreneurs decided the portage was more than just a place to pass through and began to establish homes and businesses there. Although the earliest settlers were all connected to the fur trade flowing through the Chicago Portage, over time farming and agriculture became mainstays of the area. The town that emerged, Chicago, took its name from the Chicago Portage, or, as it was referred to by the French, the *Portage de Checagou*. Later, when Jolliet's vision for a canal connecting east and west became a reality, Chicago exploded onto the world stage as one of the fastest-growing cities in America. Once that fuse was lit, land speculation and development came faster than the young city could handle.

The story of how Chicago ended up being in Illinois instead of in Wisconsin is the story of two men: an ambitious nephew and his politically astute uncle. It was the desire to keep the Chicago Portage route within Illinois that led Nathaniel Pope (the uncle) to skillfully maneuver to have the northern border of Illinois moved more than sixty miles north of where it was supposed to have been according to the Northwest Ordinance. Without that change, the history of Illinois and of the United States might have been far different.

When the Illinois and Michigan Canal opened in 1848, the Chicago Portage lost its significance as a crucial waterway. No longer needed as a water route, the land trails that converged on the Chicago Portage gained heightened importance. Canoes gave way to horses and wagons, and Native American footpaths became highways. Mud Lake was drained by landowners and was quickly developed. Within a matter of only a few years, the physical site of the Chicago Portage was threatened with extinction. The city of Chicago grew so fast that by the early twentieth century, people were not even sure where the Chicago Portage had been.

Luckily, when the Chicago Historical Society was founded in 1856, it took on the task of determining the original location of the Chicago Portage. Through research and fieldwork, an engineer and a physician were able to recover the outlines of the old Chicago Portage route. It was their work that eventually led the city to save the last remnant of the Chicago Portage for posterity, an endeavor that remains alive today.

Despite its recognition as a National Historic Site, the Chicago Portage has never received the attention or development it deserves. Plans for developing the site have been proposed since the early twentieth century, but the required funding has gone wanting. For years the site suffered at the hands of irresponsible industrial neighbors. Luckily, a group of dedicated volunteers came together to maintain the site and to advocate for developing proper facilities worthy of its historic importance.

The Chicago Portage played a significant role throughout the early history of North America. It was an important trade route for the Native Americans of the West, became a focal point for the burgeoning colonial ambitions of Europe, and provided a key to unlocking America's settlement and westward expansion. The Chicago Portage was the crossroads through which America's bounty reached the waiting markets of the world. And yet its story, still ongoing, has never been fully told—until now.

1

From Glaciers to Industrious Beavers

The origin of the Chicago Portage is bound inextricably with the geology of the Chicago area and the Great Lakes. This is a story of the almost unimaginable powers of ice and water, of glaciers, ancient lakes and rivers, and the landscape they created. Glaciers carved the basins that became the Great Lakes, and as the massive ice floes pulsed back and forth, they created new landforms at their edges. As the glaciers melted the basins filled and overflowed, flooding the land. The crushing glacial weight compressed the earth itself, and when the ice melted away, the earth rebounded, causing periods of high and low water that sculpted plains and beaches that remain embedded in Chicago's terrain to this day.

At the southwest corner of the basin that became Lake Michigan, a great outlet formed when the flowing meltwaters carved their way through earth and bedrock. The torrential flow that resulted created massive valleys reaching west and south toward the Mississippi River and the Gulf of Mexico. These processes changed the face of the earth, cutting the wrinkles and furrows that formed the Des Plaines and Chicago Rivers. Over time, the wandering courses of these two rivers created the Chicago Portage.

The story begins millions of years ago, when the area that is now home to the Great Lakes was a great tropical sea. The calcium carbonate deposits from the shells and life-forms of that sea eventually became the bedrock of the region. In time the sea was replaced by a swampy delta that in turn gave way to the Pleistocene epoch, or ice age. There were four major glacial advances during the Pleistocene. The first of these advances began about 500,000 BP (using the archaeological designation meaning "before the present"), and the last of the advances, the Wisconsin phase, spread over the area that is now Chicago beginning about 70,000 BP.[1] At its farthest reach, the Wisconsin ice extended west nearly to the Mississippi River, southwest to present-day Peoria, and two hundred miles south of Chicago to present-day Shelbyville, Illinois.[2] Estimates of the ice's thickness vary from a quarter mile to as much as five thousand feet.[3] Land around the northern Great Lakes that was compressed by the Wisconsin ice is still rising today, recovering from the crushing weight of ice that retreated thousands of years ago.

During the Pleistocene, advancing glaciers in the central part of North America followed river valleys, gouging out deep basins that became the Great Lakes. With each advance and retreat, the glaciers constructed new landforms on the underlying bedrock. In the Chicago region the most common bedrock is a limestone called *dolomite*. Although the depth of the existing bedrock rises and falls in highlands and valleys, the surface contours of the land don't necessarily correspond to those underlying forms. Rather, the area's surface terrain features were created by material deposits left by the glaciers or by the lakes that were formed when the glaciers receded.

As glaciers advance, they scour the earth before them, digging down to and in some cases into the bedrock. The assorted boulders, gravel, sand, clay, and silt thus accumulated are frozen in the ice and carried by the glacier as it advances. When the inevitable melting of the glacial ice occurs, this accumulated debris drops out and is deposited on the surface. This *drift*, so called because the material was carried to its current location from elsewhere, is an unsorted conglomerate of materials. Drift that is directly deposited by a glacier is called *till*, and drift spread and deposited by waters flowing outward from a melting glacier is called *outwash*.

Sometimes the rate of a glacier's advance will equal the rate of its melting and the glacier will seem to stop in place. Geologists call these *still stands*, and although the front of the glacier might be stationary, it is in fact the leading edge of a glacial conveyor belt that continues to bring drift to the front of the glacier where it piles up as the glacier melts. These deposits are called *moraines*, and they can be hundreds of feet thick and comprise everything from the finest clay to gigantic boulders. Immense chunks of ice breaking from the glacier fall into these deposits, creating hollows called *kettles* that eventually melt to form lakes and ponds.[4] One such moraine, the Valparaiso Moraine, played a pivotal role in the area that eventually became the Chicago Portage.

Some of the deposits left by the Wisconsin ice are more than four hundred feet thick. Conversely, in a few places along the Des Plaines River in southwestern Cook County and western Will County, the bedrock is sometimes exposed or has only a few inches of soil covering it. One such spot is on the Des Plaines River, upstream of the Chicago Portage, just north of the Forty-Seventh Street Bridge, where the bedrock rises to the surface under only a few feet of water. Such locations became important as *fords* where people, and later horses and wagons, could cross the river.

During the Wisconsin phase there were various glacial advances and retreats that contributed to the physiography of Illinois and the Chicago area. Because it was the latest of the major glaciers, the Wisconsin ice reshaped the physiography established by earlier glaciers. Of particular interest for the physiography of the Chicago area is the Woodfordian subphase of the Wisconsin phase, which lasted from 22,000 to 12,500 BP. During that time the Lake Michigan Lobe (a tongue-shaped advance from the main ice sheet) of

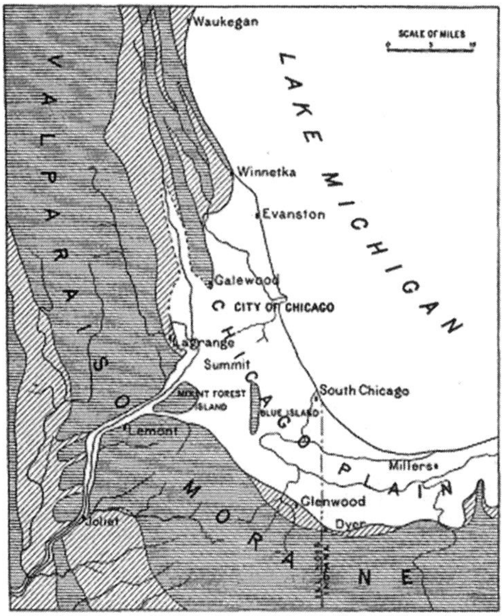

Fig. 2. The Valparaiso Moraine. From William C. Alden, "Description of the Chicago District," *Geologic Atlas of the United States*, folio 81 (Reston, VA: US Geological Survey, 1902), 1.

the Woodfordian glacier advanced over Illinois, including the Chicago area. The average rate of movement of the ice front during this time has been estimated at a third of a mile per year, and the average still stand for each of the moraine building cycles was about 190 years.[5]

About 14,500 BP, the Lake Michigan Lobe constructed the Valparaiso Moraine (fig. 2), which formed a U-shaped belt around the south end of the Lake Michigan basin through Illinois, Indiana, and Michigan.[6] The Valparaiso Moraine comprises a series of parallel ridges: a central ridge making up the main body of the moraine; an outer ridge, lower and narrower, that divides the Du Page River basin from the Des Plaines River proper; and an inner ridge, lying east of the central belt, and separated from it by the basin of Salt Creek.[7]

As the Lake Michigan Lobe melted away from the Valparaiso Moraine, Lake Chicago was formed, the first of several ancient lakes that were precursors to Lake Michigan. The glacier's regression away from the Valparaiso Moraine was not consistent, and there were periods of ebb and flow. In general, though, the Lake Michigan Lobe retreated in four phases: the Glenwood, Two Creek, Calumet, and Tolleston. At the end of the Tolleston phase, Lake Chicago ceased to be, and other lakes were formed that eventually settled into the basin we now know as Lake Michigan.

During the Glenwood phase (fig. 3), Lake Chicago reached its greatest surface area. At this phase, the surface of Lake Chicago was about 640 feet above sea level, or about 60 feet above the current level of Lake Michigan. After one or two thousand years, two drainage channels formed at the southwestern

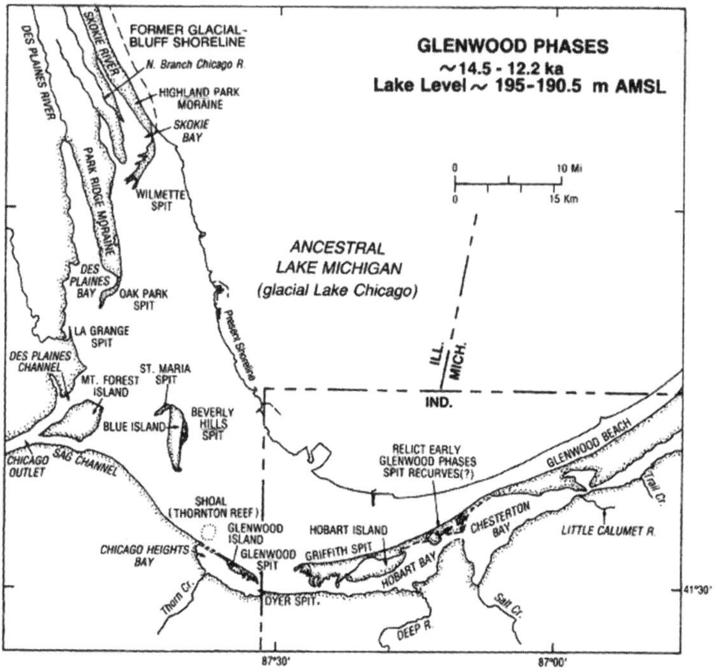

Fig. 3. Glenwood phases of glacial retreat. From Michael J. Chrzastowski and Todd A. Thompson, "Late Wisconsinan and Holocene Geologic History of the Illinois-Indiana Coast of Lake Michigan," *Journal of Great Lakes Research* 20, no. 1 (January 1994): 15. Courtesy of Elsevier.

corner of the lake in a Y shape north and south of Mount Forest Island. To the north was the Des Plaines Channel and to the south the Sag Channel. The two channels converged west of Mount Forest Island near present-day Lemont and eventually cut through the Valparaiso Moraine, creating the Chicago Outlet that then flowed south down the Des Plaines valley to the Illinois River. A tremendous torrent of water flowed through the Chicago Outlet, and the rushing waters carved out the wide valley that now contains the lower Des Plaines River.

The Glenwood phase came to an end in approximately 12,200 BP when the glacial ice retreated far enough north to allow meltwater drainage through the Indian River lowland and the vicinity of the Straits of Mackinac.[8] This increased drainage caused Lake Chicago to drop to lower than 590 feet above sea level, exposing a surface area in the Two Creeks area of Wisconsin where a mature forest of spruce, hemlock, pine, various mosses, and other plants developed. This period is known as the Two Creeks phase of Lake Chicago. With the lower lake levels of this phase, discharge through the Chicago Outlet ceased.[9] When the ice advanced again, about 11,800 BP, the northern drainage

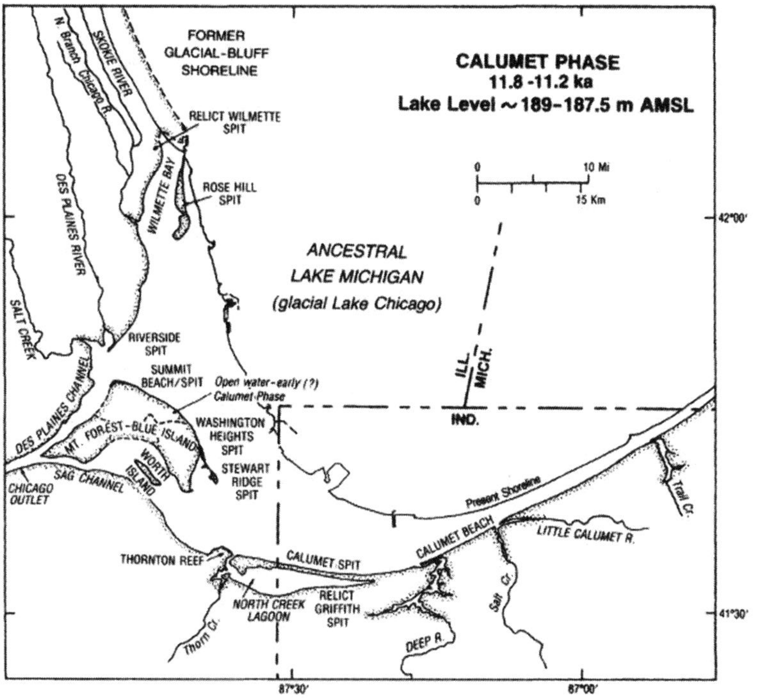

Fig. 4. Calumet phase of glacial retreat. From Michael J. Chrzastowski and Todd A. Thompson, "Late Wisconsinan and Holocene Geologic History of the Illinois-Indiana Coast of Lake Michigan," *Journal of Great Lakes Research* 20, no. 1 (January 1994): 17. Courtesy of Elsevier.

areas were cut off and Lake Chicago rose back to 620 feet above sea level, inundating the Two Creeks forest and initiating the Calumet phase of Lake Chicago (fig. 4). Today, the Two Creeks Buried Forest is a unit of the Ice Age National Scientific Reserve and was designated a State Natural Area in 1967.

With the higher lake levels of the Calumet phase, the Chicago Outlet once again became active. The Calumet phase also saw a renewed influx of water from the Huron basin into Lake Chicago, which increased the flow through the Chicago Outlet, causing it to deepen and widen. The continued erosion of the outlet dropped the Lake Chicago level to 600 feet above sea level, initiating the Tolleston phase at about 11,500 BP.[10] Lake Chicago now covered about half the area it had during the Glenwood phase, and the area that had previously been covered by the lake during the Glenwood, Two Creeks, and Calumet phases established a broad, gently sloping lake plain.

Eventually the glacier once again retreated far enough north that the waters of Lake Chicago joined those of Lake Huron, creating a new lake, Lake Algonquin.[11] In addition to the New River and Straits of Mackinac

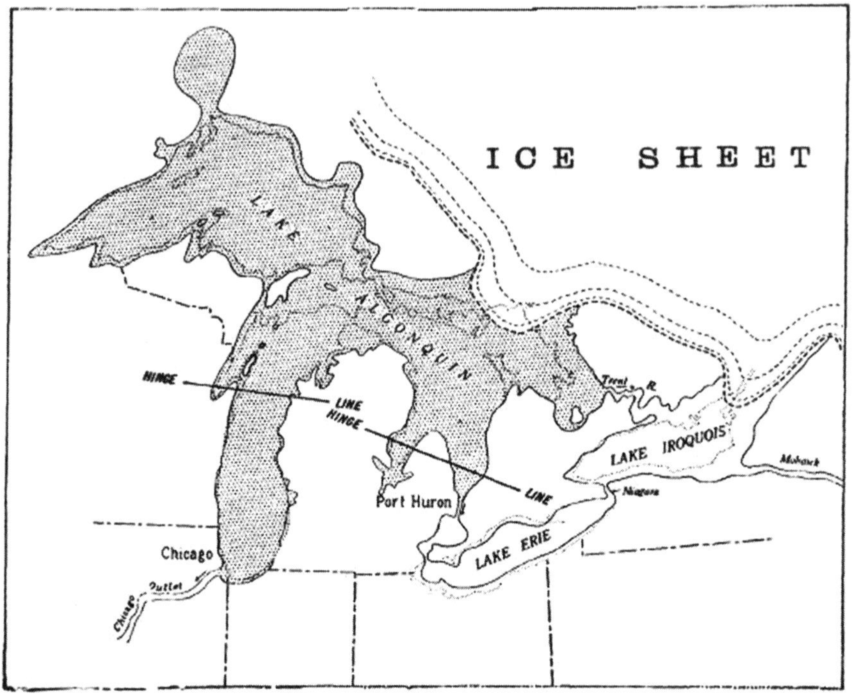

Fig. 5. Lake Algonquin, with the Chicago Outlet and outlets at Port Huron and the Trent River. From J. Harlen Bretz, *Geology of the Chicago Region: Part II–The Pleistocene*, Illinois State Geological Survey Bulletin 65, pt. 2 (Urbana: State of Illinois Department of Registration and Education, 1955), 120.

drainage that was reopened by the receding glacier, a new drainage outlet opened at the southeast end of Georgian Bay through the Trent River to a glacial lake (Iroquois) then occupying the Ontario basin.[12] With the opening of this new outlet, the lake level dropped so low that the Chicago Outlet again went dry.

As the ice continued to wane, the area containing the Trent River outlet began to uplift once relieved of glacier's crushing weight. This reduced the flow through the Trent River outlet, raising the Lake Algonquin water levels and causing the lake to find yet another source of discharge at Port Huron, down the St. Clair River into Lake Erie. With the rising waters, the Chicago Outlet also once again became functional, so there was a brief period, geologically speaking, when Lake Algonquin had three separate outlets (fig. 5). This did not last, however, and the Port Huron outlet, flowing over and through glacial drift, eventually eroded to a point that it assumed the entire outflow from Lake Algonquin, and the Trent River and Chicago Outlet discharges were abandoned.[13]

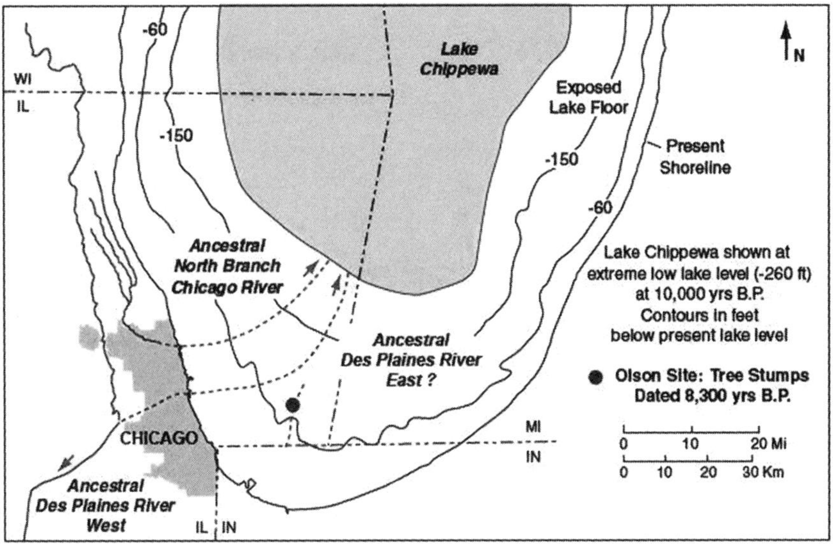

Fig. 6. Lake Chippewa. From Michael J. Chrzastowski, *The Chicago River—a Legacy of Glacial and Coastal Processes* (Champaign: Illinois Geological Survey, 2009), 13.

As the ice continued to melt in the Georgian Bay area of Ontario, it uncovered low country over which the waters found more routes of escape, likely to the Ottawa Valley.[14] Lake Algonquin dropped dramatically in depth until the water in the Lake Michigan basin reached only about 230 to 260 feet above sea level, well below the present-day Lake Michigan level. This period of low water was the end of Lake Algonquin and the beginning of Lake Chippewa (fig. 6). At its lowest point, about 9000 BP, Lake Chippewa covered only the deepest part of the Lake Michigan basin, and the shoreline was many miles northeast from where Chicago is today.[15] It was during the Chippewa phase that the southern reaches of the Chicago River were formed through subaerial erosion.[16]

As the glaciers continued to retreat northward, the Pleistocene slowly blended into the Holocene about 7000 BP. With the glaciers gone, the Georgian Bay area uplifted, closing off the prior drainage outlets and allowing the waters in the Lake Michigan and Lake Huron basins to rise again to Tolleston levels. Lake Chippewa was gone, and in its place came the Nipissing Great Lakes, which existed from about 4500 to 4000 BP (fig. 7).

The Nipissing discharged through two outlets, the Chicago Outlet and the Port Huron/St. Clair River Outlet. The latter continued to rapidly erode through the softer glacial till while the former was confined to bedrock and eroded much more slowly. When the waters dropped to 590 feet above sea level, the Chicago Outlet again went dry and Lake Algoma, the last ancient

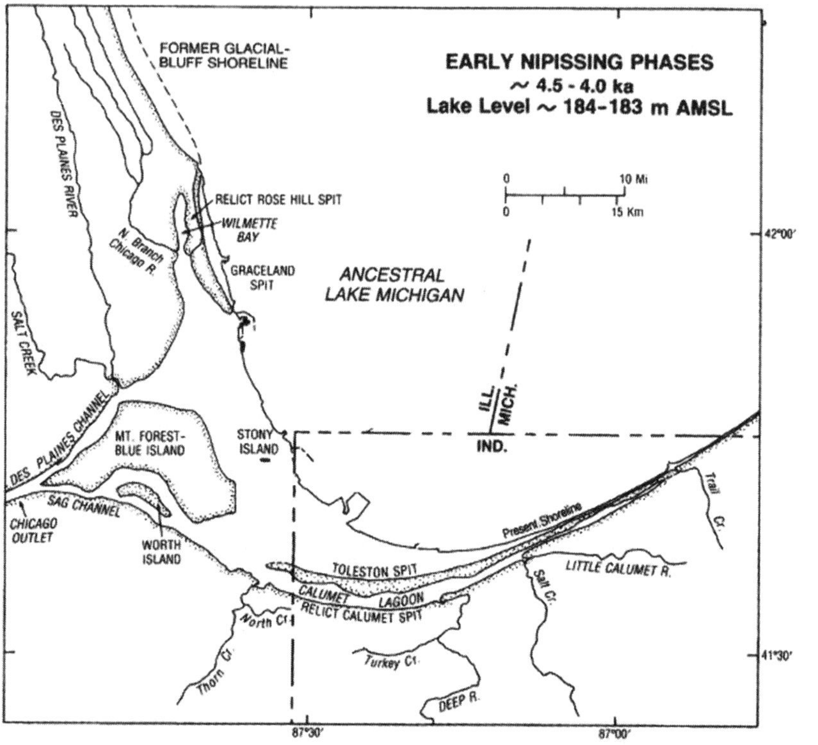

Fig. 7. Early Nippising phases. From Michael J. Chrzastowski and Todd A. Thompson, "Late Wisconsinan and Holocene Geologic History of the Illinois-Indiana Coast of Lake Michigan," *Journal of Great Lakes Research* 20, no. 1 (January 1994): 19. Courtesy of Elsevier.

precursor of the modern Great Lakes, arose.[17] Lake Algoma existed at a level of 590 feet above sea level from about 3000 to 2000 BP. The north end of Lake Algoma uplifted more than the south end, and it is likely that at higher water levels there was a small discharge through the Chicago Outlet. Eventually, however, with the continued erosion of the Port Huron/St. Clair River Outlet, the lake level dropped to 580 feet above sea level and the lake we know as Lake Michigan was established. At the same time, however, the Chicago Outlet went dry for the last time, never again to see a natural outflow from Lake Michigan.[18]

As the various phases of glaciation shaped the contours of the region, the interplay between the Des Plaines and the Chicago Rivers was also inching its way toward creating a unique spot at the southwestern corner of Lake Michigan that would have a profound effect on the peoples of North American for millennia. Slowly but surely, the pieces began to fall into place to create the Chicago Portage.

During the Glenwood phase, the Des Plaines River only existed north of the Chicago area, and the river drained directly into a bay of Lake Chicago (fig. 3).[19] During this same period, the three tributary streams that eventually formed the headwaters of the North Branch Chicago River were created. As the glacial ice retreated, it created a west-to-east sequence of moraines between which the three parallel streams developed: the West Fork North Branch formed first. then the Middle Fork and then the Skokie River. The formation of the headwater streams occurred over a time frame of about 1,500 years.[20]

As lake levels dropped during the Calumet phase, the bay into which the Des Plaines River had flowed drained away, and the upper Des Plaines River cut its way farther south, connecting to Lake Chicago at present-day Riverside. The Des Plaines channel of the Chicago Outlet was just south of this point (fig. 4 above). At the same time, the three tributary streams to the North Branch Chicago River extended their reach southward and converged to join one another, flowing together into Lake Chicago.[21]

The extremely low levels of Lake Chippewa opened up the Chicago lake plain, and the North Branch Chicago River meandered east across the lake plain to drain into Lake Chippewa. During this period, with the Chicago Outlet now dry, the Des Plaines River also might have intermittently drained into Lake Chippewa (fig. 6).[22]

During the late Chippewa phase, the mouth of the North Branch Chicago River shifted westward as the lake level rose. About 5800 BP, the mouth of the North Branch was near present-day Montrose Harbor. The lake level continued to rise, initiating the Nipissing phase and reestablishing outflow through the Chicago Outlet. Wave action along the western shore of the southern lake resulted in erosion that, coupled with a transport of sand and gravel, resulted in the formation of the Graceland Spit about 4000 BP.[23]

During the late Nipissing phase, the North Branch Chicago River discharged into a bay to the west of the northern end of the Graceland Spit (fig. 8, top left). As the spit continued to grow amid fluctuating lake levels, its central portion curved eastward (fig. 8, top right) before shifting back to the west (fig. 8, bottom left).[24]

The Graceland Spit eventually extended southward nearly seventeen miles, making it the longest such landform on the lake plain. When it reached its southern extent, it restricted and eventually blocked the lake from discharging through the Chicago Outlet. Water trapped behind the spit became the Chicago Lagoon, which over the course of the late Nipissing and Lake Algoma phases drained away through the Chicago Outlet. As the lagoon level lowered, the sand ridge of the relic Graceland Spit separated the North Branch Chicago River from the now-formed Lake Michigan. The North Branch Chicago River progressively extended south and west as it drained the lagoon until it finally joined the Des Plaines River. The Des Plaines channel of the Chicago Outlet no longer functioned to drain Lake Michigan, but it

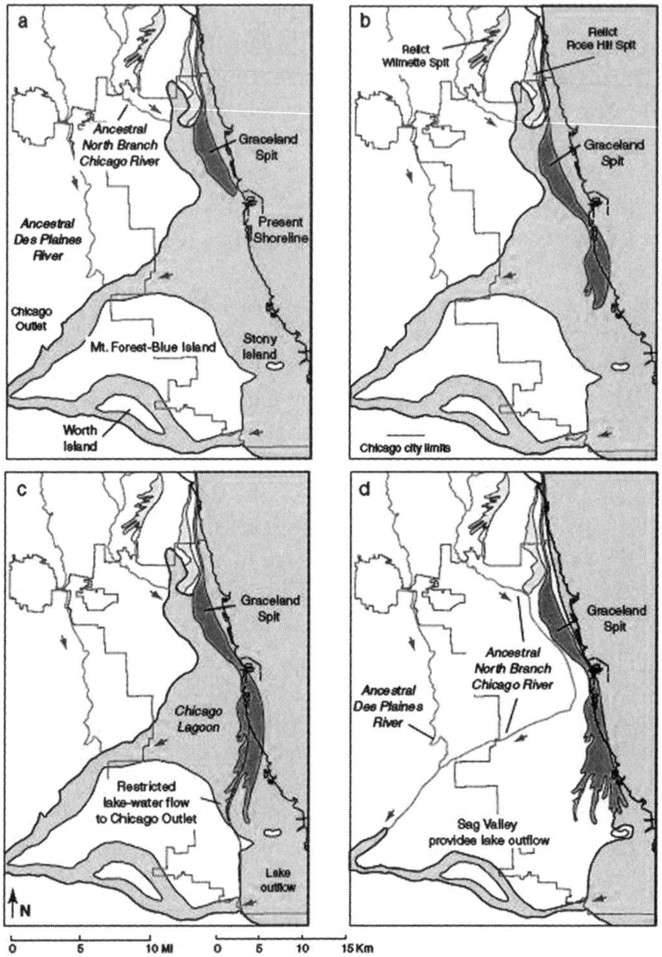

Fig. 8. Development of the Graceland Spit. From Michael J. Chrzastowski, *The Chicago River—a Legacy of Glacial and Coastal Processes* (Champaign: Illinois Geological Survey, 2009), 15.

left behind the lower Des Plaines valley through which the lower Des Plaines River now flowed. At this point, about 3500 BP, the westward-flowing North Branch Chicago River was a direct tributary of the Des Plaines River, and the high sand ridge of the relic Graceland Spit was the drainage divide between the Des Plaines River watershed to the west and the Lake Michigan watershed to the east.[25]

Over the next thousand years or so, waves slowly smoothed the western shore of the southern lake, evening out the shoreline and in the process eroding the central portion of the relic Graceland Spit that had originally extended eastward into the lake. This erosion resulted in a low spot in the remaining physical barrier between the North Branch Chicago River and Lake Michigan. The stage was set for a waterway to breach this barrier and connect the river and the lake.

Two scenarios are most likely to have created such a river-to-lake connection. The first is a flood event along the North Branch Chicago River during a time when the lake level was lower than the junction between the North Branch Chicago River and the Des Plaines River. This could have resulted in the floodwater cutting a channel to discharge into the lake. The problem with this scenario is that once the flood receded, wave action and accumulating sand would likely have closed the gap and the North Branch Chicago River would have resumed its westward flow to the Des Plaines River.[26]

A second scenario is that storm waves breached the lowland during a time of high water on Lake Michigan. This would have allowed lake water to merge with the waters of the North Branch Chicago River to flow westward to the Des Plaines River. This scenario is more likely to have had sufficient energy to erode a substantial channel connecting the North Branch Chicago River and the lake. Under this second scenario, the North Branch Chicago River would have then flowed eastward into the lake when the lake level was lower than the junction with the Des Plaines River and westward to the Des Plaines River when the lake level was higher than the junction with the Des Plaines River.[27]

However it happened, sometime around 2500 to 2000 BP, flow in what became the West Fork South Branch Chicago River reversed to drain north to join the newly cut Main Stem Chicago River and drain eastward into the lake (fig. 8, bottom right).[28] Similarly, the remaining North Branch Chicago River flowed south to join the Main Stem Chicago River and drain eastward into the lake. Thus, the three-part Chicago River we know today was established.

The Chicago area straddles the St. Lawrence Continental Divide that separates the Mississippi River watershed basin from the Great Lakes watershed basin. (There are actually two divides in the Chicago area, one on the surface that directs surface drainage, and one below the surface on the bedrock that directs subsurface drainage.) Waters east of the continental divide drain through the Great Lakes to the St. Lawrence River and then to the Atlantic Ocean, and waters west of the continental divide drain to the Mississippi River and then to the Gulf of Mexico.[29]

Although the Graceland Spit had temporarily established a drainage divide along the lakeshore that diverted waters westward, when the physical barrier separating the North Branch Chicago River and the lake was breached, the continental divide asserted itself. After the Main Stem Chicago River was established, the remaining branches and forks of the Chicago River assumed their flow eastward into the lake.

Meanwhile, the Des Plaines River was going through changes of its own. During floods, the Des Plaines River almost certainly flowed eastward into the West Fork South Branch Chicago River, and it is even possible that for a time the entire flow of the Des Plaines River might have flowed eastward to the lake in this manner.[30] At some point, however, the channel through which the Des Plaines River flowed eastward was restricted and the river backed up before turning westward to flow into the old channel that had been cut by the Chicago Outlet. One early engineer suggested that a beaver dam might have been the cause for the backing up and reversal of the Des Plaines River.[31] If so, then the earth-carving power of glaciers and the eternal winnowing of waves and wind perhaps found their final touches applied by "industrious beavers." After the Des Plaines River parted company with the Chicago River, an area of marshy land about five miles in length remained in the slough through which the Des Plaines River had once flowed. This area became known as Mud Lake, and with its appearance the story of the Chicago Portage as we know it began.

2

✦

Prehistoric Chicago

Although the Chicago Portage did not form until around 500 BCE, the area adjacent to what became the portage has a rich prehistory of glacial action, fluctuating lake levels, climate variation and associated flora and fauna diversity, and human habitation. One of the fascinating things about the prehistory of the Chicago region is how all of these variables ebbed and flowed before eventually creating the physiography and natural environment that ushered in the historic era.

The migration of prehistoric people to the area around Chicago began as far back as the Paleo-Indian period (12,000–10,000 BCE). By 12,000 BCE the glaciers had receded north beyond what is now the Canadian border, and the newly exposed land became home to a mosaic of plant life including forest, grassland, and tundra that created a habitat for animals. Once the animals appeared, it was not long afterward that bands of nomadic hunters roamed the area in pursuit of large animals such as mastodons, giant sloths, bears, caribou, and bison.[1] These were nomadic peoples who lived and traveled along the hills and moraines left behind by the glacial retreat.

As noted in chapter 1, the extent of coverage of the ancient Lake Chicago, precursor to the present-day Lake Michigan, fluctuated throughout the Paleo-Indian period. Although it is possible that Paleo-Indian peoples inhabited the lake plain at lower water phases, any evidence of their presence was subsequently lost with the rising waters. Because of this dearth of direct evidence, archaeologists can only speculate on Paleo-Indian lifeways.

The moraines that surrounded the lake plain were dotted with lakes and bogs. Archaeological evidence from a similar physiography west of Chicago suggests that Paleo-Indians inhabited the edges of major bogs and sloughs and employed a hunting strategy based on killing animals mired in the mud.[2] Although bones of large animals such as the mastodon and mammoth are usually associated with Paleo-Indian sites, it is likely that small and medium-sized game were also a significant part of the Paleo-Indian diet.

Given the sparse Paleo-Indian population of the continental United States, it is likely that the highly nomadic bands were made up of closely related nuclear families and that neighboring groups engaged in exchanging not only trade goods but also marriage partners. Stone artifacts found at Paleo-Indian archaeological sites sometimes include raw materials found far away from the locale of the sites while at the same time bearing widespread stylistic similarities. This indicates both the far-ranging movements of the Paleo-Indians and the cultural exchange of ideas inherent in intergroup trade. The craftwork and beauty of some of these trade items, such as high-quality chipped-stone projectile points and knives, further emphasize that intergroup trade was an important aspect of Paleo-Indian society.[3]

Although the Paleo-Indians were nomadic hunters, the changing climate and environment that began around 8000 BCE eventually led to a different way of life commonly referred to as the Archaic period (8000–600 BCE). As the Laurentian glacier retreated north of Hudson Bay, a new atmospheric circulation moved the winter storm track north, and the Rocky Mountain moisture shadow was extended into the upper Midwest. This change produced a wedge-shaped expanse of grassland known as the Prairie Peninsula that reached across Illinois, bordered by mixed forests to the south and deciduous forests to the north. Chicago is on the northern edge of this peninsula.[4]

As the climate warmed, the prehistoric big game animals became extinct and other previously available animals moved north out of the area. They were replaced, however, by new animals and other new food sources. Gone were the mastodon, caribou, and arctic hare, and in their place were deer, raccoons, squirrels, ducks, geese, turtles, and rabbits, to name a few.[5] Nuts and acorns became increasingly important food sources, as did fish. As the Archaic period proceeded, more and more people began to settle along the shoreline of Lake Chippewa, which was at its lowest levels during most of the Archaic period, and along rivers where nut-bearing trees lived on high ground between marshes.

As time progressed, people made the slow transition from a nomadic lifestyle to one more centered on settlements. By the Late Archaic period (3000–600 BCE), this transition led to the establishment of semipermanent settlements from which smaller groups traveled to collect seasonally available resources. This development is reflected in the archaeological evidence by two types of Late Archaic sites: large, semipermanent base camps; and small, temporary, special-activity camps. The large, semipermanent base camps also began to store food in pits for later consumption, further evidence of a diversifying diet afforded by changes in climate and environment.[6] New technologies also appeared. Spears were thrown with a catapult-like stick called an *atlatl*. Ground-stone tools such as axes were used to cut wood, and grinding stones were used to crush seeds and nuts.[7]

As people became more settled, the significance of trade became more important. Trade functioned not only as a means to obtain needed resources but also as a way to form social alliances and regulate the use of territory. There was an increased trade in ceremonial items that lacked direct practical use but were intended to establish social ties and avoid conflict among neighboring groups. It is during this period that we have the clearest evidence of long-distance trade most likely carried on via water routes. Late Archaic sites exhibit a broad distribution of copper from Lake Superior, galena from the Illinois-Iowa-Wisconsin area and eastern Missouri, New York, and Ontario, and shells from the Gulf Coast.[8]

Unfortunately, Archaic sites that might have existed in the lake plain during the low-water phase of Lake Chippewa were covered by the rising waters of the Nipissing phase, which reached its high-water mark roughly midway through the Late Archaic period. Archaic artifacts are therefore most often found on the surfaces of the glacial moraines unaffected by the Nipissing inundation. Other artifacts, however, have also been found underground on the beach ridges where sites were buried and then subsequently left behind by receding water. At the Laughton site, which is located at the Chicago Portage, Archaic materials were found a little over three feet below the surface, underneath later artifacts that were found at a shallower depth.[9]

The subsequent Woodland period is usually divided into Early (600–200 BCE), Middle (200 BCE–400 CE), and Late (400–1000 CE). Traditionally, the defining difference between the Archaic and Woodland periods was the appearance and widespread usage of pottery, which in turn indicates the increasing importance of plants and seeds as food sources. Fired-clay cooking pots were used to parch and boil seeds and greens over fires and to produce gruel from starchy seeds. This latter development was far-reaching because gruel provided an important food source during infant weaning. This improvement of infant nutrition led to higher survival rates and significant population increases by the end of the Late Woodland period.[10]

The Early Woodland period displayed many of the same characteristics as the Late Archaic period. Hunting strategies and methods were similar, as were the preferred riverine settlement sites. During the Middle Woodland period, however, extraordinary changes occurred in settlement patterns, intergroup trade, and cultural expression. The resulting culture of the Middle Woodland period remains a source of mystery and has been the subject of academic debate for decades.

The Hopewell culture existed from about 200 BCE to 300 CE and comprised groups of people who inhabited the Illinois River and Mississippi River valleys primarily in Iowa, Illinois, and Missouri. (The name "Hopewell" comes from the Hopewell farm in Ross County, Ohio, where part of an extensive earthwork was excavated in 1891.) These groups engaged in widespread and systematic trade on a level not seen in prior times. This network of exchange is called the Hopewell Interaction Sphere (fig. 9), and in the Illinois region, the Havana Hopewell played a major role in this social and trade system. Chicago was at the northeast extension of the Havana Hopewell.[11]

Apart from the extent and sophistication of the exchange network, the items of exchange were themselves unusual and included exotic materials

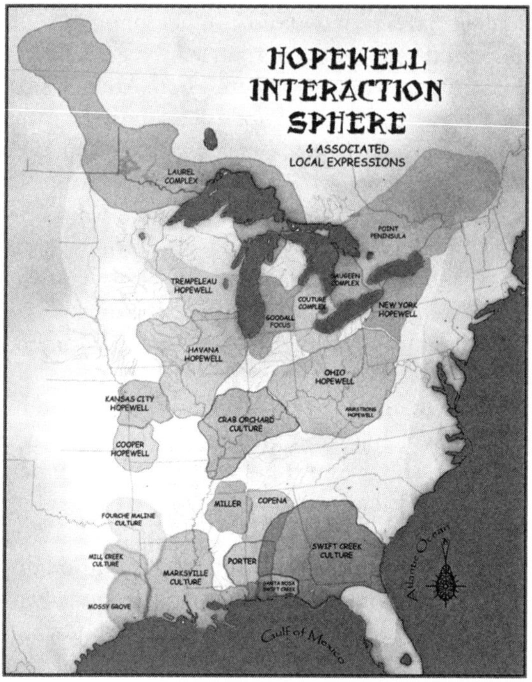

Fig. 9. Hopewell Interaction Sphere. Heironymous Rowe, February 9, 2010. Wikimedia Commons, https://commons.wikimedia.org/w/index.php?curid=9416551.

from areas far beyond the region itself, including obsidian and chert from Wyoming and Idaho. An enduring debate continues over how and why such exotic materials were acquired and used.[12] Burial mounds and ceremonial sites also appear during the Middle Woodland period, and some of the more exotic items may well have had religious significance. Analyses of Middle Woodland sites suggest a society with a division of labor based on gender and that social ranking was not hereditary but rather based on a person's ability, gender, and age, and possibly on a person's relationship to an important individual.[13]

Given the distant origins of many of the materials used by the Hopewell peoples in their artifacts and their preference for settling along rivers, it is reasonable to assume that much of the transportation of raw materials and trade goods was done on waterways. If so, it is possible that it was during the Middle Woodland period that the Chicago Portage was first regularly used as a significant trade route by the Havana Hopewell. In particular, the presence of copper from the Upper Peninsula of Michigan around Lake Superior at Middle Woodland sites throughout the Illinois River valley suggests the use of the Chicago Portage by these early traders.

For unknown reasons, the Hopewell culture began to decline around 400 CE. It is possible that as populations grew and game animals, especially larger ones, were depleted, villages began to compete more for resources, leading to conflicts. Later settlements became larger and more fortified, lending credence to this possibility. Whatever the cause, by 500 CE the Hopewell Interaction Sphere was largely dismantled.

The Late Woodland period saw significant cultural transformations. Society became even more sedentary than in the earlier Woodland periods, with people settling in small villages and camps. The bow and arrow appeared during this period. Of special significance, corn began to be used, the earliest date in Illinois falling between 600 and 800 CE.[14] Although not cultivated extensively as a staple until after 1000 CE, corn became a critical subsistence resource as a stored winter food. Also, during the Late Woodland period, effigy mounds appear, with present-day Cook County being the southeastern extent of the effigy mound tradition.[15] The mounds were sometimes, but not always, used as burial sites. They took the form of low earth and gravel structures that from an aerial perspective outline bears, panthers, birds, lizards, snakes, and turtles. The Kennicott Mounds were located on the east bank of the Des Plaines River above the present-day North Avenue Bridge. The Lake View Mounds, which took the form of a lizard or winged serpent, were located between the North Branch Chicago River and Lake Michigan.[16]

Beginning around 1000 CE, an unprecedented cultural development began in the central Mississippi River valley. Known as the Mississippian period (1000 to 1600 CE), Mississippian culture was typified by the construction of planned, permanent ceremonial centers and towns with associated hierarchical social, political, and religious systems. The Mississippians also established an extensive and sophisticated trade network.[17] In the Middle Mississippi area, which included the Mississippi valley and the river's tributaries in what are now Alabama, Arkansas, Tennessee, Missouri, western Kentucky, and southern Illinois, generalized traits included rectangular temple mounds, the pervasive use of crushed shell for tempering pottery, and, especially after 1000 CE, intensive cultivation of corn, the last of which led to settlements of unprecedented size and population.

Cahokia was the epitome of Mississippian culture. Its location across the river from what is now St. Louis was supremely advantageous, lying at the northern end of the agriculturally rich American Bottom, with the mineral-laden Ozarks to the southwest and an extensive riverine system to the north. Its location near the confluence of the Mississippi River and two of its major tributaries, the Missouri and Illinois Rivers, made it a natural gateway for trade because these rivers were the primary avenues of transportation.[18] By 1200 CE, Cahokia was the largest and most complex community—indeed, "city" is a more apt term—north of Mexico, and it remains today the largest prehistoric site in the United States.[19]

The size and sophistication of Cahokia challenges the imagination. A central arrangement of temple mounds and plazas was surrounded by as many as one hundred lesser mounds and likely hundreds of houses. The most impressive mound, Monks Mound, rose 98 feet above the floodplain and is equivalent in size to eleven football fields. Taken together, Cahokia encompassed an area of nearly six square miles.[20] At its peak, Cahokia was home to a population of approximately fifteen thousand people.[21]

Evidence of the vast trade network that emanated from Cahokia consists of the presence of exotic raw materials not regionally available, far-flung settlements displaying typical Mississippian traits, and artifacts that show Mississippian styles and motifs.[22] Similarly, the locations of settlements are indicative of the important role of trade in Mississippian culture. The Collins site, for example, is located on the Vermillion River near the headwaters of the Kaskaskia and Sangamon Rivers that in turn empty into the upper Illinois River. From there, possibly via the Chicago Portage, traders could reach Lake Michigan.[23]

The presence at Cahokia of copper from the Upper Peninsula of Michigan around Lake Superior suggests the reach of the river- and lake-based trade routes. Other than travel on foot, all transportation was by dugout canoe. (Horses were not introduced into North America until the sixteenth century.)[24] Similarly, distinctive Mississippian pottery has been found at more than forty-five sites north of Cahokia, including the Juntunen site at Bois Blanc Island in Lake Huron just east of the northeastern tip of Lake Michigan.[25] Although there is no direct archaeological evidence that Cahokian traders used the Chicago Portage, it is certainly possible given the portage's existence as a link between the Mississippi River valley and Lake Michigan. Duane Esarey draws a correlation between the proto-Winnebago tribes of the Huber phase of upper Mississippian culture (1400–1630 CE) and the Illinois Tribe in that both wanted to "straddle the routes" such as the Chicago Portage, the Calumet River, and the St. Joseph River to control trade access to the midcontinent. As Esarey puts it, "the Chicago Portage was always a big deal."[26]

For unknown reasons, Cahokia declined and was eventually abandoned around 1400 CE, and the area remained virtually uninhabited for the next fifty years.[27] However, Mississippian cultural traits are found in settlements in northeastern Illinois up until the mid-sixteenth century. What is not known is whether this incorporation of cultural traits resulted from direct migration from Middle Mississippian (1200–1400 CE) settlements farther south or whether the influence was indirectly the result of trade and more random intermingling. It is clear that reliance on corn was never as extensive in the northeastern Illinois area as it was in Cahokia and that settlements were not as large or as permanent as those in the Middle Mississippi.

The period preceding the arrival of Europeans is similarly obscure. It is not known whether the tribes encountered by the early French traders were descendants of the Middle Mississippians or whether they came from other areas. What we do know is that when the first French explorers and missionaries arrived in the region around the southern end of Lake Michigan, there was already a well-established presence in the area by the Illini, or Illiniwek, a confederation of tribes. These people spoke a language that belonged to the Native American language group known as Algonquian, and they and had likely migrated from the east.

"Illiniwek" in Algonquian means "men," and this name was intended to distinguish them from neighboring tribes in a manner intentionally derogatory to the latter.[28] The French early on modified the word to "Illinois," which became the name given by Europeans and their descendants to the river along the banks of which many Native Americans had settled, then to the territory in general, and eventually to what became the twenty-first state of the United States in 1818. At their strongest, the Illinois people had control over the entire northeastern portion of present-day Illinois. The Chicago Portage was especially important for the Illinois, not only because of the connection between the Des Plaines River and Lake Michigan but also because the western shoreline of the lake was a major overland highway for the confederation's people when traveling by land.[29] Indeed, the lake's western shoreline was so frequently used by the Illinois that Lake Michigan was generally known to early explorers as "Lake of the Illinois."[30]

We do not know how long the Illinois had been living in the region before the Europeans came. But once the French explorers, traders, and missionaries arrived, the Illinois were driven from their eponymous land. Violence erupting to the east spread quickly westward and dramatically affected Native Americans. At this point, we have arrived at the time of the first historical accounts of the Chicago Portage.

3

✦

Commerce and the Cross

This next chapter in the story of the Chicago Portage begins far away in the cold waters of the North Atlantic off Newfoundland. In the early sixteenth century, European fishermen discovered there large quantities of Atlantic cod, a much desired and financially lucrative resource. As the fishermen looked for better ways to preserve their catch for the long trip home, they eventually developed a method of "dry" fishing, which involved bringing the fish onto land, where they were dried on rocks or wooden platforms. Dry fishing quickly became the preferred method of preserving the fish because it required less salt, saved on cargo space, allowed for a longer fishing season, and resulted in a product with a long shelf life.[1]

With the advent of dry fishing, fishermen began to search for suitable harbors where they could anchor their main vessel and set up the drying operation onshore. Every day they took smaller boats out for the catch and then returned to their base to dry the fish. The best harbors were those that had ample supplies of bait as well as timber for making the fires needed for the drying process. Competition for such harbors was intense and led to more and more exploration of the coastline as well as more of a movement to the interior. After a suitable harbor was found, the fishermen would stay ashore for extended periods, and they often would return to the same harbor with each new fishing cycle.[2]

It was during their time on land that the fishermen first began to encounter and interact with the communities that already inhabited the region. A prominent aspect of this interaction was trade, and in particular the Native Americans provided beaver pelts that were made into coats by the fishermen to stave off the bitter North Atlantic cold. Throughout the first half of the sixteenth century the nascent fur trade was carried on incidentally to fishing, but it is clear that Native Americans were already accustomed to trading with Europeans by the time the French explorer Jacques Cartier sailed into Chaleur Bay in 1534. In his first encounter with the Native Americans, Cartier and his men traded knives and iron goods for pelts with members of the Micmac Tribe.[3]

Although it began as a sideline to fishing, the fur trade soon expanded into an economic engine in its own right. During the second half of the sixteenth century, demand for beaver pelts dramatically increased in Europe as felt hats became a fashion craze. For their part, the Native American peoples were glad to supply the pelts in exchange for European-made goods, especially ironware, guns, and ammunition. The fur trade intensified so dramatically that by the end of the sixteenth century, it had depleted the beaver stock in the area of the St. Lawrence River. The main tribes of that area, the Iroquois and the Huron, were soon at war with each other over hunting grounds, with the Dutch aligned with the Iroquois and the French with the Huron.

At the dawn of the seventeenth century, the fur trade had advanced to a point where demand required it to extend up the St. Lawrence and Ottawa Rivers. Warfare between the Iroquois and Huron for control of these areas escalated throughout the first half of the seventeenth century until the Iroquois finally routed the Huron in 1649–50, driving them out of the region. This conflict began a pattern of Iroquois aggression and domination that persisted for decades, eventually extending all the way to the Mississippi River and and creating significant disruptions within tribes of the region. By the middle of the seventeenth century, both the Illinois and Miami Tribes, sometimes thought to have been at one time a single tribe because of the similarity of their languages, had established settlements in the Chicago area. Both tribes were attacked by the Iroquois beginning around 1655 and after persistent repeated attacks eventually moved west of the Mississippi River around 1660.[4] A few years later the Iroquois withdrew to find other targets of opportunity, and over time the Illinois and Miami returned.

The removal of the Huron also left a vacuum in the organization of the fur trade because they had been the primary intermediaries between the French traders and the interior tribes that were providing the majority of the beaver pelts. This absence of the Huron in turn led the French to themselves push farther into the interior to try to find new trading partners.[5] For a period of time in the 1650s, the fur trade was severely impacted by ongoing Iroquois attacks on the French, with both sides vying to maintain control of the fur trade. France finally reached a breaking point in 1665 and sent a uniformed regiment to deal with the Iroquois. By 1666 the Iroquois, weakened by decades of war and decimated by diseases brought by the Europeans, had had enough, and a peace was brokered. It was a temporary peace, but it was sufficient to allow the fur trade to rebound. The fur trade reached farther west, fueled as much by the Native peoples' demand for European goods as it was by European demand for fur.

By 1670, with the Iroquois temporarily contained and the fur trade restored, the colonial territory of New France was ready to expand its reach. During the first half of the seventeenth century, explorers and missionaries had identified all five of the Great Lakes—Superior, Michigan, Huron, Erie, and Ontario—and had ventured into the areas that are now Minnesota and Wisconsin.[6] In 1634, Jean Nicolet became the first European to explore Lake Michigan, venturing as far as Green Bay, where it is possible he became the first European to be told of the portage route between Lake Michigan and the Mississippi River.[7] Nicolas Perrot was trading with tribal peoples around Green Bay in 1665. Father Claude Allouez by 1669 had explored the area around Lake Superior, and it is possible that he, too, knew of the site called Chicago as early as 1670.[8] And in 1671, Father Jacques Marquette founded the St. Ignace Mission at the Straits of Mackinac. What remained to be explored were the vast hinterlands to the south.

Of special interest to the French was the reputed existence of a great river. Members of Indigenous tribes spoke of the river, as did some more far-flung travelers and traders, but the river itself remained a mystery. Some thought it might be a route to the South Sea, while others foretold a path to gold and riches. For the missionaries, it was a gateway to large populations awaiting salvation; for the imperial minded, it promised a route by which France could claim a continent.[9]

Jean-Baptiste Talon came to New France in 1665 as an intendant; this post, appointed by a royal commission, controlled the colony's entire civil administration. He was a man of great ambition who was determined to expand France's holdings through exploration. He was especially interested in finding the great river as a possible route to the South Sea. He decided that Louis Jolliet should be the leader of an exploratory mission to locate the river and determine where it led. When the French nobleman Louis de Baude, Comte de Frontenac et Paluau arrived in New France in 1672 as vice-regent for King Louis XIV, Talon recommended Jolliet to Frontenac, and Frontenac appointed Jolliet to lead the excursion. It is possible that Claude Dablon, the superior-general of the Jesuits in Canada, recommended Jolliet to Talon, and it was also Dablon who instructed Marquette to join Jolliet as chaplain for the expedition.[10]

Jolliet was particularly well qualified to lead the expedition. As a child, he grew up near Quebec, which was then the center of the fur trade. He attended a Jesuit school where he studied philosophy and for a while intended to become a priest. He also studied music and became a skilled harpsichordist and organist. Eventually, however, he decided against the priesthood and in 1667 traveled to France, where he studied hydrography. Upon returning to New France, he became a trapper and trader, and he traveled widely through the western regions, including following the Great Lakes route to Green Bay. In his travels he learned several Native American languages and proved to be adept at interacting with Native Americans.[11]

Like Jolliet, Marquette brought a range of skills to the expedition, even if his purpose was different. From his earliest days studying for the priesthood, Marquette had been driven by a desire to bring Christianity to distant lands. He so pestered his superiors that they finally allowed him to curtail his formal studies and dispatched him to Quebec in 1666. Over the next seven years he assisted in several missions throughout the western regions and became fluent in six Native American languages. In 1671, he founded the Saint Ignace

Mission on the north shore of the straits of Michilimackinac on Lake Michigan, near present-day St. Ignace.[12]

Marquette, like Jolliet, had a keen interest in discovering the great river that could be his route to bringing Christianity to the Illinois people. He had for years gathered information on the river and in April 1670 had determined that if "the Indians who are promising to make me a canoe keep their word, we shall go down this river as far as we can."[13] He was unable to make that trip because of unrest among various tribes, so it was with great excitement that he greeted Jolliet in December 1672 when Jolliet arrived at the St. Ignace Mission with news that Marquette was to join the expedition.

Over the next five months, Jolliet and Marquette prepared for the expedition. It was clear to all that Jolliet was the leader of the group, but Marquette played a significant role in the preparations for the expedition. They gathered as much information as they could from the Native Americans who professed knowledge of the region, even going so far as to prepare a map based on these sources. The map indicated the rivers they were to use, the peoples they expected to encounter along the way, and even the purported course of the great river and the route on it that they were to take.[14]

Jolliet and Marquette were not alone on this enterprise. Five other men filled out the expedition, although their exact identities are unclear. Looking back to accounts from the turn of the twentieth century, Louise Phelps Kellogg refers to them as *voyageurs*, while Alfred Andreas says they were "one Frenchman, and four Indians."[15] Kellogg claims that only two names were certain, Pierre Porteret and Jacques Largilliers, while Francis Borgia Steck adds Pierre Moreau to the list.[16] On October 1, 1672, Louis Jolliet, François de Chavigny, Zacharie Jolliet (Louis's brother), Jean Plattier, Pierre Moreau, Jacques Largilliers, and Jean Tiberge had reached a formal agreement to undertake the expedition. It is known that Chavigny did not accompany the expedition, and the mid-twentieth-century historian Jean Delanglez is persuasive that Zacharie Jolliet did not join the group either.[17] So although only Jolliet and Marquette can be named with certainty, it is possible that the remaining five (Jolliet himself told Dablon that he had set out with "five other Frenchmen") were Porteret, Largilliers, Moreau, Plattier, and Tiberge. Of these, Kellogg notwithstanding, Porteret is least certain because he had not been part of the October 1, 1672, agreement.[18] It is unfortunate that the cloud of history obscures the names of these travelers, because they were certainly integral players in the expedition.

By the following spring, the group was ready, and on May 15, 1673, they set forth in two canoes provisioned with "Indian corn with some smoked meat."[19] They passed through the Straits of Mackinac and headed west along the north shore of Lake Michigan and then down the west coast of Green Bay, arriving at the Mission of St. Francis Xavier in early June. They then made their way up the Fox River to Lake Winnebago, which they took to the upper Fox River. Following the upper Fox River, the group arrived on

June 7 at a village that was home to the Mascouten Tribe. They spent several days among the Mascouten and also encountered some Miami and Kickapoo refugees who had fled their homes at the southern end of Lake Michigan after being attacked by the Iroquois.

At the request of the explorers, the Mascouten assigned two men who, leaving on June 10, guided the group up the river to a portage that led them to the banks of the Wisconsin River. The guides then returned to their village, leaving the expedition, in Marquette's words "alone in this Unknown country, in the hands of providence."[20] They headed southwest on the Wisconsin River, and on June 17 Marquette recorded that "at 42 and a half degrees Of latitude, We safely entered Missisipi . . . with a Joy that I cannot Express."[21] At last the great river was found.

The expedition followed the great river south, and along the way, at approximately the location of present-day Alton, Illinois, they saw paintings of two monsters on the high limestone bluffs. These figures are today called the Piasa Bird; at the time, the explorers were startled not by the figures' fearsome appearance but by the fine quality of the painting and their location high above the river.[22] After about a month, the expedition finally arrived at the mouth of the Arkansas River. At this point they decided they had gone far enough. They knew they were within a few days of the Gulf of Mexico and so had determined that the Mississippi River ran south and discharged into the Gulf of Mexico instead of turning east or west. They were also warned by the local Native American tribes, perhaps the Michigamea or Quapaw, that the Spaniards were not far to the south, and the French explorers had no doubt that they would be held captive, or worse, should they encounter them.[23]

Their minds made up, the expedition began the trip home. This time, however, they were eight in number. They were accompanied by a ten-year-old boy who had been given to Jolliet by the chief of one of the Peouarea tribes they had encountered on their trip down the Mississippi. It is possible these same Native Americans told the explorers about an alternate route back to Lake Michigan by way of the Illinois River.[24] It was tough going against the current, and it likely took the group a month to reach the mouth of the Illinois River. The group was struck with the beauty and fecundity of the Illinois River and adjacent lands, Marquette noting that "we have seen nothing like this river that we enter, as regards its fertility of soil, its prairies and woods; its cattle, elk, deer, wildcats, bustards, swans, ducks, parroquets, and even beaver."[25]

About two hundred miles up the Illinois River, the group arrived at the village of Kaskaskia, which was near what is now the town of Utica, Illinois. They were greeted warmly by the inhabitants, and Marquette promised them that he would return to their village to teach them more about Christianity. He named his mission there the "mission of the Conception among the Illinois" ("Conception" being the same name he used for the Mississippi River).[26]

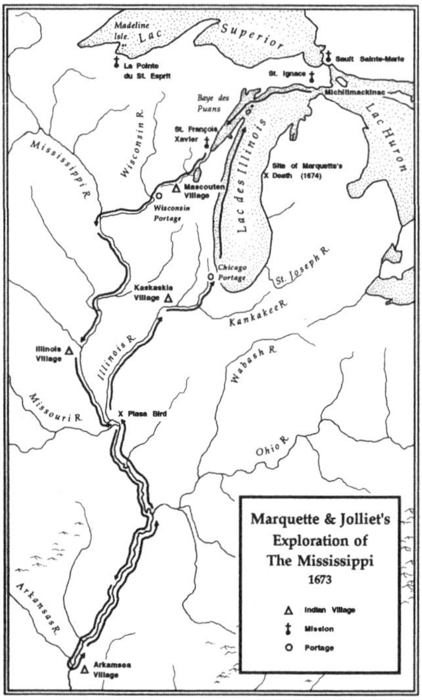

Fig. 10. Marquette and Jolliet's exploration of the Mississippi, 1673. From Charles J. Balesi, *The Time of the French in the Heart of North America, 1673–1818* (Chicago: Alliance Française, 1992), 19. Courtesy Charles J. Balesi.

When it was time to leave, one of the chiefs of the Kaskaskia, along with some of his men, guided the explorers up the Illinois River until they came to the Des Plaines River. Here the explorers headed northeast and became the first Europeans known to have crossed the Chicago Portage. Upon arriving at Lake Michigan, their Native American guides returned to Kaskaskia and the expedition headed home, arriving back at the Mission of St. Francis Xavier at the end of September 1673 (fig. 10).[27]

Having seen to the safe arrival of Marquette, whose health was declining, Jolliet may have returned to the area of the Chicago Portage and southern Lake Michigan. On a map he later drew from memory, titled "New Discovery of Several Nations in New France, in the year 1673 and 1674," Jolliet shows a river at the southeastern shore of Lake Michigan, and a hill that on the map is called "Mont Joliet." Steck opines that neither of these features could have been found by Jolliet on his return trip with the expedition earlier in 1673. Steck also finds it notable that the title of the map itself suggests the possibility of more than one trip.[28] This second trip could have been accomplished in a couple of months, which comports with Jolliet's account to Dablon that "they repaired about the end of November [1673] to the Baye des Puants."[29] It is also possible that Pierre Moreau, who likely was part of the original expedition, accompanied Jolliet on this trip. Moreau was in

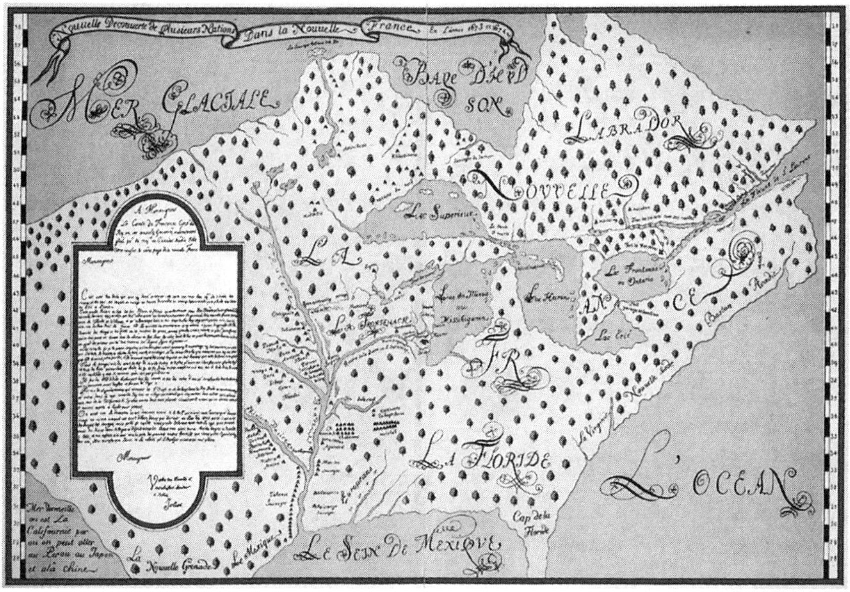

Fig. 11. *New Discovery of Several Nations in New France, in the year 1673 and 1674*, 1674. Library of Congress, Geography and Map Division, Louisiana: European Explorations and the Louisiana Purchase, https://www.loc.gov/resource/g3300.ct000655.

the area of the Chicago Portage in the winter of 1674–75 when Marquette arrived there on his second voyage.[30]

Back in Green Bay with Marquette by the end of November 1673, Jolliet set about writing an account of the expedition. He made copies of his journal and map, leaving the copies with Marquette and retaining the original. In May 1674, Jolliet set out for Quebec to report directly to Frontenac. Along the way, disaster struck when his canoe overturned as they were nearing Montreal. Jolliet's companions, including two men and the young Peouarea boy, drowned. Jolliet was cast upon a rock, exhausted and unconscious, but was saved by some fishermen. The journal and map were gone. And to compound this loss, the copies that Jolliet had left with Marquette were destroyed in a fire. All that remained to reconstruct the expedition was Jolliet's memory.

The canoe accident occurred at the end of June or in early July 1674. By July 29, Jolliet had made his way to Quebec. Frontenac lamented the loss of the journal and map, and he instructed Jolliet to write down his recollections. It was at this point that Jolliet constructed a map. Although some historians have concluded that the map *New Discovery of Several Nations in New France, in the year 1673 and 1674* (fig. 11), was made by Jolliet himself, Delanglez argues persuasively that it is in fact the work of an anonymous draftsperson and that the map actually drawn by Jolliet is lost.[31]

Fig. 12. *New Discovery of Several Nations in New France, in the year 1673 and 1674*, 1674 (detail). Library of Congress, Geography and Map Division, Louisiana: European Explorations and the Louisiana Purchase, https://www.loc.gov/resource/g3300.ct000655.

On this version of Jolliet's map, the Mississippi River is named the "Riviere Baude" in honor of Frontenac, whose family name was Baude. The Illinois River was called the "Riviere de la Divine, ou L'Outrelaise" as a compliment to Frontenac's wife—known as "La Divine" because of her beauty—and her friend Mademoiselle Outrelaise. In the detail (fig. 12), the Chicago Portage (labeled simply "Portage") along with "Mont Joliet" and the river flowing to the southeast at the southern end of Lake Michigan mentioned earlier are visible.

To supplement the map, Jolliet gave an oral account of the expedition to Dablon, which Dablon transcribed in his August 1, 1674, "Relation of the Discovery of the South Sea Accomplished by means of the Rivers of New France Transmitted from Quebec by Father Dablon, Superior General of the missions of the Society of Jesus."[32] The title notwithstanding, the expedition had not, of course, discovered a route to the South Sea. Jolliet attempted to finesse this point by asserting that it was likely that a way west could be found from a tributary or some other lake that was somehow connected to the Mississippi River. His next remark, however, presaged the actual importance of what they had found:

> The fourth remark concerns a very great and important advantage, which perhaps will hardly be believed. It is that we could go with facility to Florida in a bark, and by very easy navigation. It would only be necessary to make a canal, by cutting through but half a league of prairie, to pass from the foot of the lake of the Illinois [Lake Michigan] to the river Saint Louis [Illinois River]. Here is the route that would be followed: the bark would be built on lake Erie, which is near lake Ontario; it would easily pass from lake Erie to lake Huron, whence it would enter lake Illinois. At the end of that lake the canal or excavation of which I have spoken would be made, to gain a passage into the river Saint Louis, which falls into the Mississipi. The bark, when there, would easily sail to the gulf of Mexico.[33]

In these six sentences, Jolliet foretold the story of Chicago. The "canal or excavation" he suggested found its first form in the Illinois and Michigan Canal and was then fully realized by the Chicago Sanitary and Ship Canal. But even before these artificial waterways were created, the route traveled by Jolliet's expedition would give rise to a burgeoning trading center that eventually grew to become a great metropolis.

Marquette had not yet finished his work, and he was determined to make good on his promise to the Kaskaskia that he would return to their village to instruct them on Christianity. Before he was ready to make that second voyage, however, Marquette prepared materials, including a map, of the 1673 expedition that he sent to his superiors. The first account of what was purported to be Marquette's account of the expedition appeared in 1681 in Melchisédech Thevenot's *Recueil de voyages de Mr. Thevenot* (*Collection of the Voyages of Mr. Thevenot*).[34] This account was abbreviated, however, and the accompanying map was certainly not drawn by Marquette.

Thevenot's account was widely repeated and translated, but the open question was: On what sources had Thevenot relied? This question was answered in 1842 in Montreal when researchers found a manuscript entitled *Récit des voyages et des découvertes du R. Père Jacques Marquette de la Compagnie de Jesus, en l'année 1673 et aux suivantes* (*Story of the Voyages and Discoveries of Father Jacques Marquette of the Society of Jesus, in the Year 1673 and the Next*) among the papers of Father Felix Martin, president of the College of St. Mary.[35] The *Récit* was apparently the basis for the Thevenot account, although the map included in the *Récit* did not match the one published by Thevenot (fig. 13). The first English translation of the *Récit*, including the map purportedly drawn by Marquette, appeared in 1852 in John Gilmary Shea's *Discovery and Exploration of the Mississippi Valley: With the original narratives of Marquette, Allouez, Membré, Hennepin, and Anastase Douay* and later in 1900 in Reuben Gold Thwaites's *The Jesuit Relations and Allied Documents*.[36]

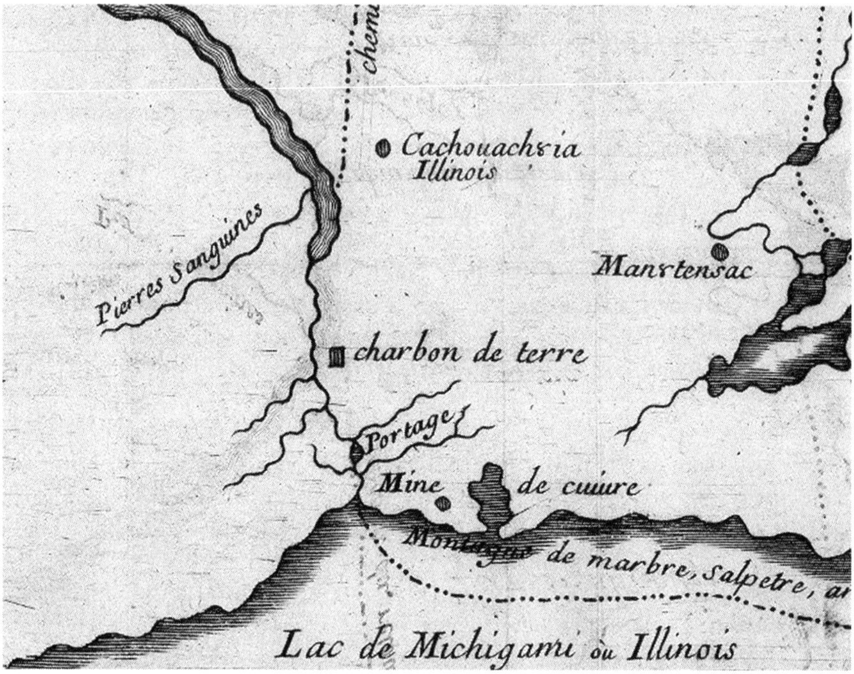

Fig. 13. Melchisédech Thévenot, attr., map of the Mississippi River, ca. 1681 (detail). https://commons.wikimedia.org/wiki/File:Marquette_and_jolliet_map_1681.jpg.

For many years, historians accepted as fact that the *Récit*, with the exception of a few missing pages that were known to have been added later, was the direct work of Marquette. In 1928, however, Steck argued that the account put forward as that of Marquette was in fact written by Dablon.[37] Steck even proposed that the account was based in part on Jolliet's journal that was believed to have been lost to fire in 1674.[38] In 1948, Delanglez agreed with Steck's conclusion that Dablon wrote the *Récit* but rejected Steck's hypothesis that it was based in part on Jolliet's journal. Delanglez thought it was more likely that Dablon had relied on a combination of his conversations with Jolliet; Dablon's August 1, 1674, letter; conversations with other explorers; and his own personal knowledge.[39] What is known for sure is that no account of the 1673 expedition is known to exist in Marquette's own handwriting.

The map is a different matter, and at least in its earliest form it is generally agreed that parts of the map included in the *Récit* are in Marquette's hand. Shea reproduced a facsimile of the map in 1852, and it is notable that Marquette shows the Chicago Portage route as a continuous line from the Illinois and Des Plaines Rivers to Lake Michigan. One possible explanation for this is that at the time the expedition crossed through the portage in late

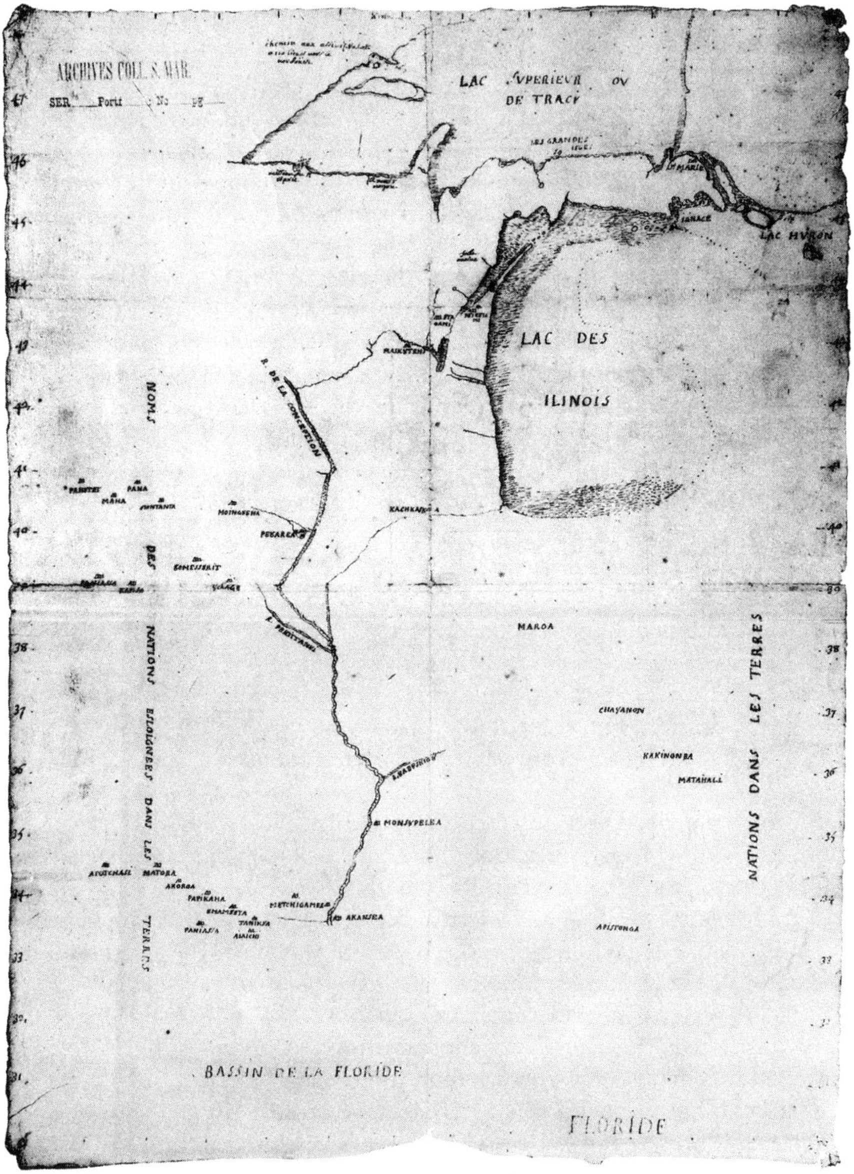

Fig. 14. Marquette map of the exploration of 1673. Illinois State Museum, Springfield.

summer 1673, it was at high water. It is also possible that the Marquette map began as the draft the expedition prepared prior to its departure in May 1673 and that Marquette then augmented the map with details as the expedition progressed (fig. 14).[40]

On October 25, 1674, Marquette set out with Porteret and Largilliers to keep his promise to the Kaskaskia.[41] They arrived back at the mouth of the Chicago River on December 12, and a few days later, they were at the Chicago Portage, where because of ice, bad weather, and Marquette's failing health, they decided to stay for the winter. They constructed some kind of shelter there, and thus began the first known sustained stay of Europeans at the site of the future city of Chicago. (The location of this camp was at the approximate location of where the current Damen Avenue crosses the Sanitary and Ship Canal.) Over the winter they were visited by two Frenchmen who were residing and trading near Kaskaskia. Marquette refers to them as "La Taupine and the surgeon." The former was Pierre Moreau, and the latter has never been identified by name. Both the Frenchmen and some local Illinois helped take care of Marquette through the long, hard winter.

Marquette's condition improved in February, but the ice persisted at the portage until late March. Marquette then encountered the vicissitudes of the portage that would be confirmed by many future travelers:

> On the 28th, the ice broke up, and stopped above us. On the 29th, the waters rose so high that we had barely time to decamp as fast as possible, putting our goods in the trees, and trying to sleep on a hillock. The water gained on us nearly all night, but there was a slight freeze, and the water fell a little, while we were near our packages. The barrier has just broken, the ice has drifted away; and, because the water is already rising, we are about to embark to continue our journey.[42]

Marquette arrived at Kaskaskia on April 10.[43] His health allowed only a short stay before his party began the long trip back to St. Ignace. They passed again through the Chicago Portage but this time crossed Lake Michigan and headed northward up its eastern shore. There Marquette's illness finally overcame him. He died on May 18, 1675, and was buried near present-day Ludington, Michigan. As an indication of the great respect he had earned among the Kaskaskia, two years later, on May 18, 1677, members of the tribe disinterred Marquette's remains and took them to St. Ignace, where Marquette's remains were reinterred on June 9, 1677.[44]

The next European known to cross the Chicago Portage was Claude Allouez, who was appointed after Marquette's death to continue the mission at Kaskaskia. Allouez left Green Bay with two companions in October 1676, but the weather closed in on them and they wintered until February 1677 with a local Potawatomi tribe. When they could finally continue their travels, they did so in a most unusual way. Instead of launching their canoe in water, they set out upon ice, using a sail and a favorable wind to continue their trip. They met other obstacles along the way, however, and it was not until late April that they "entered the river that leads to the Ilinois."[45] They were met there by a large group of Kaskaskia and continued on to their village, arriving on April 27. Allouez remained among the Kaskaskia for a short time, departing on his return trip via the Chicago Portage in early May. He returned again the next year with the intention of remaining for an extended period, but there is no record of this trip.[46]

The period of the next five years is significant, if obscure. France had attempted to regulate the fur trade since the days of Samuel de Champlain in the early 1600s, with varying degrees of success. In the 1670s, Talon had issued orders against illegal trading, and these efforts were furthered by Frontenac when he convinced Louis XIV to declare the death penalty for anyone trading without permission of the governor. Thus arose the *coureurs de bois*, who defied these laws and regulations and continued to trade illegally throughout the territory. While the official effort was to require the western tribes to bring their furs to Montreal, the *coureurs de bois* thwarted this effort by going straight to the source to trade with the tribes directly. Even worse, from the official French perspective, the *coureurs de bois* were more than happy to trade with the British because they got better prices for their goods from the British than from the French.

Frontenac, frustrated by the incursion of the *coureur de bois*, wanted to extend the official trade beyond the St. Lawrence to the western territories and so sought out explorers who shared his imperialistic ambitions. One such man was René-Robert Cavelier de La Salle. With Frontenac's blessing, La Salle constructed Fort Frontenac in 1673 for the express purpose of controlling the fur trade. La Salle was present at the fort during the years 1674–79, and during that time he made two trips to France to further his and Frontenac's interest in extending France's reach into the North American interior. It is possible that during this period La Salle also made trips to the west, perhaps as far as Illinois. Certainly, during his trip to France in 1677, La Salle displayed a considerable knowledge of the Midwest and was able to convince the court of the value of expanding French interests in the area. He arrived back in Quebec in 1678 with authorization to explore and settle the region. He also had a patent from the crown to conduct trade in the region south of the Great Lakes.

In September 1679, La Salle and fourteen men set out to make good on his grand vision. They made their way in four canoes from Green Bay down the western shore of Lake Michigan, passing the locations of the future cities of Milwaukee and Chicago. They rounded the lake's southern end and then headed up the eastern shore to the mouth of the St. Joseph River. At the same time, La Salle's lieutenant and friend, Henri de Tonty, took twenty men and headed down the eastern shore of Lake Michigan from Green Bay, also bound for the St. Joseph River. While waiting for Tonty to arrive, La Salle built a small fort near the mouth of the river and named it Fort Miami.[47]

After Tonty arrived on November 20, the combined party ascended the St. Joseph River to a portage that connected to the Kankakee River near the site of the current city of South Bend, Indiana. They then took the Kankakee

River to the Illinois River and on to Kaskaskia, and then on to Lake Peoria, where they encountered a village of the Illinois people. La Salle convinced the Illinois to allow the construction of a fort, and over the winter of 1679–80, La Salle's party built the first known permanent structure built by Europeans in Illinois. The Illinois people called the fort Checagou, while La Salle named it Fort Crevecoeur.[48]

In March 1680, La Salle left Tonty in charge of Fort Crevecoeur and returned to Montreal. While La Salle was in Montreal, Tonty left Fort Crevecoeur to establish another fort at Starved Rock. In Tonty's absence, the men at Fort Crevecoeur mutinied, burned down the fort, and deserted. Things then went from bad to worse for Tonty, now left with only five men, when the Iroquois, despite the nominal peace agreement between them and the French, attacked the village at Starved Rock in September 1680. Wounded during the attack, Tonty and his men escaped the siege and made their way back to Lake Michigan, this time following the Illinois River to the Des Plaines River and almost certainly crossing the Chicago Portage to reach the lake.[49] They made their way up the western shore of Lake Michigan and finally were taken in by a band of friendly Potawatomi south of Green Bay. They spent the winter of 1680–81 there and eventually made their way back to Mackinac in June 1681. La Salle, who had been in search of his friend, arrived shortly thereafter and, typical of this driven man, immediately began making plans for the excursion that would be his greatest achievement—traveling down the Mississippi River to its discharge point into the Gulf of Mexico.

By December 1681, both La Salle and Tonty had convened at Fort Miami, ready for their great expedition. It was a big group, totaling fifty-four persons, composed of twenty-three Frenchmen and thirty-one Native Americans from the Abenaki and Mohegan Tribes (eighteen men, ten women, and three children).[50] They set out in two groups, Tonty leaving on December 21 going "in canoes to the River Chicaou, where there is a portage which joins that of the Islinois."[51] The advance group camped at the Chicago Portage, where they waited for La Salle and his group. On New Year's Day 1682, La Salle arrived at the mouth of the Chicago River but was detained for a few days by the weather. He was finally able to join Tonty at the Chicago Portage on January 6. This was likely the first time La Salle had been at the site of the future city of Chicago, but it is possible that he might have come ashore in the vicinity during his trip down the western lake shore in 1679.[52]

With the exploring party assembled, it made ready to continue southward. As Tonty recounted, the waters at the portage and adjoining rivers were frozen, so the party "made sledges and dragged our baggage to a point thirty leagues below the village of the Islinois, and there, finding the navigation open, we arrived at the end of January at the River Mississipy."[53] The explorers entered the Mississippi River from the Illinois River on February 6, 1682, and headed south, reaching the Gulf of Mexico on April 9, 1682, thereby becoming the first Europeans known to have traveled the length of the Mississippi River from the north to its discharge into the Gulf of Mexico. La Salle proclaimed formal possession under the name "Louisiana" of all the territory even remotely connected to the Mississippi River, "from the Alleghenies to the Rocky Mountains; from the Rio Grande and the Gulf to the farthest springs of Missouri."[54]

The explorers then set out on their return trip. Early on, La Salle fell ill, so Tonty reluctantly went on without him, arriving back in Mackinac in July. La Salle recovered from his illness and finally arrived in Mackinac in September. From there La Salle sent Father Zenobe Membré to Paris to officially report to Louis XIV on the discovery of the Mississippi River.[55]

With the Mississippi valley now nominally in France's possession, La Salle sought to advance his grander plans of consolidating the fur trade in that area. A continuing obstacle to these plans was the enduring threat of more violence by the Iroquois, who were a constant menace to both other Native American tribes and Europeans throughout the valley and especially at its northern reaches around Kaskaskia and Starved Rock. Since the attack in 1680, there had been constant rumors of an impending Iroquois war. Frontenac moved to quiet the situation by calling together a great council in Montreal that was attended by delegates of the northwestern tribes. Frontenac gave permission to the tribes to defend themselves against the Iroquois but said that they should not initiate attacks against the Iroquois because he still hoped he could broker a lasting peace. Unfortunately, at this critical stage of negotiations, Frontenac was recalled to France and replaced as governor in October 1682 by Joseph-Antoine Le Fêbvre de La Barre. La Barre was woefully unprepared for the delicate diplomacy required and completely reversed Frontenac's approach, encouraging the northwestern tribes to attack the Iroquois and requesting more men and arms from the king so that the Iroquois could be subdued by force.[56] La Barre's approach threw the entire territory into disarray, and war with the Iroquois now seemed inevitable.

Accordingly, La Salle and Tonty set about preparing for the violence to come. La Salle had a grand vision for the Mississippi valley as a French colony and saw it as having vastly more potential than the northern settlements in New France. He possibly had this vision in mind when he and Tonty chose Starved Rock as the location for a new fort. La Salle envisioned the location as a future center of trade that could connect the Gulf of St. Lawrence and the Gulf of Mexico. He also saw it as a natural settlement that could bring together the northwestern tribes and French settlers. In the current circumstance, however, it was an ideal spot to act as a bulwark against the Iroquois and possible future incursions by the British settlers to the east who already were looking to the riches and resources of the west.

During the winter of 1682–83, La Salle and his men built a fort on the acre-wide top of Starved Rock, 125 feet above the water's edge and accessible only by a narrow pathway up the sheer face of the rock. They called the fort St. Louis in honor of the canonized French king Louis IX.[57] Over time,

Tonty and La Salle brought together four thousand warriors from numerous tribes to live there, the entire village surrounding the fort numbering twenty thousand people.[58]

While establishing Fort St. Louis as the primary point of defense, La Salle also sent men to build a fort at the Chicago Portage during the winter of 1682–83. Not nearly as substantial as Fort St. Louis, the portage outpost was a small house surrounded by a stockade. Although called Fort Checagou, it was never regularly garrisoned.[59] Other than the temporary hut that Marquette had constructed in the winter of 1674, this was the first structure built by Europeans at the Chicago Portage, and, as the early twentieth-century historian Milo Milton Quaife puts it, if "a sojourn of several months be regarded as establishing a residence, its builders, André Eno and Jean Filatreau, deserve remembrance as the first white residents of Chicago."[60] The establishment of this outpost emphasized the importance of the portage to La Salle's greater plan of colonizing the Mississippi valley because the portage provided the essential bridge between the Mississippi River and Lake Michigan.

La Salle had hoped to draw French settlers to Fort St. Louis, but his prospects foundered when Frontenac, his staunch supporter, was recalled to France and replaced by La Barre, who was hostile to La Salle's efforts. So great was La Barre's dislike of La Salle that the new governor determined to recall La Salle to Quebec and take possession of Fort St. Louis for himself. To accomplish this, he commissioned Olivier Morel de La Durantaye to summon La Salle to Quebec. Aware that the new governor spelled trouble for his future plans, La Salle wrote a letter in April 1683 appealing directly to La Barre, telling him that the Iroquois menace was growing and that he needed arms and ammunition to defend Fort St. Louis, and asking La Barre to allow settlers to come to the fort. La Salle sent Eno and Filatreau with this letter to Montreal in hopes of appeasing La Barre and obtaining the needed arms and ammunition.

In May came rumors that the anticipated aggression by the Iroquois had begun. La Salle moved quickly to gather the Miami from around St. Joseph who were preparing to flee the Iroquois and convinced them to come to Fort St. Louis. From the St. Joseph vicinity and southward, La Salle assembled about 4,500 Miami who made their way around the southern end of Lake Michigan and up the western coast. They arrived at the Chicago Portage in May and then by degrees made their way from the portage to Fort St. Louis.

La Salle stayed at Fort Checagou in May and June, which at the time was occupied by one of his men, Jacques Cauchois, and a Native American whose name is unknown. While there, La Salle wrote a second letter to La Barre, dated June 4, beginning with the note "Du portage de Checagou 4 juin, 1683." This was probably the first document wholly written at the portage, and in it La Salle reiterated the need for men, supplies, and especially arms and ammunition. Although largely deferential, La Salle could not at one point refrain from admonishing La Barre:

> Monsieur, it is in vain that we risk our lives here and that I exhaust myself to fulfill the wishes of His Majesty, if, at the settlements below, all the measures are thwarted which I take to procure success, and if on far fetched pretexts those are kept back who go to obtain the supplies without which we cannot defend ourselves. It is useless for the King to permit me to build forts and to do what is necessary for the accomplishment of my design, if I am prevented from bringing arms, powder and lead here.[61]

La Salle gave the letter to Cauchois, who traveled to Quebec to deliver it to La Barre. The latter did nothing in response to aid La Salle—indeed, La Barre even gloated over being able to detain La Salle's men from returning to Fort St. Louis. La Barre was so roused by his dislike of La Salle that he claimed the discovery of the Mississippi River to be a lie and eventually dispatched Morel de La Durantaye and his lieutenant, the chevalier Louis Henri de Baugy, with orders that La Salle was to immediately vacate the West and return to Quebec.

Morel de La Durantaye and de Baugy left Quebec in April 1683 and arrived at the foot of Green Bay in late summer. At that point Morel de La Durantaye stayed at the mission there and de Baugy set out for Fort St. Louis, doubtless by way of the Chicago Portage.[62] In the meantime, La Salle had determined that help was not forthcoming from La Barre, so he decided to take his case directly to Louis XIV in France. He set out from Fort St. Louis in late August and headed up the Illinois River toward the Chicago Portage. He was about thirty-four miles from the fort when he encountered a party coming downstream—it was de Baugy, who delivered the harsh commands from La Barre. La Salle's worst fears were realized, but he nonetheless treated de Baugy courteously and even gave him letters of introduction to Tonty wherein La Salle instructed Tonty to welcome de Baugy.

La Salle continued to the Chicago Portage and there wrote a letter "at Checagou" dated September 1, 1683, to the inhabitants of Fort St. Louis. In the letter La Salle expressed his gratitude for their fidelity and assured them that he was confident that Louis XIV would do right by them. He said he would return in the spring and that in the meantime they should obey La Barre, even if he ordered them to leave the fort. He dispatched the letter to his faithful followers and set sail for France.[63] He never returned to Illinois.

While La Salle was at the Chicago Portage in late 1683, he wrote the most detailed description of the portage to that point. In it he differed from Jolliet as to the relative ease by which the Chicago Portage could be traversed. Their differences had much to do with the water levels that prevailed at the time of their passing. We can see from the Jolliet and Marquette maps of the 1673 expedition, and their accompanying accounts, that the portage was almost a continuous water route when they came through. Marquette's map shows a continuous line from the Des Plaines River to Lake Michigan, while Jolliet's more accurately shows a narrowing stream through the portage. On his second trip through the portage, Marquette experienced first ice and then high waters. So, their experiences of the portage were based on it being a mostly water route, which made crossing it by canoe relatively easy. This ease of passage possibly influenced Jolliet's prescient remark concerning the viability of digging a canal to connect the Chicago River and the Des Plaines River.

La Salle's impression of the Chicago Portage was quite different from that of Jolliet and Marquette because La Salle had passed through the portage several times during different seasons and was aware of how the water levels fluctuated significantly during the year. He also was very familiar with the St. Joseph River–Kankakee River–Illinois River route, which he personally preferred over that of the Chicago Portage. In 1680, La Salle pointed out that goods brought to "Checagou" in larger vessels would have to be reloaded onto canoes because in summer only canoes could navigate the Des Plaines River for a distance of about forty leagues (a French league in La Salle's period was about 2.4 statute miles).[64] This assessment ran contrary to Jolliet's claim that there was only a quarter of a league interruption before reaching open water.[65] La Salle's report is the first recorded use of the place-name Chicago. His spelling as "Checagou" was a mistaken French translation of a Miami-Illinois word used to designate the portage between Lake Michigan and the Illinois River. The word referred to the wild garlic that was abundant in the area.[66]

La Salle returned to his description of the Chicago Portage in 1683 and extended his opinion about its efficacy as a trade route:

> There is an isthmus which is at 41 degrees 50 minutes elevation from the pole on the west of the Lake of the Illinois [Lake Michigan], where one goes by a channel [main portion and south branch of the Chicago River] formed by the juncture of several small streams or gullies of the prairie. It is navigable about two leagues to the edge of this prairie at a quarter of a league distant towards the west. There is a little lake [Mud Lake] which is divided in two by a beaver dam, about a league and a half from which there runs a stream, which after having twined in and out about half a league across the rushes, falls in to the Chicago river [Des Plaines River], and from there into the river of the Illinois. When this lake is full, either from great rains in summer, or from the floods of the spring, it is discharged also into this channel which leads to the Lake of the Illinois, whose surface is seven feet lower than the prairie where is situated this lake. The River of Chicago does the same in the springtime when its channel is full. It discharges by this little lake a part of its waters into the River of the Illinois, and at this time should one make a little canal of a quarter of a league, says Joliet, from the lake to the basin which leads to the Illinois river ships could in the summer enter into the river and descend

> to the sea. That might perhaps happen in the springtime, but not in the summer, because there is not enough water in the river as far down as Fort St. Louis where the navigation of the Illinois river begins at this season and extends as far as the sea. It is true that there is still another difficulty which this ditch which one would make could not remedy. It is this: The lake of the Illinois always forms a sandbank at the entrance of the channel which leads to it. I doubt very much, in spite of what anyone says, whether this could be cleaned out or cleared away by the force of the current of the Chicago river when it was made to flow therein, since much greater currents in the same lake cannot do it. Moreover, the utility of a canal would not be very great, for I doubt when everything should succeed if a boat could overcome the great floods which the currents cause in the Chicago in the springtime. These are much heavier than those of the Rhône [river in France]. Again, navigation would be for only a short time, at most for 15 or 20 days in the year, after which there is no longer any water. What confirms me still further in the thought that the Chicago river could not clean the mouth of the canal, is that when the lake is filled with ice, it blocks up the most navigable mouths at this time, and when ice is formed there is no longer water in the Chicago river to hinder blocking this canal with sand. Also I would not have made mention of this way of communication, if Joliet had not proposed it without sufficiently examining the difficulties.[67]

La Salle concluded, contrary to Jolliet, that the Des Plaines River was not navigable even for canoes in times of low water. He believed that "it would be easier to transport by land the goods from Fort St. Louis to the lake, making use of horses which it is easy to procure there."[68]

It is possible that La Salle's disagreement with Jolliet about the best trade route was also based on personal interests. La Salle had been granted a patent to carry out trade in the region south of the Great Lakes and was not permitted to carry out trade north of that area. It was thus in his interest to cultivate trade routes south down the Mississippi River rather than dwell on a canal that directed trade northward toward the St. Lawrence. It is also possible that the disagreement was more of a political nature. There were two competing interests in New France politics. On the one hand was the Jesuit faction, which had a very large following among the merchants who were engaged in the fur trade. Jolliet was closely aligned with this faction. On the other hand were those who wanted to open up a new region for the fur trade south of the Great Lakes. La Salle and Frontenac represented these interests. Add to the political ramifications La Salle's general dislike of the Jesuits (it was mutual), and there were ample reasons for him to part company with Jolliet's views.[69]

The winter of 1683–84 at Fort St. Louis was a tense one, with Tonty and de Baugy at odds. By spring the Iroquois, who had been threatening since the previous year, finally decided to attack Fort St. Louis, in part because they believed La Barre would not come to the aid of the fort owing to his enmity for La Salle. Tonty and de Baugy learned of the approaching war party on March 20, 1684, and sent a canoe to Mackinac asking Morel de La Durantaye for reinforcements. The next day began a six-day siege, with the Iroquois at times trying to storm the fort. But they were no match for the trained soldiers within the fort led by Tonty and de Baugy, who put aside their differences and fought side by side to repulse the attack. Defeated, the Iroquois made do with capturing some of the surrounding village's inhabitants from other tribes who had not been able to take shelter within the fort, but even these prisoners escaped and made their way back to safety. The Iroquois in turn were pursued by war parties from members of the tribes at the fort, leading to further casualties for the Iroquois.[70]

Morel de La Durantaye did not arrive at Fort St. Louis until May 21. He led a group of sixty Frenchmen, supposedly to help in repelling the Iroquois, who had been defeated two months prior. Morel de La Durantaye's real purpose was to deliver orders from La Barre that Tonty was to leave Fort St. Louis and turn sole command of the fort over to de Baugy. Mindful of La Salle's orders to obey the governor no matter what, Tonty acquiesced and left the fort to make his way to Quebec. His distasteful work at Fort St. Louis concluded, Morel de La Durantaye went to the Chicago Portage, where he rebuilt and enlarged Fort Checagou and left there a garrison that remained for several years.[71]

In 1684, La Barre embarked on a plan that would lead to his being recalled in disgrace to France. Throughout the early parts of the year, La Barre had his representatives work to build a coalition of the western tribes that he was determined to use to vanquish the Iroquois once and for all. This became the first war party of Native Americans to traverse the Great Lakes at the direction of Europeans. At the same time, La Barre made the mistake of contacting the British governor of New York to ask him to stop providing the Iroquois with weapons. The governor promptly warned the Iroquois of the coming offensive and sold them even more weapons than usual. La Barre's forces never got beyond the eastern end of Lake Ontario where, with most of his men sick, he signed a peace treaty with the Iroquois that basically wrote off the western territory in exchange for promises from the Iroquois that the St. Lawrence region would be free from attack. Upon hearing of La Barre's misadventure, King Louis XIV immediately recalled him, and in August 1685, the new governor, the Marquis de Denonville, took his place.

Meanwhile, La Salle was in France, where he successfully made his case to Louis XIV for the colonization of the Mississippi valley. In April and again in July 1684, the king wrote La Barre directly, ordering him to restore all properties that had been taken from La Salle and appointing La Salle commandant of the entire region from Fort St. Louis down the Mississippi River to Mexico. At the same time, Tonty was appointed governor of Fort St. Louis.

It was probably with some measure of vindication that Tonty arrived back at the fort in June 1685 and reclaimed his command from de Baugy.[72]

During de Baugy's tenure, relationships between the Miami and Illinois had deteriorated, and it took Tonty considerable effort and expense to resolve the difficulties. During the summer, rumors reached Fort St. Louis that La Salle had shipwrecked in Florida and was in need of help. Tonty resolved to go to Mackinac to get more information on his friend. Tonty arrived at Mackinac in the autumn, where he learned that La Barre had been replaced by Denonville. He also received there a letter from Denonville asking Tonty to report to him so they could discuss how to handle the ongoing difficulties with the Iroquois. Denonville also relayed that La Salle had gone by sea in search of the mouth of the Mississippi River.[73] Tonty decided he would first go to the aid of La Salle and then retrace his steps to report to Denonville. Tonty left Mackinac on November 30, 1685, but ice impeded his way by water and he and his companions were forced to complete the journey by land, finally arriving "at the Fort of Chicacou, where M. de La Durantaye commanded."[74]

It is not clear whether Tonty's reference to the "Fort of Chicacou" refers to the original "fort" that La Salle's men built in the winter of 1682–83 and that was rebuilt and enlarged by Morel de La Durantaye in 1684 or if it was an entirely new structure built by the Jesuits. In addition to the fort commanded by Morel de La Durantaye, a separate fort was also present in the vicinity of the Chicago Portage that was built during the summer of 1685. When La Salle and Tonty were reinstated as being in control of Fort St. Louis and the Mississippi Valley, the Jesuits, who were largely opposed to La Salle's efforts, decided to move their headquarters for the Illinois country to the vicinity of the Chicago Portage, again recognizing the portage as the primary route to the west.[75] The Jesuit opposition to La Salle's efforts was so deep that some even advocated for destroying Fort St. Louis as a way of breaking La Salle's relationship with the tribes that had settled there.[76] In any event, the Jesuits built a fort near the mouth of the Chicago River in 1685. Allouez was successful in wooing some of the Miami from Fort St. Louis to the new settlement at Chicago. Jean-Baptiste-Louis Franquelin's map of 1684 shows a settlement of eighty Miami warriors, situated just west of the fork of the two branches (fig. 15), and Edward G. Mason estimates that the total population might have been as high as four hundred people.[77]

According to Mason, other tribes were also persuaded to move to the vicinity of the new fort, and, pursuant to an order from La Barre, Morel de La Durantaye was placed in command. So, it is possible that Tonty's reference was to this fort and not the smaller structure first built in 1682–83. Quaife, however, maintains that Tonty was mistaken in saying that he arrived at Fort Chicacou but rather arrived at Fort Miami in St. Joseph and that Morel de La Durantaye was in command there, not Chicago.[78] Quaife's basic argument is that (1) Tonty would not have taken the route along the western coast of Lake Michigan in November but would have instead gone down the eastern

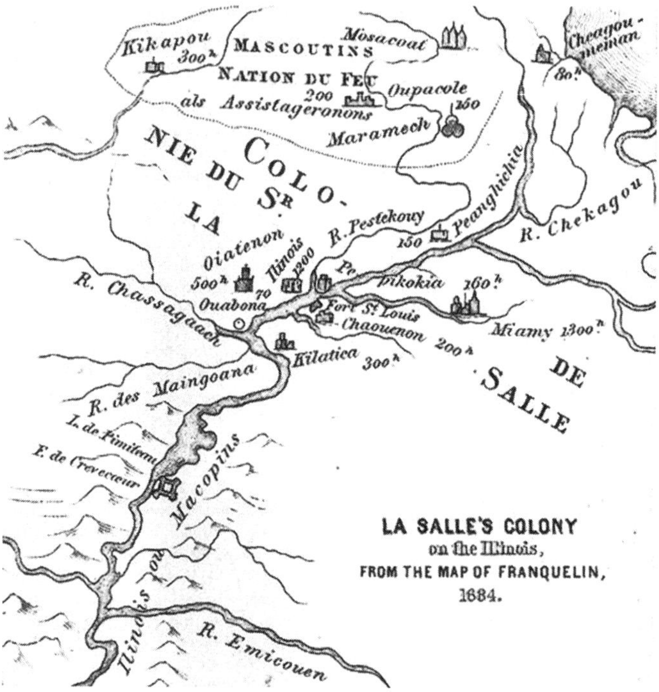

Fig. 15. Detail of Jean-Baptiste-Louis Franquelin's 1684 map showing La Salle's colony on the Illinois. Illinois State Museum, Springfield.

coast to St. Louis, (2) Tonty makes reference to traveling 120 leagues before having to set off on foot, and that distance doesn't comport with a trip down the western coast, and (3) Henri de Joutel does not mention a fort at Chicago during his two visits there.

Conversely, Quaife himself reports the construction of the first "fort" at the Chicago Portage in 1682–83 but does not consider it a proper "fort" because of its size and lack of regular garrisoning.[79] Joutel reports a Jesuit outpost at Chicago in 1685. On not only his 1684 map (fig. 15) but also his 1685 map (fig. 16), Franquelin shows "Checagou" on the west bank of the South Branch Chicago River. His map of 1688 (fig. 17), however, clearly depicts "Fort Chécagou" on the east bank of the South Branch nearer the mouth of the Chicago River—this was likely the structure built by the Jesuits.

Quaife's conclusion that no "fort" stood at Chicago in 1685 or earlier seems more a matter of semantics than fact. Indeed, a document from 1723 prepared by Alphonse de Tonty and other heirs of Henri de Tonty specifically refers to private expenditures made by Tonty "in the construction of the forts Pimitouy, The Rock, and Checagou."[80] The reference to "Checagou" is likely to the structure built in 1682–83 because Tonty was not building

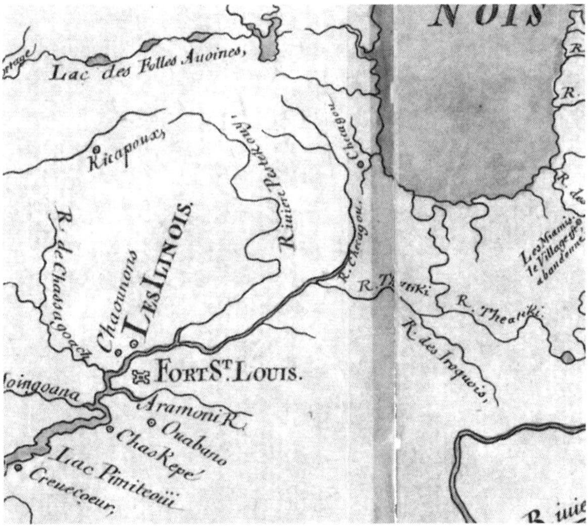

Fig. 16. Detail of a map of New France showing the location of "Checagou." Jean-Baptiste-Louis Franquelin, *Amérique septentrion.lle [i.e. septentrionale]: Composée, corigée, et augmētée, sur les iournaux, mémoires, et observations les plus justes qui en ón' etes.tes en l'année 1685 & 1686, par plusieurs particuliés*, 1685 (detail). Library of Congress, Geography and Map Division, https://www.loc.gov/item/2002622263/.

Fig. 17. Detail of a map of New France showing "Fort Chécagou." Jean-Baptiste-Louis Franquelin, *Carte de l'Amerique Septentrionnale: Depuis le 25, jusqu'au 65° deg. de latt. & environ 140, & 235 deg. de longitude*, 1688 (detail). Library of Congress, Geography and Map Division, https://www.loc.gov/resource/g3300.ct000668/.

forts in the Chicago area after that.[81] As for Joutel not making a reference to a "fort" in 1687, he does reference a "post" at Chicago at that time.[82] There is also no support for the claim that Morel de La Durantaye was ever in command of Fort Miami in St. Joseph. So it does seem that there were at least two structures, whether or not one deems them worthy of being called "forts," in Chicago in the seventeenth century, the first built in 1682–83 and then rebuilt and enlarged by Morel de La Durantaye in 1684, and a second structure built by the Jesuits in the summer of 1685. The first structure was at the Chicago Portage and the second near the mouth of the Chicago River. As a final point regarding this latter structure, the Treaty of Greenville makes specific mention of "One piece of land six miles square, at the mouth of the Chicago River, emptying into the southwest end of lake Michigan, where a fort formerly stood."[83]

Throughout 1686 Tonty made excursions looking for La Salle. Finally giving up hope of finding his friend, he made his way to Montreal to meet with Denonville. During the year Tonty had traveled more than five thousand miles by foot and canoe, twice traversing the continent between the Gulf of Mexico and the lower St. Lawrence. After conferring with Denonville and agreeing on a plan to once and for all deal with the Iroquois menace, Tonty returned to Fort St. Louis. The following year an army of regular troops from France, a group of soldiers and traders from New France, and Native Americans from the western tribes amassed and attacked and defeated the Seneca, one of the tribes of the Iroquois. This attack failed to win the peace, however, and only led to further attacks of retribution by the remaining Iroquois.

Tonty had no way of knowing that while he was preparing for war with the Iroquois, La Salle had been murdered in Texas by fellow explorers. Following La Salle's death, a small group from his party made their way north to Fort St. Louis. The group included the Abbé Cavelier (La Salle's elder brother), Colin Cavelier (La Salle's nephew), Father Anastase Douay, a mariner named Teissier, and Henri de Joutel. The group arrived at Fort St. Louis in mid-September 1687. They had agreed among themselves, primarily at the behest of the Abbé Cavelier, to keep La Salle's death a secret until the group had returned to France.

Also at Fort St. Louis at this time was Allouez, who had taken ill. He was quite agitated to hear that La Salle might soon appear at the fort and discover the efforts of Allouez and the Jesuits to undermine his efforts to colonize the Mississippi valley. It was at this time that Allouez told Joutel of the Jesuit fort at Chicago. Because of the dark secret they kept, Joutel and the others were eager to make their way to Quebec so they might sail to France. They stayed at the fort only three days before leaving on September 18, bound for the Chicago Portage. It took them a week to get to the portage, and then storms kept them encamped there for another eight days before they finally set out on Lake Michigan. The weather and waves, however, were too much for them, and they were forced to return to the portage, where they made a cache of their belongings, stored their canoe on an elevated platform, and then returned to Fort St. Louis.[84]

Tonty arrived back at Fort St. Louis from the war with the Iroquois on October 27, 1687, and throughout the fall and winter of 1687–88, the Abbé Cavelier and his men persisted in their lie that La Salle was still alive. Eager to leave before word to the contrary reached the fort, they pushed on as soon as possible when the weather improved, leaving Fort St. Louis on March 21, 1688. Because of the swift current, the party had to wade in the water and pull their canoes much of the way, and Joutel injured his foot. He would later say that he suffered more on that trip than at any other time in his travels. They finally arrived at the Chicago Portage eight days later to find that their belongings had been pillaged and that only Native Americans were present at the post, the French garrison of Fort Checagou apparently not having returned from the campaign against the Iroquois. Once again weather detained Joutel's party. The group was poorly prepared, and they were especially short on provisions. Fortunately, according to Joutel, "Providence provided us with a kind of manna" in the form of maple sap, which they boiled and added to their cornmeal.[85] It was not until April 8 that they were finally able to depart. This time their trip north was successful, and they made their way to Quebec and set sail for France on October 9, 1688. When they arrived, the Abbé Cavelier made his way to Paris to reveal the death of La Salle. Tonty finally learned the truth about La Salle's death in September 1688 when Jean Couture and two Native Americans arrived at Fort St. Louis with the tragic news.[86]

Joutel later wrote a detailed description of the area from Fort St. Louis to the Chicago Portage, and he correctly identified the continental divide:

> We [Joutel and the Abbé Cavlier] continued to travel until Thursday the 25th [of March 1687] when we arrived at the place called Chicagou, which according to what we were told, took its name from the quantity of garlic which grows in the woods in that region. There is there a little river which is formed of the waters that drain from a great prairie or field at this place, and which takes its course towards the lake named, as I have said elsewhere, Illinois or Michigan. About three or four leagues away on the other side of the great prairie, the waters discharge into the Illinois river and form that. It seems that this place must be the highest between the Gulf of Mexico and St. Lawrence river, since the waters flow from that place in one and the other direction, so that the higher they are the less distance must be portaged, for in navigation of this kind, the canoe or boat must be carried, as well as the clothing; there is no way of escaping that task.[87]

Like Jolliet before him, Joutel also recognized the potential for creating a canal at the Chicago Portage, noting that it would "be easy to make a junction of these two rivers."[88]

By 1689, the eastern half of the Mississippi valley had become an integral part of France's empire in North America. The western regions had been explored and mapped, and forts, outposts, and missions had been established. The French had successfully negotiated peaceful relations between many of the western tribes and the European settlers and traders. And the Chicago Portage route had become the preferred gateway connecting the Gulf of Mexico and the St. Lawrence River—all because in 1673 Native Americans had shown Jolliet and Marquette the Chicago Portage.

Despite this initial success, the French hegemony over the fur trade soon faced serious challenges. The latter part of the seventeenth century was marred by persistent attacks by the Iroquois and increasing conflict with the British, who more and more longed for the resources and riches of the western territories. Frontenac returned to Quebec for his second term as governor in October 1689 and was faced with turmoil spreading from the colony to the western frontiers. The Chicago Portage remained a major point of concern, with Sieur de Mantet commanding at Fort Checagou to keep an eye on the Miami who resided there. The Miami were known to have ties with the western Iroquois, who loathed the French, and also to have leanings toward trading with the British.[89] The pressure from the British was exacerbated when war was declared between France and England (King William's War, 1689–97) that extended to the North American continent.

From 1690 to 1693, the situation in the Midwest became so perilous for European traders that the fur trade was suspended. During that time, not a single trading canoe made its way to Montreal. In 1693 Frontenac sent word to Fort St. Louis that it was essential to restore the trade route, and the intrepid Tonty and Perrot put together a flotilla of canoes to bring the much-needed trade to Montreal. This effort reopened the fur trade for a while, but then came devastating news that on May 21, 1696, King Louis XIV had issued an edict revoking all trading licenses and prohibiting colonists from transporting any goods to the western territories.[90] With this action, the western territories were in effect handed over to the missionaries, who were the only ones allowed to remain legally under the terms of the edict.

This edict was nominally an attempt by the king to drive up the price of beaver furs by limiting their supply. But it also reflected a deep and ongoing rift in the political situation of New France that divided into two main factions. On the one hand were imperialists like Frontenac and La Salle, who saw the western territories as ripe for colonial expansion. On the other hand were the Jesuits, who had long opposed imperialistic designs and instead focused on their desire to convert the Indigenous peoples to Christianity. The Jesuits also saw the fur trade as fostering wanton and reckless conduct among traders and tribes alike and were especially affronted by the degree to which the latter were being exposed to alcohol. This political divide continued for as long as the French attempted to exert their influence in the western territories.

Frontenac tried to lessen the impact of the edict by delaying its enforcement, but by 1698 all of the western outposts, including Fort Checagou, were abandoned, and French trade in the western territories withered. Only Fort St. Louis was granted an exception because of the long and singular service of Tonty, but even he was put under such constraints that his trading efforts became unprofitable, and he left Fort St. Louis in 1698. Frontenac died on November 28, 1698, having initiated a process that eventually led to a peace treaty with the Iroquois and western tribes that was finalized by Frontenac's successor, Louis-Hector de Callière, in 1701. But even with success in achieving the long-sought peace, the era of French expansion in the west was largely over.

In 1696, Father François Pinet traveled from Mackinac to Chicago to minister to the Miami who had settled there in 1687. Because of the Miami settlements and the traffic that regularly traveled through the Chicago Portage, Pinet decided to establish the Mission of the Guardian Angel at Chicago. Although the mission's exact location has been debated, it was possibly a small house on the North Branch Chicago River. Pinet had barely begun his work when he was ordered by Frontenac to abandon the mission. Pinet obeyed but promptly appealed to Bishop François-Xavier de Montmorency Laval, and through Laval's intervention Pinet was allowed to return in 1698.

Later that year an interesting group visited the Chicago Portage. Before coming to New France in June 1658 as its first Roman Catholic bishop, Laval had founded a seminary to train priests and missionaries. Although the Jesuits had already established their presence in the upper Mississippi valley, Laval was determined to send missionaries to the lower Mississippi valley, where he envisioned a vast population ready for salvation. His goal was finally realized in the summer of 1698 when he sent forth three of his seminary priests to minister to the tribes in the lower Mississippi valley. The group was led by François Jolliet de Montigny, and he was joined by Father Antoine Davion and Father Jean-François Buisson de St.-Cosme. Luckily for them, they met Tonty when they were in Mackinac preparing for their trip and he agreed to accompany them in their travels.

They left in early September 1698, skirted the western shore of Lake Michigan, and arrived in Chicago in late October. They were welcomed there by Pinet, with whom they stayed a few days before making their way through the Chicago Portage. St.-Cosme left a detailed description of his travels down the western shore of Lake Michigan, his time in Chicago, and the group's passage through the Chicago Portage.

Of the mission established by Pinet, St.-Cosme reported:

> Their house is built on the bank of a small river, with the lake on one side and a fine and vast prairie on the other. The village of the savages contains over a hundred and fifty cabins, and a league up the river is still another village almost as large. They are all Miamis. Reverend

> Father Pinet usually resides there except in winter, when the savages are all engaged in hunting, and then he goes to the Illinois. We saw no savages there; they had already started for their hunt.[91]

According to Quaife, Pinet followed this pattern of staying in Chicago during the summer when the Miami were there and then wintering in Peoria. Quaife wryly concludes that Pinet was Chicago's first regular commuter.[92] Pinet left the mission in 1700 or 1701 to minister to the tribes around St. Louis. The mission was continued for a year or two after that by Father Jean Mermet and then closed.

As to their crossing through the portage in late October 1698, St.-Cosme says:

> We started from Chikagou on the 29th, and slept about two leagues from it on the little river [South Fork Chicago River] that afterward loses itself in the prairies. On the following day we began the portage, which is about three leagues in length when the waters are low, and is only one-fourth of a league in the spring, for then one can embark on a small lake [Mud Lake] that discharges into a branch of the river of the Illinois [Des Plaines River], and when the waters are low a portage has to be made to that branch.[93]

At this point, St.-Cosme says that they had only portaged half of their supplies when they realized that a young boy who was traveling with them had gone missing. Days were lost as the party, along with the priest at the mission and "some Frenchmen who were at Chikagou,"[94] searched for the boy. (The boy eventually found his way back to the mission at Chicago thirteen days later.) Of note in St.-Cosme's telling is the reference to the Frenchmen. It suggests that Louis XIV's edict had not succeeded in driving all the French traders and hunters from the region and that the Chicago Portage remained the epicenter of travel from the Mississippi valley to Lake Michigan and beyond.

One final document concerning the Chicago Portage comes by way of Father Jacques Gravier, who was present with Pinet at the Mission of the Guardian Angel in 1700. In a letter to Father Jacques de Lamberville dated February 16, 1701, and "sent from Fort Mississippi, 17 leagues from its discharge into the Mexican Gulf or sea," Father Gravier writes, "I received on my return from Michilimachinack the letter that you did me the honor of writing to me by way of the Mississippy, addressed to Father Aveneau, who sent it to me at Chikagoua—whence I started in 1700, on the 8th of September, to come here."[95] Although not conclusive, this letter suggests that Father Gravier and other Jesuits regularly used the Chicago Portage route to reach their missions along the Mississippi River.

The conclusion of the Iroquois wars brought a respite to the western territories. But the combined effect of the wars, the French edict against trade, and Jesuit resistance had more or less emptied the territories of outsider trade and inspiration. The European explorers who had opened and mapped the wilderness were gone, and European visions of empire and salvation waned. With peace came a void of outsiders and interest, and the "heroic epoch when great discoveries and great adventures occurred was over."[96]

4

The Eighteenth-Century Background

As the eighteenth century dawned, the western regions of New France were in disarray. With the legal French traders, hunters, and officially sanctioned soldiers and garrisons withdrawn, intertribal attacks once again increased. The Iroquois, although nominally restrained by the peace of 1701, continued to play the French against the British, constantly stirring discord wherever possible. The vacuum that had been feared by Frontenac and the imperialists with the enforcement of the French king Louis XIV's edict of 1696 materialized, and attempts to direct trade directly to Montreal were hampered by the continued presence of the illegal fur traders known as the *coureurs de bois* (runners of the woods) who continued to trade directly with the western tribes.

Facing this dismal reality, the officials of New France, many of whom still clung to Frontenac's vision of a thriving colony in the the Midwest and Mississippi Valley, devised a new plan that they hoped would remain out of reach of bureaucrats in France. No longer able to spread French influence widely across the territory, they decided instead to focus their efforts on developing two or three major strategic centers. The idea was to place significant military strength at these points to counteract British incursions into the region, while also making them safe and welcoming settlements for French colonists and members of allied Native American tribes.

To further this plan, three locations were selected and some of the most exceptional talents of New France were enlisted. The first step was the founding of a French colony in Louisiana to safeguard the mouth of the Mississippi River south of present-day New Orleans. For this task, Pierre Le Moyne, Sieur d'Iberville, was selected. He sailed for the Gulf of Mexico in 1699 and barely arrived in time to claim Louisiana for the French ahead of a British excursion attempting to do the same for England. A similar race was on for Detroit, the second target, and in 1701 Antoine Laumet de La Mothe, Sieur de Cadillac, along with Henri de Tonty's younger brother Alphonse, established a post and colony there just as the British were contemplating the same move. Tonty and his partner François Dauphin de La Forest completed the trifecta as they reasserted French claims on the forts at Lake Peoria, Fort St. Louis, and Chicago. Thus, as Phelps Kellogg concludes, at the start of the eighteenth century, the French had laid claim to the "keys to the interior of North America—the three great centers of modern American life: New Orleans, Detroit, and Chicago."[1]

On October 13, 1697, the intendant of New France, Jean Bochart de Champigny, Sieur de Noroy et de Verneuil, wrote to Louis XIV that Tonty and La Forest had a warehouse at Chicago and that Champigny was concerned they were carrying on illegal fur trading with the local tribespeople.[2] Champigny also noted that Tonty's cousin, Pierre-Charles de Liette, was in command at Chicago.[3]

As regards de Liette, Quaife puts him at Chicago helping La Forest run the trading business that Tonty and La Forest had assumed after La Salle's death. Quaife says de Liette spent four years at Chicago "among the Miami" from 1698 to 1702.[4] In his memoir, de Liette refers to the Illinois country as the "finest that is known anywhere between the St. Lawrence River and that of the Mississippi." He also gives a detailed description of the Chicago Portage:

> The Chicago is a little river only two leagues long bordered by prairies of equal width. This is the route usually taken to go to this country. At this river a portage is made, of a quarter of a league in low water and of an arpent [approximately 193 feet] in high water. A tiny stream half a league long issues from two little lakes that extend a league and a half, at the end of which, on the rising ground at this point, a short portage simply of one's baggage is made. When the water is favorable you re-embark at once, but when it is low you must carry it a league.
>
> This is called the Portage of the Oaks; and it requires much effort to propel the boat in this streamlet, which empties into the river which the French call the Illinois [Des Plaines River]. However, this is not the Illinois, as we only come to that stream twenty leagues farther on. The passage is very difficult on account of the low waters which render this river virtually impracticable, since travellers ordinarily reach this region only in summer or autumn. There are ten places where for half a league it is necessary to take out half of the baggage, and very often to remove it entirely, until the deep water is reached. Sometimes you are also compelled to carry the canoe.[5]

Like La Salle, de Liette, through his tenure at the portage, was able to see how conditions such as water depth and the length of portage varied depending on the season.

As part of the effort to consolidate French power, the French also attempted to force various tribes from their traditional locations to new ones chosen by the French. These efforts met with varying degrees of success, but by the early part of the eighteenth century, the Illinois and Miami had left the area around the Chicago Portage. The Potawatomi had taken their place, moving south from their earlier location in what is now southern Wisconsin. This artificial reorganization of the tribes did not bode well, and conflicts inevitably arose. In 1706, Father Jacques Gravier, who had served with François Pinet at the mission in Chicago and had succeeded Claude Allouez as head of the mission to the Illinois, was gravely wounded by a member of the Peoria Tribe. Tensions were so bad that the Chicago Portage route once again became unsafe, and it was largely abandoned as a trade route by the few French traders still in operation.[6]

Although travel by the French through the Chicago Portage was dramatically curtailed, one exception is notable. Joseph Kellogg was a boy of twelve when he was captured in 1704 by Mohawks during a raid on Deerfield, Massachusetts, during Queen Anne's War. He remained with the tribe for a year before being turned over to the French, with whom he stayed the next ten years. During that period, he traveled and traded alongside the French and became accomplished at Native American languages and dialects. In 1710, along with six Frenchmen, he was part of a trading expedition to the Mississippi River, thereby becoming the first known North American–born white New Englander to see that river. To reach the Mississippi River, the party used the Chicago Portage route where, according to Kellogg's account, they

> carried their canoos over Land a full League to a branch of the River Hinois, and this is called the Chigaquea.
>
> About the head of the River Hinois are fine large Savannahs or meadows of forty miles in Length some of the richest Land the world affords. This River Hinois is one of the great Rivers that falls into Mifsisippi and runs a Course of one hundred &thirty Leagues before it empties itself into Mifsisippi. Into this River Hinois comes the River Miamis or St. Joseph, as the French call it, ifsuing from the Lake Hinois.[7]

In his account, like those of previous explorers, Kellogg goes on at length about the natural beauty and abundance of the area, "some of the richest Land the world affords."[8]

In addition to the friction caused by attempts to relocate Native American tribes to satisfy French interests, another serious conflict arose in the late seventeenth and early eighteenth centuries that over time seriously weakened the French hold on the western territories. The Fox Tribe had grown dissatisfied with the nature of the French trade, and in particular with the French intention to trade with the Sioux, who were long-standing enemies of the Fox. To curtail this trade, the Fox shut down access to the Fox-Wisconsin Rivers route used by the French to reach the Mississippi River. Thereafter ensued nearly fifty years of often bloody conflict between the French and the Fox, a conflict that expanded to include intertribal warfare as well. Although in the end the French defeated and nearly exterminated the Fox, the toll of the conflict in lives and resources seriously weakened the French by the time the Seven Years' War with the British began in 1754.

In 1714, the Fox attacked the Illinois, and the French decided to destroy the Fox. The French governor, Philippe de Rigaud, Marquis de Vaudreuil, devised a plan whereby warriors from the Miami, Ouiatanon, Illinois, and Detroit Tribes would rendezvous at the Chicago Portage in the summer of 1715 under French leadership. At the same time, a force comprising *coureurs du bois*, the Ottawa, and the northern tribes would assemble at Mackinac. The forces would then converge in a concerted attack on the Fox.

Thus conceived, the plan quickly fell apart. A measles outbreak killed many of the Ouiatanon while they were en route to Chicago. The French in attendance divided their forces, one contingent staying with the stricken Ouiatanon to ensure their arrival at Chicago and another contingent heading out to rally the Illinois and lead them to Chicago. When the Ouiatanon group finally arrived at Chicago, the Illinois and Detroit forces who were supposed to be there had not arrived. The group had also been promised that canoes would be delivered from Mackinac, but these, too, were missing. When another measles outbreak erupted, the Ouiatanon deserted the French and returned home, and the remaining French made their way to Starved Rock. Meanwhile, the other French contingent had collected the Illinois warriors and led them back to Chicago, arriving in mid-August only to find neither reinforcements nor the promised canoes. After waiting for a few weeks for the other French contingent to arrive, the Illinois departed, and the remaining French made their way back to Starved Rock only to find their missing comrades there.

Meanwhile, the *coureurs du bois* had assembled in Mackinac, but the canoes and other supplies that had been promised never arrived from Montreal, and so they, too, dispersed. Unaware of the foregoing debacles, the Detroit warriors arrived in Chicago. Finding nobody there, they made their way to Starved Rock expecting to find the rest of the forces, but upon arrival not even the French were there, having fallen ill and retired to Kaskaskia. The Detroit were able to convince some of the Illinois to join with them and some Huron in a raid against the Mascouten and Kickapoo, which were allied with the Fox. Finally, in November, the assembled forces attacked the Mascouten, inflicting serious casualties and taking prisoners. While making their retreat after the battle, the Detroit force was set upon by the Fox. The Detroit force claimed a victory in this encounter, but there is no way to verify this claim. Ultimately, though, the elaborately conceived campaign of the French to eradicate the Fox failed.[9]

Another similar effort by a combined French and Illinois force, again advancing through the Chicago Portage, was carried out against the Fox in 1728, but it, too, failed to have significant impact.[10] Such conflicts continued well into the eighteenth century.

In 1721, Pierre François-Xavier de Charlevoix traveled to New France to examine the French colonies and report back to the French king Louis XV.

Charlevoix recounted his travels in a series of letters to the Duchess of Lesdiguieres. It is clear that Charlevoix had knowledge of the Chicago Portage route. In a letter written from the "Fort on the River St. Joseph" on September 14, 1721, he wrote:

> It is now three days since I set out from this place for Chicagou, by coasting along the south shore of Lake Michigan; but we found the Lake so stormy that we resolved to return hither and to seek out some other way to reach Louisiana. Our departure is fixed on the 16th, and I am going to make use of this delay of two days to continue my account of the customs and traditions of our Americans.[11]

A few days later, on September 17, he referred again to the Chicago Portage route:

> I believe I gave you to understand in my last that I had two routs to chuse, in order to gain the country of the Illinois; the first was by returning to lake Michigan, coasting along the southern coast, and entering the little river at Chicagou. After ascending five or six leagues up this river, there is a passage to that of the Illinois, by means of two carrying places, the longest of which is not above a league and a quarter; but being informed that at this season of the year there is not water sufficient for a canoe, I have taken the other route, which has likewise its inconveniences and is far from being agreeable, but it is more certain.[12]

The "other route" referred to by Charlevoix was the St. Joseph River to Kankakee River to Illinois River route. There is no evidence that Charlevoix ever used the Chicago Portage route.

With the Chicago Portage and Fox-Wisconsin routes effectively closed to French trade during the first half of the eighteenth century, the center of French commercial activity shifted southward, where the French increasingly came into conflict with the British, who were determined to gain access to the riches of the Mississippi Valley. The British were well aware of the French trade routes, as can be seen by a detailed description of the routes given in a "Representation of the Lords Commissioners for Trade and Plantations to the King upon the State of His Majesties Colonies & Plantations on the Continent of North America, dated September the 8th 1721." After tracing the routes from the St. Lawrence River through Lake Erie and Lake Huron, it references the route through the Chicago Portage to the Mississippi River:

> From the lake Huron they pass by the Straight Michillimackinack four leagues, being two in breadth, & of a great depth, to the lake Illinois; thence 150 leagues on the lake to fort Miamis, situated on the

> mouth of the river Chigagoe; from hence came those Indians of the same name, viz' Miamis, who are settled on the forementioned river that runs into Erie.
>
> Up the river Chigagoe they sail but 3 leagues to a passage of ¼th of a league; then enter a small Lake of about a mile [Mud Lake], and have another very small portage, & again another of two miles to the river Illinois, thence down the stream 130 leagues to Mississippi.[13]

Weakened by its long conflict with the Fox, the French were ill equipped to effectively compete against the British and their Native American allies in the Seven Years' War. In 1763, the Chicago Portage passed into the hands of the British, ending France's formal possession of the area. Despite the nominal transfer of possession, however, French influence in the area, particularly on the flow of trade, remained strong. In 1766, British Captain Harry Gordon reported that the French were carrying on trade "all around . . . by Land and by Water; 1st up the Mississippi and to the Lakes by the Ouisconsing, Foxes, Chicagou, and Illinois Rivers."[14] In 1773, a British entrepreneur named William Murray connived to purchase "Chicagou or Garlick Creek" outright from the local tribes and persisted in his claim to owning the Chicago Portage until the US Congress finally absolutely denied his claim in 1801.[15]

The Chicago Portage assumed a different kind of importance during the American Revolution (1775–83) when the British expressed repeated concerns that the American forces might use the Chicago Portage to attack British outposts.[16] In October 1778, British Lieutenant Governor Henry Hamilton relayed intelligence garnered from an Ottawa chief to General Frederick Haldimand, governor of Quebec, that the Americans intended to send six hundred troops to Chicago.[17] On May 2, 1779, British Major Arent Schuyler De Peyster similarly informed Haldimand that the Americans were reported to be at Chicago.[18] Although De Peyster subsequently said the reports were not true, he remained concerned that the Americans might come up the Illinois River and through the Chicago Portage to mobilize at Chicago for an attack up Lake Michigan on Mackinac.[19] On May 8, 1779, British Captain Dederick Brehm wrote to Haldimand over fears that the American general George Rogers Clark might use the Chicago Portage route to attack the British:

> After considering the situation of Major de Paister [De Peyster] I apprehend he runs more risk from Chicagu by the Illinois River, than Capt. Larnould, as your Excellency will have and yet see, what precautions and means Col. Bolton has taken and is still constant sending party's towards Tuscarowas, and Fort Pitt to harass and disturb their proceedings but Clark having reduced Vincennes as early as February may have time to attack de paister by the above mentioned River, if the least preparation has been ordered by him at his leaving the Illinois.[20]

In a follow-up letter dated May 12, 1779, Brehm notified Haldimand that Brehm intended to take supplies to Mackinac "by the way of the Illinois & Chicago Rivers over Lake Michigan."[21]

Prior to Hamilton's capture by the Americans at Vincennes, he had devised a plan to attack the Americans at Kaskaskia. In the winter of 1778, he sent orders to Captain Charles Langlade to gather a force of Native Americans for an attack in the spring. Langlade was to proceed from Green Bay down Lake Michigan and through the Chicago Portage to the Illinois River and then to Kaskaskia. At the same time, Charles Gautier de Verville, a Canadian who was employed by the British during the Revolutionary War to recruit Native American allies for the British, was to gather a Native American force from the upper Mississippi and descend that river to Kaskaskia. Not knowing that Hamilton had been taken prisoner in February 1779, Langlade did as he was told and got as far as Milwaukee before learning of Hamilton's capture. Upon hearing this news, his force refused to proceed any farther. Verville got as far as Starved Rock before his force also disbanded.[22]

In 1779, the British sent a raiding party to attack the trading post of Le Pé, located where present-day Peoria now stands. It had been a significant trading post for the French, who still resided there and were supportive of the American cause. The French had built a stockade at Le Pé, and De Peyster, the British commandant, feared the Americans might make use of this stockade and the route north through the Chicago Portage to attack the British. The raiding party was led by Verville. The soldiers in the raiding party were almost all Native Americans from various tribes. The raiding party left Mackinac and came down the west coast of Lake Michigan, through the Chicago Portage, and then down the Illinois River. They caught the French by surprise, destroyed the stockade, and then retraced their steps back through the Chicago Portage and up the lake to Mackinac.[23]

A more serious military action was contemplated by the British the following year. Spain and England were at war, and Patrick Sinclair, the new lieutenant governor who had taken over for De Peyster at Mackinac, had devised a plan for a comprehensive attack designed to sweep the entire area from Canada to Florida and thereby destroy the Spanish and American powers in the region of the Mississippi Valley. Just as in the earlier failed actions conceived by the French against the Fox, Sinclair envisioned an elaborate and multipronged operation:

1. From Pensacola in the south, British forces would advance on lower Louisiana;
2. A Native American force including Sioux warriors would descend the Mississippi River to Natchez;
3. A combined force of British, Sac, Fox, and other Wisconsin tribes would assemble at the Fox-Wisconsin Portage and, joining forces with the tribes from the upper Mississippi, advance to St. Louis;

4. Langlade would gather a force at Chicago to travel by way of the Chicago Portage and to make his attack by the Illinois River on St. Louis;
5. Another British force would "watch the plain" between the Wabash and Mississippi Rivers; and
6. A British force from Detroit under the command of Captain Henry Bird would engage the American forces of General George Rogers Clark at the Falls of Ohio, where Clark had set up a base of operations.[24]

By May 1780, Sinclair was ready to begin the operation, and on May 2 a force of about one thousand men began the descent down the Wisconsin River. Unknown to him at the time, the Spanish governor of New Orleans, Don Bernardo De Galvez, was already making significant advances against the British that culminated in the taking of Pensacola in May 1781.[25] Also unknown to the advancing force was that St. Louis had been alerted of the pending attack and had made preparations to defend the city. The battle was joined on May 26, and St. Louis successfully repelled the invading force. The Spaniards later said they lost twenty-nine men, and Sinclair numbered their losses at sixty-eight. Although the invading force killed or imprisoned many farmers in the surrounding countryside, the attack against St. Louis failed.

Having failed in its mission, and possibly upon hearing that General Clark was in Cahokia with an armed force, the British began their retreat. The retreating forces took two routes, one up the Mississippi River and one overland to Lake Michigan and on to Mackinac.

The attack on St. Louis might have turned out differently had Captain Langlade been able to take part. An undated letter apparently written in 1780 and possibly written by several British military officers to Captain Langlade outlined the project as it was intended to unfold:

> Sir: You are commanded to put your detachment on land as near Milwaukee as the circumstances will permit and without losing time to get across the land in order to gain the first village of Illinois which is named Peoria. You will send by canoes as much provision as you will find necessary by the River Chicago, taking good care not to overload your canoes and that they are sufficient in number to carry your detachment to Cahokia, the village opposite St. Louis.[26]

Fortunately for St. Louis, the invading force did not wait for Langlade. By the time Langlade began making his way down the Illinois, the battle at St. Louis was over. Upon hearing that John Montgomery with 350 American troops was advancing up the Illinois River, the force retreated back up the Chicago Portage to Lake Michigan, where it was rescued by two boats sent from Mackinac.[27] The story of this part of the retreat was related by Sinclair in a June 4, 1780, letter to a Colonel Bolton:

> The Sloop Felicity with a small Vessel, private property, went into Lake Michigan on the 29th Ultimo to land a Party of Canadians and Indians, who go by the Illinois River to second the attack of a Thousand Traders, Servants and Indians, sent down the Mississippi in obedience to my Lord George Germain's Circular Letter. . . . The Two Vessels are returned from Lake Michigan with a part of the Indians & Volunteers on the attack against the Illinois, scarcity of Provisions obliged them to return by different Routes, some by the Mississippi, some through the Country between Lake Michigan and that River, and some as directed by Chicagoe.[28]

In a letter sent the next month, on July 8, Sinclair expanded on this story to Haldimand:

> Sir—I have the honour to inform your Excellency that the two vessels sent into Lake Michigan have returned.
>
> They fortunately carried from this a force sufficient to enable the Party retiring from the Illinois by Chicago to pass with safety through a Band of Indians in the Rebel Interest & to embark in security, Some in canoes & some on board the vessels. The others retired in two Divisions, one by the Mississippi with Monsieur Calvé, who allowed the prisoners taken by the Sacks & Outagamies to fall into the hands of the enemy. The other Division penetrated the country between Lake Michigan & the Mississippi & are arrived here with their prisoners. Two hundred Illenois Cavalry arr'd at Chicago five days after the vessels left it.[29]

The reference to the arrival of two hundred cavalry at the Chicago Portage is likely a reference to Montgomery and his men, although they had stopped their advance at Peoria.[30]

In a letter dated April 24, 1782, Guilhaume La Mothe, a captain in the British militia in Detroit, proposed a planned attack against the Illinois, again by way of the Chicago Portage:

> Leaving Detroit with a small army of & some neighboring Indians, Sauteux, Hurons & Misthey will come by land to St. Josephs a journey of eight or ten days. They after having taken the poux [Potawatomi] Nation, who are settled on this river they will come to the branch of the Chicagoust & the Quinquiqui to try to get the Indians of the small fort of Milanaquis & another village, who have appeared, till the present to give their services to the Illinois & Lately conducted a party to St. Joseph who took the Commandant placed there by Governor St. Clair. As the two villages are the refuse of all the malefactors of all the other nations of which the

> two chiefs are Dougurne Sauteux, the one named Segurnac & the other Macquivois who have their families near Michilimackinac & it would be easy for the leader of the party to send them with the belts & we would by these means keep back the intelligence which they would have given to the enemies. During this time we could bring the barges & ammunition & go to join the little army at the entrance of the Chicagous where is a portage of half a league in good weather, in this way we could come without difficulty to the Illinois.[31]

Although there is no record of this plan being advanced, it shows once again the strategic importance of the Chicago Portage in the minds of the British.

With the Treaty of Paris in 1783, the Chicago Portage became an American possession, although for years this was more a matter of nominal ownership than actual control. The British were slow to retire from the West, and the British and French fur trade continued for years after the signing of the treaty. Tensions remained high—in a February 6, 1791, letter, William Burnett, an American trader, wrote, "Those that has any property in the country are in a very precarious situation, and will be until times take a change, which I hope will be soon. The Pouwatamies, at Chicago, has killed a frenchman about twenty days ago."[32] Nevertheless, the British persisted in trading with the Native Americans. One account tells that two canoes of merchandise were traded between the British and the Potawatomi at Chicago in the winter of 1792 and that twenty more canoes passed through Chicago heading for the Illinois River, eight to trade with the Potawatomi, eight with the Mascouten, and four with the Kickapoo.[33] It is possible that there was a substantial settlement of Potawatomi at Chicago during this time because a July 19, 1794, letter from Captain La Mothe to Superintendent of Indian Affairs John Chew notes that "there is likewise at Chikagoe Fifty Indians died of the Small Pox which alarms the Indians much in this post."[34] While keeping up this now-illicit trading with the Native Americans, the British did their best to incite the tribes in western New York and those west and north of the Ohio River to resist the newcomer Americans. By 1794, the British were openly encouraging the tribes to attack those Americans.

Conflict between Native Americans and the Americans of European extraction continued until 1795, when the Native Americans finally acknowledged defeat. In the ensuing Treaty of Greenville, the US government for the first time explicitly recognized the significance of the Chicago Portage to the future of the western frontier. The treaty specifically provided that the Native Americans ceded to the United States "one piece of land six miles square, at the mouth of the Chicago River, emptying into the southwest end of lake Michigan, where a fort formerly stood."[35] The treaty went on to guarantee that the Native Americans would do nothing to impede the free travel by the newcomer Americans "from the mouth of Chicago, to the commencement of the portage, between that river and the Illinois, and down the Illinois river to the Mississippi."[36]

During negotiations for the Treaty of Greenville, the British were still plotting to find ways to thwart western expansion by the United States by building depots at the various portages, including the Chicago Portage.[37] Although these British outposts were never built, the British persisted in their efforts to sow discord between the Native American tribes and the US forces. By so doing, the British hoped to maintain control of the fur trade and to create a buffer of Native American tribes hostile to the United States as a way of protecting the British colonies in Canada. These British efforts to undermine US interests continued until, and possibly contributed to, the War of 1812.

There is no evidence that Native Americans had permanent settlements at the Chicago Portage until after the arrival of the Europeans.[38] Similarly, during the early years of French use of the portage, the only semipermanent residents were hunters and traders, soldiers temporarily garrisoned at a fort, and missionaries. All these groups were transient, and the Chicago Portage was more a place that people passed through than a place where people stayed over time. The next step for the Chicago Portage was for it to become a place where people wanted to stay, a place for people to call home. When hostilities with the Fox came to an end, it was time for the portage's namesake, Chicago, to become a reality.

Recall from chapter 2 that from the time of Jacques Marquette's first stay at the Chicago Portage with Pierre Porteret and Jacques Largilliers in the winter of 1674, a succession of French traders, soldiers, and missionaries had a presence there. Even in 1674, Marquette was visited by Pierre Moreau and "the surgeon," who apparently were residing in the area, even if only in a transient manner. André Eno and Jean Filatreau built and inhabited a post there in the winter of 1682–83, and Olivier Morel de La Durantaye enlarged that post the following year, leaving a small garrison there that remained for several years. In 1685 the Jesuits built yet another post at the Chicago Portage as a headquarters for their missionary efforts in the Illinois territory, and in 1698 François Pinet established the Mission of the Guardian Angel that remained active until the early eighteenth century. And we know from Jean-François Buisson de St.-Cosme's account in 1698 that there already were Frenchmen present at the Chicago Portage, although again we don't know in what manner of residence. Pierre-Charles de Liette was also in command of the fort in Chicago in the early eighteenth century, and according to his own account, he spent four years there.[39]

Quaife points to at least two other possible early residents of Chicago, although their reputed presence rests solely on oral tradition. The first account is from John Reynolds, the fourth governor of the state of Illinois, who served from 1830 to 1834. Reynolds describes a French woman named La Compt whom he knew for thirty years and who claimed to have lived in Chicago with her husband, Pilette de Sainte Ange, as early as 1765.

Reynolds says that she was born at St. Joseph in 1734 and grew up having close relations with the Potawatomi and other local tribes from her infancy. She lived at Mackinac before coming to Chicago, and after some period at Chicago, around 1770 she moved to Cahokia, where she lived until her death at the age of 109.[40] Assuming this account is true, La Compt and her husband would have been among the earliest settlers at Chicago not connected to a military or religious purpose. According to Reynolds, she "possessed a strong mind, with the courage and energies of a heroine."[41] He attributes her with quelling numerous attacks by the local tribes on the French and Americans from 1781 to 1795, often going personally to stay at surrounding tribal villages where she "never failed to avert the storm and prevent bloodshed."[42]

The next possible known settler at Chicago might have been a fur trader named Guary, Guarie, or Guillory. This story comes to us from Gurdon Saltonstall Hubbard, who visited the Chicago Portage area in 1818 as a young apprentice to the fur trade. While there, he was told by Antoine Deschamps and Antoine Beson, two old fur traders who had been passing through the portage on a yearly basis since 1778, that a fur trader named Guarie had a trading house, "enclosed by pickets" on the west bank of the North Branch of the Chicago River.[43] According to the old traders, the North Branch was then known as "River Guarie," and the South Branch as "Portage River." The old traders pointed out the remnants of cornfields they said had been cultivated by Guarie, and Hubbard said the fields were "distinctly traceable, though grown over with grass."[44]

Although this story comes primarily via oral tradition from Hubbard, Quaife notes that when Major Stephen Long's expedition came through the area in 1823, the historian for that expedition recorded the name of the North Branch as "Gary River," presumably on the basis of being given that name by a local resident. Quaife suggests that the trader in Hubbard's story could have be Jean Baptiste Guillory, who was engaged in the fur trade at the St. Joseph and Illinois Rivers during the American Revolution. In 1778 Guillory was licensed to convey two canoeloads of trade goods to "Illinois via St. Joseph," and later documents show him active at St. Joseph in 1779–80.[45]

Ulrich Danckers cites a few other early traders and transient settlers at the Chicago Portage. In May 1770, Jean Orillat, a wealthy trader from Montreal, financed two canoes to travel through "Chiquagoux" under the direction of Jean Baptiste St. Cyr. Records show they took no trade goods but did have two hundred pounds of chocolate. Danckers suggests it was likely an exploratory expedition to see whether a trading post might be warranted. In 1776, Col. George Morgan, who had been appointed as Indian agent by the Continental Congress, issued safe-conduct passes to "the French people in Chicago" to visit Pittsburgh, although the names of these people are not recorded. And In 1782, Jean Baptiste Gaffé of Cahokia sent boatloads of goods to Chicago, so presumably he had a trading post there. In a November 6, 1783, letter to

General Haldimand from Philippe-François de Rastel de Rocheblave, the last governor of Illinois country under the British, Rocheblave mentions that his wife and family were "at Chikagou." Danckers suggests they could have been in residence at Gaffé's trading post.[46]

The first settler for which we have firm documentary evidence as having established what was intended to be a permanent residence in Chicago was Jean Baptiste Point de Sable, generally agreed to be the founder of Chicago.[47] Although there are various accounts of his birth and early life, none are supported by contemporaneous evidence.[48] The first definite account we have of him is in October 1778, when he was managing a trading post at Michigan City. He was associated in this endeavor with Pierre Durand and Michel Belleau. Durand had come up the Illinois River and through the Chicago Portage in October 1778 only to determine that, because of the lateness of the season, he could not make the trip the rest of the way to Canada. In a report to Governor Haldimand, he recounted how he took two canoes of goods to "Baptiste point Sable, free negro," at Michigan City (Durand referred to the location as being at the mouth of the *Rivière du Chemin*). After making his way back through the portage, Durand wintered at Cahokia and Kaskaskia.[49]

The following spring, Durand sent Belleau to retrieve the goods he had left with Point de Sable only to discover that Point de Sable had been arrested by the British as an American sympathizer and that the British had taken all of Durand's goods.[50] A "Corporal Tascon" took Point de Sable to Lieutenant Thomas Bennett, who was camped at St. Joseph, and on August 9, 1779, Bennett wrote to Major De Peyster that "Baptiste Point au Sable I have taken into custody, he hopes to make his conduct appear to you spotless."[51] In a follow-up report on September 1, 1779, Bennett noted that "since his imprisonment [Point de Sable] has in every respect behaved with becoming a man in his situation, has many friends, who give him a good character."[52] The familiarity by which Bennett referred to Point de Sable suggests that he was known to both Bennett and De Peyster prior to his arrest. Years later, De Peyster referred to Point de Sable as "a handsome negro, well educated and settled in Eschecagou."[53] At the time of his arrest, however, Point de Sable was located at Michigan City, not Chicago.

Point de Sable was held by the British for a year, during which time he sufficiently proved his loyalty and abilities such that he was assigned to manage the estate of Governor Patrick Sinclair, who had taken over from De Peyster in October 1779. By this time, Point de Sable was married to a Potawatomi woman named Kitihawa (later Christianized to Catherine) and had two children, a girl named Suzanne and a boy named Jean. Point de Sable ran the Pinery, as Sinclair's estate was called, until 1784, when Point de Sable moved to Detroit with his family.

It was at Detroit that Point de Sable met William Burnett, a successful and influential trader who had a trading post at St. Joseph.[54] Although he never lived in Chicago, Burnett is nonetheless a significant character in the history of the Chicago Portage and its namesake city. Burnett ran a wide-ranging trading business and, among many others, he employed Jean Lalime and John Kinzie, both of whom played a big role in early Chicago history. In 1782, Burnett married Kakima, a Potawatomi woman who because of family ties was already familiar with the business of trading, and together they built an impressive trading operation at St. Joseph that included a large house, a barn, storehouses, a blacksmith shop, and a bakery.[55]

Like many other Native American wives of traders, Kakima was an integral part of the business. In addition to managing the trade business whenever Burnett was away on trade missions, she was a skilled farmer who cultivated fields of corn and wheat in addition to apple, peach, quince, and cherry orchards. She also packed maple syrup in containers that were suitable as trade goods. Burnett and Kakima benefitted mutually from their close relationship, her extended family providing a ready-made trade network, and Burnett's business provided her family with goods and services they desired. Burnett was well aware of the importance of his partner, and upon returning from his wintering post to St. Joseph in February 1790, he wrote that "his Indian woman" had "done on her part in the trading very, very well."[56]

Burnett also had a business relationship with Point de Sable and may have been instrumental in facilitating Point de Sable's move to Chicago sometime between 1784 and 1788 to establish a farm and trading post at the mouth of the Chicago River to take advantage of the active trade flowing through the Chicago Portage. Several pieces of evidence suggest such a business connection between Point de Sable and Burnett. In a letter dated August 24, 1798, Burnett discusses the coming construction of Fort Dearborn in Chicago and states that "I have a house there already."[57] Later, in 1800, when Point de Sable sold his property at Chicago to Lalime, who was an agent of Burnett's in the fur trade, Burnett was one of the witnesses to the bill of sale. Further, it appears from the bill of sale that Point de Sable had an "account" with Burnett and that Burnett also loaned money to Lalime for the purchase of Point de Sable's property. The bill of sale, which was recorded with the Wayne County Register of Deeds in September 1800, reads in part:

> I, Jean Batiste Point Sable by these presents certify to have sold of my own free will and consent all my property belonging to me at Chicago, and I further oblige myself to deliver to Mr. Jean Lalime or his representatives all the articles above mentioned according to the inventory made at Chicago on May 7, 1800, for the sum of 6000 livres of twenty coppers and [empty space] livres, which sum I acknowledge to have received as being the balance of my account with Wm Burnet of St. Joseph and the said Wm. Burnet obliges himself to pay the balance of the sale to J. Bte. Point Sable for Jean Lalime after having delivered all the articles mentioned in the above inventory . . .[58]

Whether the "house" that Burnett refers to in his letter was the farm and trading post occupied by Point de Sable or a separate structure is unknown, but the existence and specificity of the Point de Sable bill of sale suggest that Point de Sable owned the property being transferred. If so, then Burnett's "house" might have been a separate property. The original bill of sale is still on file at the Wayne County Register of Deeds in Detroit. A later typewritten copy was made of the bill of sale and is also on file there.

In her history of Fort Dearborn, Ann Durkin Keating concludes that Burnett was a supplier to Point de Sable and also accepted payments and extended credit on Point de Sable's behalf.[59] This view is given further credence by the fact that after Lalime purchased Point de Sable's property in 1800, the property was apparently abandoned for several years. This suggests that it was actually Burnett who purchased Point de Sable's property, using Lalime as the nominal purchaser. The bill of sale indicates that the sale of the property allowed Point de Sable to clear his account with Burnett while also giving Burnett a clear interest in the property as the person who advanced the balance of the purchase price on Lalime's behalf. The property was unoccupied in 1803 when Lalime returned to live in it in anticipation of the building of Fort Dearborn.

In 1790, Hugh Heward journeyed through the Chicago Portage on his way to the Mississippi River. His journal entry for May 10 and 11 recited:

> Monday May 10th 1790 Stopt at Point Sables. Entered with the Cannots [canoes] & begun to hull com & bake Bread & arranged everything for next Morning left the Cannots at point Sables &took his Purogue [pirogue] bought of him 41 lb Flour & baked in Bread for 25 & 29 lb pork @ 2/8 the whole amount to £ 5. 10. 8 & paid him with 13 Yds. 4/4 cotton.
>
> Tuesday May 11th 1790 Engaged five Indians to help us over the Carrying place with the periogue & paid them two handfuls of powder each. Duarrier this Morning very saucy & abuseful about getting Salt. I promised to requite him for it—a Showery day & Wind at West the Carrying place about 1/2 a Mile got over nearly at Mid Day.—from thence passed in the Run &small Lake [Mud Lake] to the River deplain [Des Plaines River] &course turning nearly South West a very wet afternoon & heavy thunder arrived at the River deplain said to be fifteen Miles & camped.[60]

The items described in this entry suggest that Point de Sable's main business was farming and providing food and provisions to the traders passing through the Chicago Portage. It also appears that Point de Sable's farm was substantial. Quaife arrives at a similar conclusion by examining the inventory included with the bill of sale when Point de Sable sold his property in 1800:

> Besides the [main house] . . . (22 by 40 feet in size), there were numerous outbuildings: two barns, 24 by 30 and 28 by 40 feet, respectively; a horsemill, 24 by 36 feet; a bakehouse, 18 by 20 feet; a poultry-house, a workshop, a dairy, and a smokehouse, each of smaller dimensions. The equipment included 8 axes, several saws, 7 scythes, 8 sickles, 3 carts, and a plow. There were 2 mules, 30 head of full-grown cattle, 2 calves, 28 hogs, and 44 hens. A moment's reflection will suffice to show that these figures indicate an extensive civilized establishment. One does not build and equip a mill and a bakehouse unless he has grain to grind and flour to bake. Corn might be bought from the Indians, but to have wheat for his mill Point Sable must have raised it himself. This, and the cutting of hay for his livestock, explains the use to which his seven scythes and eight sickles were put. We are now ready to perceive the significance of Point Sable's transaction with Hugh Heward, his chance visitor of 1790. Evidently the wheat field, the mill, and the bake house had all been developed prior to that year. Evidently, too, Point Sable produced the lumber used in the erection of his buildings: 8 axes, 1 plank saw, 1 large ripsaw, 1 crosscut saw with 7-inch blade, 1 cooper's handsaw, and a kit of carpenter's tools, tell their own story. Noticeable in this connection is the inventory item "1 horse stable—all the wood for a barn." This can only mean that prior to selling his establishment Point Sable had planned to erect a third stable, and had already manufactured the lumber for it.[61]

Quaife adds that because Point de Sable was still a trader and was likely gone from Chicago for extended periods, he must have employed a number of workers at his farm. If so, then these workers were among the first regular residents of Chicago.

Suzanne Point de Sable married Jean Baptiste Pelletier in 1790, and they resided in Chicago. On October 8, 1796, they had a daughter, Eulalie.[62] We can also estimate, if we assume Susanne was in her early to mid-teens when she was married, that her father was probably born around 1750.

Point de Sable sold his property in May 1800 and left Chicago that fall. Keating speculates that the visit to Chicago in the spring of 1800 by General Arthur St. Clair, then the governor of the newly established Northwest Territory, might have influenced Point de Sable to move away from Chicago (Keating even suggests that St. Clair might have stayed with Point de Sable during his visit). The increasing assertion of American authority was creating tension among the local tribes. In addition, Point de Sable's wife and daughter had died prior to 1800, and without their help, it is possible that Point de Sable simply could not continue to maintain the property and his business.[63] In any event, Point de Sable moved to St. Charles in Spanish Upper Louisiana (present-day Missouri), where he lived until his death in 1818.

Point de Sable was not alone in Chicago. In 1790, the husband and wife Antoine and Archange Ouilmette moved to Chicago and built a home west of Point de Sable's property. When he first moved to Chicago, Antoine, who was French Canadian, was employed by the American Fur Company, and his business seems to have involved farming, trading, and running a transportation service for traders crossing the Chicago Portage. He kept oxen for the crossings by which he transferred goods along the portage road and pulled boats to the Chicago River. He also had horses and other farm animals, including sheep that he used to furnish wool to the soldiers and their families at Fort Dearborn. He was a significant provider of goods and services to Fort Dearborn, supplying the garrison with meat and fuel while at the same time operating a fairly extensive trading business with Native American peoples north of Chicago all the way to Canada.[64] In addition to his own personal business, he also sometimes worked for John Kinzie, and an entry in Kinzie's account book for June 14, 1806, shows that Kinzie paid Ouilmette fifty dollars to transport goods over the Chicago Portage to the fork on the Illinois River.[65]

Archange Ouilmette was a French-Potawatomi woman, born Archange Marie Chevalier to François and Marianne Chevalier. The Chevalier family was very successful in the fur trade of the Great Lakes in the mid-eighteenth century, and Antoine and Archange had ready access to her family's existing trade relations. Like most of the Native American and Mètis wives of the early traders, Archange played an indispensable role in the family business, tending to all aspects when Antoine was away on his trading adventures. When the US garrison fled Fort Dearborn in 1812, the Ouilmette family remained safely behind because of Archange's family ties. In 1814, Alexander Robinson, who became chief of the Potawatomi, came to Chicago, and he and the Ouilmettes cultivated the fields in the area where the fort had stood before it was burned down in 1812, raising corn that they subsequently sold to the US soldiers when they returned to rebuild the fort in 1816.[66] The Ouilmette family remained a staple in the growing settlement of Chicago for the next thirty-six years, and Antoine and Archange raised a family of eight children there before they moved north and became the founders and namesake of present-day Wilmette.[67]

And so at the close of the eighteenth century, the seeds of a future city had been sown along the banks of the Chicago River. But the frontier was still a frontier, and the new Americans were a long way from consolidating their power in the region. The fur trade remained dominated by French and British traders, and even the Spanish continued to play a role in the region. In 1790, Governor St. Clair was directed by the US Congress to issue a report on the situation generally in the Northwest Territory, and in particular on the state of trade. In late 1790, St. Clair issued his report to President George Washington and said in part:

> The commerce of the Illinois country is of some importance in itself, but more so when considered as connected with the Spanish side of

> the Mississippi. The villages on that side of the river having been originally settled by the French, and under the same government as that part which is now in the possession of the United States, the connection between them is still very intimate, and favors a commercial intercourse which, though illicit, might be carried on by the citizens of America without risk. It is carried on at present without risk, but is, unfortunately, almost entirely in the hands of the British. Even much the greatest part of the merchandise for the trade of the Missouri River is brought from Michilimackinac by that of the Illinois, partly by the Spanish subjects themselves, and partly by British traders. The manner is this: The Spanish subjects either introduce them at once in consequence of a secret connection with their commandants or they are brought down to Cahokia and landed there, and afterwards carried over to St. Louis, as opportunities can be found. What is brought by the British traders, the Spanish subjects purchase and pay for on the American side, taking all the risk that attends the introducing them into their own country upon themselves. The furs in which these goods are generally paid for (deer skins answering better than furs at the New Orleans market), are carried to Canada by the same communication, that is to say, up the Illinois river, up the Chicago, and from thence by a small portage into Lake Michigan, and along that lake to Michilimackinac; or from the Chicago up the river Au Plain [Des Plaines River], and by a portage into the same lake.
>
> In the spring of the year the waters of the Michigan and the Chicago rise each to such a height that the intermediate space is entirely overflowed, and is passable by the vessels in use there, which are bark canoes, but which carry a very considerable burden, and are navigated by three or by five persons.[68]

The need to establish control over the Chicago Portage and the trade flowing through it was apparent to the Americans, and doing so became a recurring theme in the early years of the nineteenth century. It was time for the Americans to take the reins of western expansion, and the Chicago Portage would play a significant role in these efforts.

5

✦

Fort Dearborn

Well in advance of the 1795 Treaty of Greenville, the United States was fully aware of the importance of the Chicago Portage as a key to trade and expansion in the west. Writing in 1781, Thomas Jefferson predicted, "The *Mississippi* [River] will be one of the principal channels of future commerce for the country westward of the Alleghaney."[1] He went on to specifically identify the Chicago Portage as the route to this great river from Lake Michigan:

> The *Illinois* is a fine river, clear, gentle, and without rapids; insomuch that it is navigable for batteaux [small boats] to its source. From thence is a portage of two miles only to the Chickago, which affords a batteaux navigation of 10 miles to its entrance into Lake Michigan. The Illinois, about 10 miles above its mouth, is 300 yards wide.[2]

Pursuant to Jay's Treaty in 1794, the British formally withdrew from their northwest posts in the summer of 1796. This action, in conjunction with the ceding of the Chicago Portage to the United States by the Native Americans under the Treaty of Greenville, prepared the United States to assert control over this vital trade connection. With the threat of attacks from the resident tribes officially removed, there was a significant expansion by US settlers into the region north of the Ohio River. By 1800, this area was so well settled that it was ready for statehood, so in 1800 the Congress divided the Northwest Territory into two sections. Two years later, the easternmost section was admitted to the United States as the state of Ohio. The western section became the Indiana Territory under the control of Governor William Henry Harrison. In the following years, US settlers continued to slowly advance north and west into this territory.[3]

At the time of this expansion, the United States had only two outposts from which it could exert direct control and influence, Detroit and Mackinac. It was from these two locations, widely separated, that the young nation had to try to protect new settlers from Native American attacks while also policing the actions of traders and settlers themselves. In addition, the British, who might have technically relinquished their northwest posts, remained committed to maintaining their control of the lucrative trade of that region and of inciting tribes against the United States. All of these factors impressed upon the United States the need for a western fort at Chicago to maintain control of the area and provide a critical communications bridge between Detroit and Mackinac.

It isn't clear exactly when the idea for a fort at Chicago was conceived, or by whom, but certainly there was already speculation about the coming of a fort in August 1798 when US trader William Burnett wrote to his suppliers in Montreal:

> In the course of last winter, I wrote you that it is expected that there will be a garrison at Chicago, this summer, and from late accounts, I have reason to expect that they will be over there this fall; and should it be the case, and as I have a house there already, and a promise of assistance from headquarters, I will have occasion for a good deal of liquors, and some other articles, for that post. Therefore, should there be a garrison at Chicago this fall, I will write for an addition of articles to my order.[4]

Despite whatever information Burnett might have received, the fort did not materialize for another five years. In March 1803, Secretary of War Henry Dearborn directed that an officer and six men be sent from Detroit to Chicago to determine the best route to be taken, to ascertain the "disposition of area Indians to this intrusion through their territory," to determine the ability of local traders to supply the larger company of soldiers who were to follow, and to select a staging site at St. Joseph for the soldiers until final arrangements were made at Chicago.[5] Upon arriving at St. Joseph, the advance party consulted with Burnett, who recommended that Jean Lalime be made the first interpreter at the fort. Lalime was literate and spoke fluent French, English, and Potawatomi. He also had close ties to the Potawatomi because of his marriage to a Potawatomi woman, Nokenoqua, with whom he had a child. Dearborn accepted the recommendation and appointed Lalime as interpreter. It turned out to be a fateful appointment.

The advance party was led by Captain John Whistler, who was also selected to be the commander of the new fort. Upon arriving at Chicago, the party found that a sandbar at the mouth of the Chicago River made it impossible for any vessel larger than a canoe to pass. They also found there the homes of Jean Baptiste Point de Sable and Antoine and Archange Ouilmette on the north side of the river. Whistler determined that the land opposite these homes on the south side of the river was the proper spot for the fort. The land elevation was higher there, about eight feet above the river, the highest ground in the area. The river itself was about thirty feet wide and more than eighteen feet deep of "dead water."[6]

Whistler returned to Chicago with a band of soldiers on August 17, 1803. Most of the troops had followed the overland route that Whistler had determined in the spring, while the schooner *Tracy* brought Whistler's family, the rest of the soldiers, and supplies—including two small cannons. The ship was unlike anything the local tribes had ever seen, and two thousand Potawatomi gathered to see the "big canoe with wings."[7] This number might have included the tribe from the Calumet region, the tribe to which Archange Ouilmette belonged.

Construction began in the fall of 1803, and Whistler issued his first report from the newly named Fort Dearborn in December of the following year. While the surveying and construction of Fort Dearborn were under way, other events were taking place that significantly affected the unfolding history of early Chicago. In 1803, the Louisiana Purchase cemented American control of the Mississippi River and added the port city of New Orleans and the vast Louisiana Territory to the United States. This acquisition heightened the importance of the Chicago Portage as the connecting point between the Gulf of Mexico and the Atlantic Ocean. At the same time, William Henry Harrison, the governor of the Indiana Territory, managed to negotiate two land acquisitions, one from the Kaskaskia and the other from the Sauk and the Fox, that succeeded in bringing land just west of Chicago at the Fox River and south of Chicago at the Kankakee River under US ownership. With these acquisitions, the United States was slowly but surely boxing in the Potawatomi in a manner that eventually led to violence and bloodshed. Although the United States had told the Potawatomi that Fort Dearborn would protect them from the incursion of American settlers, over time Fort Dearborn became for the Potawatomi a symbol of American betrayal.[8]

It is beyond the scope of this work to relate the general history of Fort Dearborn, but there are a few particulars that pertain more directly to the interplay between the fort and the Chicago Portage.[9] Without the Chicago Portage, it is likely that there never would have been a Fort Dearborn—or, indeed, a Chicago. Without the portage, the Chicago River was but a small, sluggish inlet from Lake Michigan that led to nowhere. But with the portage, the Chicago River became the entry point for US western expansion and trade. Fort Dearborn contributed to both by providing a safe place, or so it was thought in 1803, for settlers and traders alike. In addition to the fort itself, Whistler built two other structures on the south bank of the river west of the fort. The first was a US Indian Agency house, which was built in 1805 and charged with the responsibility of handling relations with the tribes of the region (fig. 18).[10] The first appointed Indian agent in Chicago was Charles Jouett, an experienced and skilled diplomat who had been at Detroit before coming to Chicago. Although the local Potawatomi were not allowed inside Fort Dearborn, they were welcome at the agency house.

Assisting Jouett in his duties was Jean Lalime. Together they made an effective team. Jouett was respected by the Potawatomi as a fair and honest man,

Fig. 18. Fort Dearborn and the US Indian Agency House, 1805. Courtesy of the Chicago Architecture Center.

and Lalime brought his knowledge of the local tribes, his fluency in their language, and his family connection to the Potawatomi through his wife. The Lalimes at this point were living across the river next door to the Ouilmettes, and Nokenoqua Lalime even came to work for Jouett and his wife, Elizabeth, as their housekeeper. The relationship between the Jouetts and the Lalimes became more than professional, and the goodwill they shared enhanced their effectiveness.

As the United States continued to acquire land from local tribes, the Potawatomi became more uneasy and distrustful. This increasing pressure made Fort Dearborn a fragile and dangerous place. Tensions were made worse by the British, who continued to foment bad blood between the Potawatomi and the Americans. An early flash point was reached in June 1807 when the British warship *Leopard* fired on and then boarded the US frigate *Chesapeake* in what many observers now see as a precursor of the War of 1812. With tensions already high, and with the British fanning the flames in the region, Jouett and Lalime were central to at least temporarily stabilizing the situation in Chicago.

Charles Jouett suffered a personal tragedy when Elizabeth died, leaving him with sole responsibility for their three-year-old daughter. The Lalimes helped Jouett through this hardship, and Jouett eventually remarried and attempted to resettle his family at Chicago. So close were the families that when Jouett's new wife gave birth to a son, he was named Charles Lalime Jouett. Sadly, the infant died a few months later, and the Jouetts decided to leave Chicago in 1810. Jouett's departure did not bode well, as tensions in the region remained high.

The second building added to the Fort Dearborn complex was a US trading house. Trading houses, also called "factories," were established by Congress after the signing of the Treaty of Greenville with the express purpose of providing US goods to the Native American tribes at a fair price. Unfortunately, that goal was often not achieved, and this failure contributed to the factory system eventually being abolished in 1823. An ancillary goal of the factories was to keep furs out of the hands of British traders.

In 1808, Secretary Dearborn appointed Matthew Irwin as the third "factor" to run the Chicago factory. Irwin was a talented young man, but he had no experience in the fur trade or with how to set prices for the goods he received from the government. As with the agency house, an underlying purpose of the trading house was to obtain and preserve good relations with the local tribes, a daunting and challenging task for even a more seasoned and experienced trader. Irwin was fortunate, however, that once again Jean Lalime stepped into the picture. In addition to working as an interpreter for the fort and as an associate to agent Jouett, Lalime helped Irwin. With his long experience as a trader and his respect among the Potawatomi, Lalime was integral in establishing fair and equitable trade with the local tribes.

Lalime was aware of the tensions created by the US military presence at Fort Dearborn. Although alongside Jouett he was able to forge favorable relations with the local tribes, and with Irwin he was able to ensure fair dealing and competitively priced goods, there was no getting around the mixed signals being sent to the Potawatomi, which included "offering friendship and building a fort; promoting peace and threatening war; offering gifts and taking land."[11] It was only a matter of time before the tensions came to a head.

In the spring of 1804, John Kinzie, his wife, Eleanor, and her daughter Margaret (by her first husband, Daniel McKillip, a British officer who had died fighting the Americans at Fallen Timbers in 1794) moved to Chicago from St. Joseph. Eleanor had been captured at age nine by a Seneca war party and remained captive for four years before her father, John Lytle, secured her release. Her familiarity with Native American customs that resulted from this captivity served her and Kinzie well as they embarked on their life together in Chicago.

John Kinzie already had long experience in the fur trade before coming to Chicago. He was a man of malleable allegiances, having been solidly aligned with the British for thirty years before coming to Chicago. During and after the Revolutionary War, he proclaimed himself pro-American, but the facts of his life suggest that his loyalties were more matters of convenience and expediency than conviction. Much of what we know about Kinzie comes from a book written by Juliette Kinzie, wife of eldest son John H. Kinzie. Her book, *Wau-Bun: The Early Day in the Northwest*, was published in 1873 and contains an account of the Kinzie's life in Chicago as related to her by Eleanor Kinzie. Not surprisingly, the book portrays John Kinzie in a positive light and generally demeans anyone with whom he ever had a disagreement. It is also often factually in error and is best read more as a period piece than as history.

According to *Wau-Bun*, the Kinzies moved into the former home of Point de Sable upon their arrival in Chicago, and the book also claims that Kinzie purchased that property while still at the trading post he ran on the St. Joseph River near present-day Niles, Illinois. Although no written record of this transaction exists, it does seem likely that Kinzie owned the property in Chicago. *Wau-Bun* inexplicably names the purchaser of the Point de Sable property as Le Mai, another trader located at Chicago, instead of Lalime, an unusual mistake given the Kinzie family's connection with both men. In any event, Lalime lived in Chicago from 1804 until 1812, and during that time apparently Lalime never laid claim to the Point de Sable property. Similarly, if one takes the position that Burnett had a financial interest in the property, he, too, never attempted to interfere with Kinzie's occupancy of the property.

Kinzie established a successful and far-reaching trading business in Chicago with his half-brother, Thomas Forsyth. In addition to their personal trading business, Kinzie and Forsyth established a lucrative, if sometimes questionable, business relationship with Fort Dearborn. This business with the fort led to Chicago's first murder in the killing of Lalime by Kinzie. But to understand this murder, one must understand its background and context.

The factory at Fort Dearborn was one source of trade goods for soldiers at the fort. The other source was through a sutler—that is, a local trader who was designated by the base commander and given a monopoly over providing goods to the soldiers. The sutler could set whatever prices he deemed appropriate, which in the case of Fort Dearborn were often higher than those charged by traders in the public market. The suttle system was rife with opportunities for corruption, and too often officers received more beneficial pricing than the rest of the men.

From 1805 to 1809, the designated sutler at Fort Dearborn was Whistler and Cooper, the former being John Whistler Jr., the son of Captain Whistler, commander of the fort, and the latter being the fort's surgeon mate, Dr. John Cooper. The newly appointed factor, Matthew Irwin, found this situation rightly problematic, and on December 30, 1809, Irwin wrote to the newly appointed secretary of war, William Eustis, that regarding Whistler and Cooper, "No check, exists, in their dealings, against extortion!"[12] Irwin accused Whistler and Cooper of charging higher prices to soldiers at the fort than those charged by local trader John Kinzie, and he pointed out that Captain Whistler, Lieutenant Seth Thompson (Whistler's son-in-law), and Surgeon Mate Cooper made up three-fourths of the officers at the base. He also noted that Cooper had been offered a bribe of $2,000 if he relinquished his claim to the partnership with John Whistler Jr.[13]

Despite the seriousness of these charges, Captain Whistler and the involved officers were never charged with wrongdoing. Instead, Captain Whistler was reassigned to Detroit and Captain Nathan Heald took his place. Cooper left the army in early 1811, and Thompson fell ill and died in March 1811.[14]

If Irwin thought he had carried the day, his hopes were dashed when on January 12, 1812, Heald appointed Kinzie and Forsyth as the new, exclusive sutler for Fort Dearborn. By January 19, Irwin wrote Eustis to report that the suttle system was again corrupted. He accused Kinzie of receiving smuggled guns and ammunition from the British and insinuated that Heald's appointment of the new sutler was "not granted from disinterested motives."[15]

The situation at Fort Dearborn quickly became polarized. On one side were Captain Heald and two officers, Lieutenant Linai (sometimes spelled "Linah") Helm and Ensign George Ronan, all of whom conspired to protect Kinzie and Forsyth and keep them in place as the sutler. On the other side were Irwin and surgeon's mate Isaac Van Voorhis, who viewed the suttle arrangement as corrupt and unjust. Ronan had graduated from West Point, and Van Voorhis from the College of Physicians and Surgeons in New York City, but both were inexperienced, and Fort Dearborn was their first posting. Lieutenant Helm, although experienced, was John Kinzie's son-in-law.[16] In a letter to Eustis on May 16, Van Voorhis wrote, "In favour of Lt. Helm nothing earthly can be said; if there be any thing striking in him it is ignorance."[17] In the middle between these two camps was Lalime, who worked with the factor Irwin and also had had long dealings with Kinzie.

Irwin and Van Voorhis continued to press their case with Eustis in the ensuing months. In a March 10 letter, Irwin wrote that although officers were receiving goods from Kinzie and Forsyth at cost, the rest of the soldiers were paying 25 to 50 percent more than they should be paying. Irwin also said that Kinzie and Forsyth had offered a $400 per year bribe to someone in Washington to obtain the appointment as sutler. Irwin went further, accusing Kinzie and Forsyth of having provided ammunition to the Native Americans fighting against the United States during the American Revolution and that one of them had even refused to save the lives of US captives during the war by giving a few quarts of whiskey to the Native Americans, instead saying that "he would not sacrifice his property for the sake of a few d——d 'Americans.' "[18]

The situation at Fort Dearborn worsened in April, when a party of Winnebago killed two settlers at a farm owned by James Leigh that was near the fort. Within the pressure cooker of the outpost, Helm and Kinzie called for blood. In an April 16 letter to Eustis notifying him about the killing of the settlers, Irwin reported that some friendly tribes who lived near the fort were ordered away, while "propositions were openly made to murder them as well as some French persons (with Indian wives) who have, ever since they have been here, manifested peaceable dispositions." He identified Helm and Kinzie as the instigators of these threats and also noted that because of the killings, the factory at the post had been closed, a decision he thought hurt relations with the friendly local tribes but benefited "a few pretended Americans," who while trying instigate violence against the Native Americans were simultaneously reaping the benefits of the factory being closed through their private trading posts.[19]

It is not known whether the "French persons (with Indian wives)" included Jean and Nokenoqua Lalime. But in two letters to Eustis, one written on May 15 by Irwin and one on May 16 by Van Voorhis, it becomes clear that Lalime was in the crosshairs. In his letter, Irwin relates that Kinzie, Helm, and Ronan continued to try to inflame the soldiers at the fort against the Native Americans, and in particular states that "Ensn. Ronan threatened to Shoot the Interpreter [Lalime], and very lately Lt. Helm swore 'he would take the scalp of the Factor' [Irwin]."[20] Irwin concluded his letter with a litany of past charges against Kinzie, concluding that they all pointed to "the dangerous Character of the man."[21]

Van Voorhis in his letter echoed Irwin's sentiments, pointing to the "unofficer-like and extravagant conduct" of Helm and Ronan in trying to constantly incite violence against the Native Americans in the region and the French at Chicago. He accuses Helm of giving "secret instructions" to and "inflaming" the soldiers at the fort, of saying he might "murder Indians" and "take the scalps of a respectable, and other persons here."[22] Van Voorhis notes that Heald had arrested Helm for such conduct but that Helm was released when he apologized. For his part, Ronan had "openly threatened to shoot the Frenchmen and Indians at this place who were apparently the most friendly."[23] Van Voorhis characterizes Kinzie as two-faced, calling Native Americans who came peaceably to Fort Dearborn to trade "damned rascals" while his own traders did business with unfriendly tribes such as the Winnebago "in their own country."[24] In early June, Van Voorhis again wrote Eustis, this time saying that "I have not only been threatened by Lt. L. T. Helm, who is the son-in-law to Mr. Kenzie [*sic*], in the presence of his Father-in-law and others, but from him have been handed a challenge from Mr. Kenzie himself." Citing Kinzie's "sinister character," Van Voorhis asked Eustis to transfer him from Fort Dearborn.[25]

Such reports clearly showed that Lalime was in danger. The situation came to a head when Helm argued with Lalime about Irwin and the factory, with Helm offering to "give a very handsome treat" if the factory were to be abolished. Van Voorhis was present at this argument and in a June 30 letter to Eustis wrote that Lalime had taken the side of the factory against Helm and Kinzie and "defended the pure motives and just dealings of the Institution."[26]

On June 17, 1812, Kinzie killed Lalime outside the gates of Fort Dearborn. Accounts vary, but it seems that both men were armed for a fight. Lalime, the older and smaller of the two, had a pistol, and Kinzie carried a knife. Kinzie was grazed by a bullet and then stabbed Lalime, killing him instantly. According to Van Voorhis, the argument between Helm and Lalime about Irwin and factory had led to the killing, which Van Voorhis termed "a perfect assassination."[27] Both Irwin and Van Voorhis witnessed the fight.

The wounded Kinzie retreated to his quarters within the fort, where he was tended to by his wife. He remained there several hours, and, according to a July letter from Irwin to Eustis, upon learning that Irwin had witnessed the killing, Kinzie said that he was "a lost man."[28] Both Irwin and Van Voorhis claimed that Helm and Ronan helped Kinzie escape from the fort to hide in the woods and that they supplied Kinzie with provisions, including wine.[29] Both claimed that Heald did little if anything to try to apprehend Kinzie, and Irwin wrote that despite the fact "the Citizens were anxious an inquest should be held in the [Lalime's] body," a group of soldiers led by Helm "carried it away by force."[30] Van Voorhis and Irwin feared for their own lives following the killing of Lalime. Irwin requested that Heald provide him with protection, but Heald refused. Instead, Irwin moved in with Van Voorhis for mutual protection.

A few days after the killing, Heald received a letter from Eustis directing Heald to "regulate the sutlers, so as to prevent impositions from exorbitant charges."[31] Heald, Helm, and Ronan were "considerably agitated" that Irwin had reported the suttle irregularities to Eustis. In an ominous move, Heald claimed that he had heard of the whereabouts of Kinzie and ordered Irwin to accompany Ronan, just the two of them, at night, to go apprehend Kinzie. Fearing for his life, Irwin refused. In retaliation, Heald ordered Irwin out of Van Voorhis's quarters, said that the garrison would offer him no protection, and, in a particularly petty move, destroyed Irwin's garden.[32] It became clear to Irwin that he had to get away from the fort, and on July 5 he left for Mackinac under the excuse that he had to find a new interpreter to replace Lalime. He arrived at Mackinac on July 16, and the next day the British took the fort there in the first military action of the War of 1812 in the West. Irwin was taken prisoner and transferred to Detroit. It was there he learned that General William Hull had ordered the evacuation of Fort Dearborn.[33]

The foregoing account of what might be the first murder among White settlers in Chicago is based on archival documents, many of which were not available to the public until the 1940s.[34] The contemporaneous accounts of Irwin and Van Voorhies vary substantially from the account handed down through the years by the heirs of John Kinzie. In Juliette Kinzie's telling, Ronan was "a gallant young officer," Van Voorhies was a coward, and Lalime was "insanely jealous" of Kinzie's success as a trader.[35] In the Kinzie version of events, Lalime was lying in wait for Kinzie and attacked him with a knife. Kinzie, in self-defense, killed Lalime and then turned himself in to Heald. A trial was held and Kinzie was acquitted.[36] The only other account from the Kinzie side comes from Victorie Porthier, a family servant of John Kinzie, who years after the event told historian Alfred T. Andreas that Kinzie and Lalime came out of the fort together at sunset and then the fight ensued. According to Porthier, Kinzie was unarmed and Lalime had both gun and knife. Lalime shot Kinzie, Kinzie grabbed him, Lalime pulled a knife, they both "fell down together," and Lalime "was stabbed by his own knife."[37]

Within weeks of Lalime's death, Irwin wrote to Eustis that he feared Kinzie was trying to provoke a war with the Native Americans to cover up his crime.[38] In October 1812, Irwin reiterated this charge:

> I cautioned the Capn by letter, on more than one occasion, to beware of an individual (John Kinzie) that I had every reason to believe a british emissary, and who, I had been informed, had supplied the Prophet [Tenskwatawa] and his party with ammunition at different periods, and was known to have done the same thing during former Indian Wars. But, to my regret, I found this man had obtained so great an ascendency over the Captain as to render my efforts unavailing, and I also found they were connected in many improper concerns. The plots entered into by this man to destroy friendly Indians—the methods he had taken to inveigle the Officers (with the exception of the Surgeon's mate) into improper concerns—his bold and menacing conduct to the Citizens, if they dared to doubt his intentions—all tended to convince me that he felt an interest in bringing about an Indian War. Should he not have been instrumental in the fate of Chicago, I shall be much deceived, because if he fulfilled his part as emissary, he had it much in his power to preserve his own life by destroying the Witnesses to the murder of Lalime.[39]

There is no evidence to support Irwin's charges that Kinzie conspired to bring about a war with the Native Americans or an attack on Fort Dearborn. Commenting on Irwin's charge, Quaife noted that "to those who subscribe to the traditional estimate local to Chicago which pictures Kinzie as a kind of demigod, Irwin's charge that in addition to being a murderer and a traitor he contrived the massacre of the garrison and settlers in order to destroy the witnesses of his crime will come as a distinct shock."[40]

The same day that Kinzie killed Lalime, the US Congress declared war on the British, formally launching the War of 1812. Just as tensions had been escalating between the United States and Britain, so, too, the relations between the Native Americans in the West and the United States had been deteriorating. The increasing pressure on the Native American sovereignty and way of life from the waves of settlers arriving from the east gave rise to a strong nativist backlash that agitated for the removal of all European settlers and the reestablishment of a traditional Native American lifestyle. Inspired by Tenskwatawa, whom whites called the Shawnee Prophet, and given force by Native American leaders such as Tecumseh (Tenskwatawa's brother) and Main Poc, Native Americans in the Midwest and Canada widely embraced this desire to reclaim their land and traditions. By 1812, tensions were high, and the fuse was lit when the British took Mackinac on July 17, 1812, in the first military action of the War of 1812 in the region.[41]

On August 9, 1812, Captain Heald received the following order from General Hull dated July 29, 1812:

> It is with regret I order the Evacuation of your Post owing to the want of Provisions only a neglect of the Commandant of [word illegible—possibly Detroit].
>
> You will therefore Destroy all arms and ammunition, but the Goods of the Factory you may give to the Friendly Indians who may be desirous of Escorting you on to Fort Wayne & to the Poor & needy of your Post. I am informed this day that Makinac & St. Joseph will be Evacuated on acct of the scarcity of Provision & I hope in my next to give you an acct. of the Surrender of the British at Malden as I Expect 600 men here by the beginning of Sept.[42]

It is notable that Hull's order is direct and unambiguous. An alternate narrative, put forward by Lieutenant Helm in 1814 and later reiterated by Eleanor Kinzie, was that the order said "to evacuate the fort, if practicable, and, in that event, to distribute all the United States' property contained in the fort, and in the United States' factory or agency, among the Indians in the neighborhood."[43] The Kinzie account has John Kinzie, who had been allowed to return to Fort Dearborn by Heald with the express order that he be allowed to "live unmolested with his family,"[44] wisely advising Heald that (1) he should not evacuate the fort but rather stay and wait for reinforcements, or (2) if Heald wanted to evacuate, it should be done immediately, perhaps while the Native Americans were dividing up the provisions to be given to them from the factory.[45] The implication of this version of events is that the ensuing events of August 15 occurred because Heald failed to follow Kinzie's advice.

Heald followed Hull's order, with the addition that he also destroyed all the whiskey at the fort and required Kinzie to also destroy all arms, ammunition, and whiskey held at his trading post. It is possible that the destruction of these items sparked the violence that followed.[46] In any event, Heald evacuated Fort Dearborn on the morning of August 15. The party was led by a former army captain, William Wells, and behind him were fifty-five soldiers, twelve civilian militiamen, nine women, and eighteen children. When the column was about a mile and half from the fort, it became apparent that there were several hundred Potawatomi waiting in ambush. Heald ordered his soldiers to attack, and thus ensued the Battle of Fort Dearborn. The fighting lasted only about fifteen minutes but was intense and bloody. In the end, fifty-two members of the evacuating party were dead—Wells, twelve soldiers, all twelve militiamen (who had been defending the party's two wagons, in which most of the children had been riding), two women, and twelve children. It was estimated that the Potawatomi lost fifteen warriors.[47]

Among the dead were Ronan and Van Voorhies. Kinzie was spared because of the protection of Black Partridge and Topinbee, Potawatomi chiefs. Kinzie's family had not been part of the evacuation; Eleanor and the children were safely offshore in a small boat when the battle occurred. Captain Heald, who was wounded, met with the Potawatomi chief Black Bird and agreed to surrender after receiving promises that survivors would be spared; Heald and his wife, Rebekah, who also had been wounded, thus were spared.[48] Lieutenant Helm was captured and while being taken back to the fort passed by the bodies of those killed in the battle. He feared that he had seen his own wife's decapitated body but was relieved to find her alive and well once he arrived back at the fort.[49]

The next day, the Potawatomi divided up the captives, burned Fort Dearborn to the ground, and dispersed. Some of those captured died while in captivity, but most were eventually ransomed and returned to their families.[50] Kinzie and his family were taken to St. Joseph as captives of Topinbee, where they joined Heald and his wife at the Burnett trading post. Captain Heald and his wife escaped to Mackinac.[51] The Kinzies were eventually allowed to go to Detroit, where they were turned over to the British. They stayed there until eventually returning to Chicago in 1816.[52] Lieutenant Helm and his wife were separated after the battle, but he was successfully ransomed and was eventually reunited with his wife in New York in the spring of 1813.[53]

Just as during the Fox Wars, the trade through the Chicago Portage was greatly reduced during the War of 1812. Only the Ouilmettes were able to safely stay at the portage during the fighting, thanks to Archange's close relations with the Potawatomi. Indeed, Archange and her sister, Sheshi Buisson, are credited with saving the lives of several people during the Battle of Fort Dearborn and its aftermath. Alexander Robinson, a trader who had a house on the South Branch Chicago River, hid out in the Ouilmette home during the battle. Sergeant William Griffith, a soldier who had been sent back to retrieve medical supplies from the fort only to be cut off from the evacuating party because of the battle, was taken captive by Topinbee, who then told him to go hide across the river beyond the Ouilmette and Kinzie houses. Griffith instead crawled through a window to get inside the Ouilmette house. When Archange discovered him, she had him discard his military uniform and don "a suit of deer skin with belt, moccasins and pipe, like a French engage."[54]

A few days after the battle, a party of warriors appeared at Chicago. Black Partridge was especially concerned about the safety of Margaret Helm because she was married to a military officer. He quickly had her dress like a Métis woman and took her to Archange for protection. Archange and Sheshi were afraid the disguise would not be enough, so they hid Margaret under the edge of a large featherbed. Sheshi then sat on the other side of the bed and took up work on a patchwork quilt. Although the warriors searched the Ouilmette house, they did not find Helm. Archange and Sheshi had likely saved another life.[55]

The War of 1812 and the Battle of Fort Dearborn represent a turning point in American history. Although some of the old-time traders, John Kinzie among them, longed for a return to the life that existed before the war, including reestablishing the Native American tribes in their former locations, such was not to be. The days of Native American sovereignty in the Midwest and the Mississippi Valley were coming to a close, and a new era of American expansion was about to begin. And once again the Chicago Portage was to play a key role.

6

The Métis Effect

In 1803, when American troops arrived in Chicago to build Fort Dearborn, there were four established properties supporting the trade along the Chicago Portage owned by French traders and their Potawatomi wives: Antoine and Archange Ouilmette; Jean and Nokenoqua Lalime; François and Marie Therese Le Mai; and Louis and Angelique Pettell.[1] We have met the Ouilmettes and Lalimes in chapters 4 and 5. Not much is known about the Le Mais and Pettells other than they were traders. We also know that Louis Pettell at times did business with John Kinzie and that Pettell and his son, Michael, were among the militiamen killed at the Battle of Fort Dearborn.[2] A map of Chicago in 1812, after the battle, shows the locations of the Ouilmette and Kinzie homes, the fort, and the battleground (fig. 19).

The fur trade was substantial in the early days of the nineteenth century, and the Chicago Portage was heavily used. In response to an account of the quantity of furs that were passing through Fort Dearborn, Colonel Jacob Kingsbury wrote to Captain John Whistler in the fall of 1804 that "I had no idea of there being so extensive a trade carried on in that quarter."[3] Entries from John Kinzie's account book further show the extent of the trade passing through the Chicago Portage. On June 14, 1806, Kinzie charged Ouilmette for hiring a wagon and oxen to transport goods to the forks of the Illinois River. Three weeks later Kinzie charged Hugh Pattinson and Company for the labor of four men for six days each to pull boats up the river, and for the portage of 156 packs of peltries (animal skins). In July 1807, Kinzie transported forty-six packs across the portage for James Aird, and later that month he charged Auguste Chouteau almost forty pounds for transporting goods. In July 1808, Chouteau paid Kinzie $256 to carry 128 packs from Mount Joliet to Chicago.[4] Although only a few families had established homes at the portage in the opening years of the nineteenth century, it was nonetheless an active hub for the fur trade.

Life at the Chicago Portage was a family affair. It was through the Native American wives of the traders that critical trading alliances were made, and it was through the French traders that Native Americans became increasingly familiar with European customs and mannerisms. While the men focused

Fig. 19. Chicago in 1812. From Alfred T. Andreas, *History of Chicago from the Earliest Period to the Present Time* (Chicago: Alfred T. Andreas, 1884), 1:81.

on trading, the work of farming and maintaining the households fell to the women. In addition to raising food for their families, the women tended to cows, horses, and sheep (and, in the case of Ouilmette, oxen). These activities often produced surplus goods that could be sold to raise funds for their husbands' trading adventures. And, perhaps just as important as their practical contributions, the close-knit community of the Potawatomi wives brought stability to the nascent settlement through the tumultuous years of the late eighteenth and early nineteenth centuries.

The marriage of Native American women to French traders was not a matter of the women "marrying out" of their tribes so they could be with successful traders. Rather, the men were "marrying into" a tribe's kinship network. It was the women who were the key to the traders' success. For the tribes of the West, trade always existed within the context of kinship, and the status of a trader's Native American wife could spell the difference between success and failure. This was true from the very first settlers in Chicago. Both Jean Baptiste Point de Sable and his colleague William Burnett were certainly dependent on their wives, Kitihawa and Kakima. As Susan Sleeper-Smith puts it:

> Both men owed their prominence and success to the kin networks of the indigenous communities into which they had married. Theirs was an indigenous universe where economic success depended on the role that their Potawatomi wives played in the fur trade. The extensive kin networks and agricultural and trading skills of these Native women allowed both Du Sable and Burnett to winter among the Potawatomi,

to acquire the choicest furs, and to be absent from their trading posts for prolonged periods of time.[5]

Although both the French and the British manipulated the Native American populations and saw them primarily as a means to an economic end in the context of the fur trade, neither country evinced a desire to completely replace the tribes with European settlers. Although the French and British periodically sought to relocate various tribes for perceived strategic purposes, both the French and the British recognized that without the Native American populations, there would be no fur trade. The Native Americans realized, for the most part, that the Europeans were there to stay and that the tribes benefited from European goods and technology.

The French, perhaps because they arrived first, were more sophisticated and open in their willingness to meet the Indigenous populations on what Richard White termed a "middle ground" of a "jointly invented world" that would be beneficial to both groups.[6] The marriages between French traders and Native American women produced numerous Métis (French for "mixed-blood") children. These children embodied the "middle ground" by literally blending the languages, cultures, and worldviews of their parents. The Métis were especially important in negotiating the political, economic, and social differences between the Native Americans, the Europeans, and, later, the self-proclaimed Americans. The Métis community grew to dominate Chicago and much of the Great Lakes region during the first decades of the nineteenth century.

With the protection offered, or at least thought to be offered, by Fort Dearborn, the area around the Chicago Portage provided a secure home for the growing Métis community. Among the first to come were Louis Buisson, a French Canadian trader with ties to Peoria, and his wife Sheshi Buisson, who was the sister of Archange Ouilmette. They lived to the north of the Chicago River along Lake Michigan and raised at least five children there.[7]

Jean Baptiste Mirandeau, a blacksmith, and his Ottawa wife, along with some of their ten children, came to Chicago in 1810. Mirandeau was also skilled at gun repairs and did an active business at Fort Dearborn until returning to Milwaukee shortly before the Battle of Fort Dearborn. Over time, several of the Mirandeau children worked for the Ouilmettes and Kinzies. Another family hailing from Milwaukee were the LaFramboise, who moved back and forth between the two locations after the founding of Fort Dearborn. François LaFramboise came from a family of traders and was married to Shaw-we-no-qua, a Potawatomi woman. After 1803 they lived along the east side of the South Branch Chicago River, where they raised five children. Like the Mirandeaus, the LaFramboise family returned to Milwaukee after the attack on the Leigh farm in 1812 and did not return to Chicago until 1817.

Jean-Baptiste Beaubien was taken in as an apprentice at age eight by Joseph Bailly, a strongly pro-British trader married to a French Ottawa wife, who provided Jean with a basic education, an introduction to the Ottawa and Potawatomi languages, and the workings of the fur trade. While working for Bailly, Beaubien first visited Chicago in 1804 and later moved there permanently in 1811, building a house on the east side of the South Branch Chicago River. He was married to an Ottawa wife who died soon after giving birth to his first daughter, Marie, and in 1807, Beaubien remarried to Mah-naw-bun-no-quah, a Potawatomi who was either the sister or daughter of Shabbona, a Potawatomi chief.[8] Their son, Charles, later married Josette LaFramboise, daughter of François, and left Chicago with the LaFramboise family after the attack on the Leigh farm. When he returned to Chicago, Beaubien bought the Leigh farm, the first of many property acquisitions. Beaubien was a major property owner in the growing Chicago of the 1820s and 1830s and became a colonel in the Sixth Regiment of the Illinois Militia. Beaubien is an excellent example of the impact that the burgeoning Métis community had in the early days of Chicago.

A similar example exists in Alexander Robinson, son of a Scottish father and an Ottawa Métis mother. Like Beaubien, Robinson was trained by Bailly in the fur trade. Although illiterate, Robinson could speak fluent Ottawa, Potawatomi, Ojibwa, French, and English. In 1800, at age eleven, Robinson was working for Bailly at St. Joseph, where he met John Kinzie. One account puts Robinson at Chicago in 1809, and he was certainly there in 1812 when he was protected by Archange Ouilmette during the Battle of Fort Dearborn, as recounted in chapter 5. In 1812 he had a house on the east side of the South Branch Chicago River just south of the LaFramboise home.

It was Robinson who aided in the rescue of Captain Nathan Heald and his wife, Rebekah, following the Battle of Fort Dearborn, taking them by canoe to St. Joseph. Robinson returned to Chicago around 1815 and assisted Ouilmette in tending to the fields around the site of Fort Dearborn, which had been burned to the ground after the battle. In 1816, when Kinzie returned to Chicago, Robinson was living with his first Native American wife on the north side of the Chicago River. His second wife, Catherine Chevalier, was the sister of Archange Ouilmette and Sheshi Buisson and daughter of François Chevalier, a Potawatomi chief. Upon François's death, Robinson was appointed chief of the United Potawatomi, Ottawa, and Chippewa. Like Jean-Baptiste Beaubien, Robinson lived a long, active, and influential life in Chicago.[9]

As can be seen from the foregoing account, the Métis community was one of interwoven kinship and business connections. Everybody was in the fur trade, and everybody was where they were because of the essential role of the Chicago Portage in that trade. As historian Jacqueline Peterson puts it, they were "united by blood, occupational survival, common values, and the river."[10] As more Native American women married French traders, and as their families grew and intermarried, a new culture emerged that was neither Native American nor French but something new. As White observes, the

Native American and French worlds "melted at the edges and merged."[11] Over time, whether something was deemed "Native American" or "French" became unclear and, more important, irrelevant. What mattered was a common life of kinship and trade relations that served the interests of both groups.

Both the Native Americans and the French who inhabited the areas around the Chicago Portage benefited from the blended world they created. The French traders found a home among the complex kinship relations and rituals of the Native American tribes of which they became a part through marriage and progeny, and the tribes were rewarded with technologies and goods that far surpassed what they had at their disposal. The presence of the French brought immediate advances—knives replaced sharpened rocks, and guns replaced lances and arrows.

But underlying this surface stratum of relationships based on the fur trade was a starker reality. Yes, the Europeans adopted certain aspects of Native American social interaction and kinship practices to advance their commercial interests, but for the most part the Europeans retained their own cultural foundation. This was not the case for Native American tribes, observes Peterson:

> The arrival of the European fur trade . . . had a profound effect on the Indian conception of time and spatial integrity. All the land, even regions of which the Great Lakes tribes had neither heard nor seen, was said to "belong" to Frenchmen and Englishmen. The natives must have thought them vain, these God-like white men who set their linear-progressive stamp on times and places as yet unknown and who vied with one another for the "protection" of their "primitive" wards. Europeans had no respect for the cyclical stores of nature; nor did they respect the spiritual knowledge of the "savage." They scoffed at the notion that nature's vicissitudes were personally directed—for good or for evil—toward humans. Natural phenomena were to be understood and then controlled.[12]

Although the Native American tribes benefited from European goods and technology, Peterson continues, "the disintegration of stable and coexisting tribal structures was the necessary price of the formation of a new social order."[13] The breakdown of social norms resting on the oral traditions left the tribes without a context into which to place the newly arrived items and ideas brought by the Europeans. The Europeans did not just bring material things that the tribes had never seen, they also brought a worldview completely at odds with the enduring traditions of Native American tribes. The tectonic cultural shift was not only technological but metaphysical, and although European technology brought immediate benefits, the associated weakening of the tribes' cultural and spiritual foundations was catastrophic. As Peterson so eloquently puts it, "Indian magic lost face to the gun."[14]

The increased reliance on European goods also disrupted long-existing traditions. Potters, weavers, basket makers, stoneworkers, and planters became less important to the tribe, and their social status was diminished. Traditional patterns of kinship recognition and social norms were destroyed by intermarriage with Europeans, who often refused to follow the moral precepts of the tribes. Acceptance of Métis chiefs confused and weakened the integrity and power of clan identification. The relentless search for peltry to feed the insatiable appetite of the fur trade fragmented villages and kin groupings and destabilized respect for tribal boundaries that were necessary for peaceful coexistence.

The Métis effect therefore had positive and negative implications for both Native Americans and the French. The new culture resulted from a series of disruptions experienced by the western Native Americans driven by the explosion of the fur trade in the seventeenth and eighteenth centuries. First came the fur trade wars of the mid- to late seventeenth century, when the Iroquois pushed westward in search of new sources of fur. The Potawatomi, Miami, Fox, Sauk, Huron, and Erie tribes all were displaced by this onslaught, and as fellow refugees, they became more accustomed to intertribal reliance and cooperation, relationships that were facilitated by the rituals of kinship and trade. The Miami, especially, suffered a great deal of upheaval with regard to their settlements at the Chicago Portage, first being pushed west by the Iroquois in the 1650s only to return in the 1690s before being displaced again, finally, to the Maumee and Wabash valleys in the early eighteenth century.[15]

After the Iroquois came the French and then the British. There was a common bond between the western tribes and the French or the British—they all, for the most part, accepted that their separate desires could not be obtained through force. The Native Americans knew they could not repel the Europeans even if they wanted to, and the Europeans knew that their livelihoods as traders depended on the trade networks of the western tribes who, not incidentally, vastly outnumbered the Europeans. Battles might be won, and peace treaties signed, but at least as far as the western tribes, the French, and the British were concerned, they were all in it together.

The Métis community at Chicago faltered during the Fox wars but afterward reemerged stronger than ever. In the 1740s the Potawatomi moved south from Wisconsin to establish permanent villages in the Chicago area and were soon joined by the Chippewa and Ottawa. These tribes formed the primary Native American components of the Métis community in Chicago, especially the Potawatomi. From 1790 to 1833, the Métis were the majority of inhabitants at the Chicago Portage and the environs that later became the city of Chicago.

Although armed aggression between the revolutionary Americans and the British ended with the Treaty of Ghent in 1815, the British persisted in their attempt to maintain control over the fur trade. Writing to Acting Secretary of War A. J. Dallas on June 20, 1815, Lewis Cass, governor of the Michigan

Territory, emphasized the need for the Americans to reestablish the post at Fort Dearborn:

> There are three great channels of communication, by which traders may introduce the goods into the Mississippi and Missouri Country from the British dominions. One is by the way of Chicago, and down the Illinois. Another by way of Green Bay up the Fox River down the Ouisconsin. This has been the great thoroughfare along which goods have been taken. Immense quantities have been smuggled to the Mississippi and it is calculated that not more than one third part of those sold in the Indian Country, every [year] pay duties. The establishment of a post at Green Bay and at Prairie du Chien will close this line of communication. Another at Chicago will effect the same object upon the Illinois. There will, then remain a route to be taken, which has heretofore been little used. It is up a small river which enters lake Superior near the Grand Portage and along a number of small lakes with portages to heads of the Mississippi. I am informed by intelligent men that this is the only route, after closing those by Chicago and Green Bay which is practicable.[16]

John Kinzie joined Cass in advocating for the reestablishment of Fort Dearborn at Chicago. In a letter to Cass, he pointed out that the Native Americans who were still hostile to the United States had taken to having a seasonal rendezvous at Chicago in the spring and that a military presence there could help deter their aggression and reduce the influence of the British. He emphasized that Chicago was "all important to the Illenois Country as it is the key of communication" and made the case for its strategic, long-term importance:

> The hostility of those tribes is owing to their intercourse with the traders of S. W. Company [South West Fur Company—a British enterprise located in Montreal], whose intercourse and of course whose policy is to render them inimical to all American traders, from what I have already said the importance of establishing a military post at or near the place of their general rendezvous will at once present itself the spot which is most important and which will possess the greatest advantages is that on which Fort Dearborn formerly stood as those tribes generally rendezvous there in the Spring consequently a garrison would be necessary to reduce trade and intercourse with them to a system and to prevent frauds and misrepresentations from the agents of another government whose interference will ever keep them hostile to the United States—
>
> As the navigation of those waters will in a few years become an object of great importance to the U. States as at present boats of several tons burthen can pass from Lake Michigan into the Mississippi

> River there being only four and half feet difference in the elevation of the two waters. Therefore it would be politick to adopt measures in due time that will secure the friendship of the hostile and fix that of the wavering.[17]

The arguments of Cass and Kinzie carried the day, and by the end of 1815, the United States had decided to rebuild Fort Dearborn.

In the spring of 1816, Captain Hezekiah Bradley landed at Chicago with his detachment and set about rebuilding Fort Dearborn. He found Robinson and Ouilmette there and engaged them and their families to help the soldiers establish a garden. Work on the fort progressed quickly and included the building of a new Indian agency house and a factory (trading house). By the end of 1816, Major Daniel Baker had arrived to take command of the completed fort. Charles Jouett returned to Chicago briefly as Indian agent, and Jacob Varnum was named the factor (Varnum had preceded Matthew Irwin as factor at the first Fort Dearborn).

Jouett returned to Kentucky in 1817, and Kinzie lobbied heavily for the job as Indian agent. The Kinzies had returned to their old home in 1816 and attempted to reenter the fur trade but with limited success.[18] Kinzie was eventually named both interpreter for the new fort and Indian subagent, the salaries for which supplemented his trading business. President James Monroe named Alexander Wolcott the new Indian agent and before long, Wolcott grew close to the Kinzie family. Wolcott eventually married Kinzie's daughter Ellen Marion in 1823. Kinzie's son, John Harris Kinzie, married Wolcott's niece, Juliette Magill, in 1830.[19]

About the same time that the Kinzies moved back, Lieutenant Linai Helm and his wife, Margaret (another of John Kinzie's daughters), also returned to Chicago. So, for a while in 1818, Chicago had a familiar look, much as had existed before the Battle of Fort Dearborn. The Kinzie and Ouilmette families were in their old places, a new Fort Dearborn offered stability and protection, an Indian Agency house and a factory persisted in their efforts to serve and placate the Native American tribes in the area, and trade flowed through the Chicago Portage. But this sense of familiarity belied a deeper fact that the times were changing, and these changes would eventually lead to the end of the Métis community in Chicago.

The nature of the fur trade had transformed significantly in the years following the Battle of Fort Dearborn. The biggest change came with the advent of John Jacob Astor's American Fur Company. Astor created a global trading company that he operated from New York City. He was instrumental in obtaining the abolition of the United States factory system in 1822, and before long his American Fur Company was the dominant player in the fur trade.[20]

Astor assigned Ramsay Crooks and Robert Stuart to direct his operations in the western Great Lakes, including Chicago. In 1818, the American Fur

Company hired more than one hundred young men from the Lake Champlain region who had grown up around Canadians and knew how to speak French. One of these young men was Gurdon Saltonstall Hubbard, who started as a clerk but eventually became superintendent of the Illinois River trading posts.

Each autumn, from its headquarters in Mackinac, the American Fur Company sent out a "brigade" of trading outfits heading for the various trading posts throughout the West. The Illinois brigade consisted of about a dozen boats, each manned by a half dozen *voyageurs* and carrying about three tons of merchandise. In addition to the *voyageurs* were the traders and their families, so the Illinois brigade numbered around one hundred people.

The Illinois brigade would make its way down the eastern shore of Lake Michigan and then around the southern shore to Chicago, where it crossed over the Chicago Portage and headed down the Des Plaines River to the Illinois River. Once it reached navigable water on the Illinois River, the brigade would break up into smaller groups that made their way to the various trading posts along the Illinois River and its tributaries. The traders passed the winter trading with the Native Americans, and then in the spring the route was reversed, this time the boats being laden with furs.[21]

Hubbard was part of one of these brigades when he first came to Chicago in October 1818. In his autobiography he described the Chicago Portage and how difficult it could be to cross it in times of low water:

> Mud Lake drained partly into the Aux Plaines [Des Plaines River] and partly through a narrow, crooked channel into the South Branch, and only in very wet seasons was there sufficient water to float an empty boat. The mud was very deep, and along the edge of the lake grew tall grass and wild rice, often reaching above a man's head, and so strong and dense it was almost impossible to walk through them.
>
> Our empty boats were pulled up the channel, and in many places, where there was no water and a hard clay bottom, they were placed on short rollers, and in this way moved along until the lake was reached, where we found mud thick and deep, but only at rare intervals was there water. Forked tree branches were tied upon the ends of the boat poles, and these afforded a bearing on the tussocks of grass and roots, which enabled the men in the boat to push to some purpose. Four men only remained in a boat and pushed with these poles, while six or eight others waded in the mud alongside, and by united efforts constantly jerking it along, so that from early dawn to dark we succeeded only in passing a part of our boats through to the Aux Plaines outlet, where we found the first hard ground. While a part of our crew were thus employed, others busied themselves in transporting our goods on their backs to the river; it was a laborious day for all.

> Those who waded through the mud frequently sank to their waist, and at times were forced to cling to the side of the boat to prevent going over their heads; after reaching the end and camping for the night came the task of ridding themselves from the blood suckers.
>
> The lake was full of these abominable black plagues, and they stuck so tight to the skin that they broke in pieces if force was used to remove them; experience had taught the use of a decoction of tobacco to remove them, and this was resorted to with good success.
>
> Having rid ourselves of the blood suckers, we were assailed by myriads of mosquitoes, that rendered sleep hopeless, though we sought the softest spots on the ground for our beds.
>
> Those who had waded the lake suffered great agony, their limbs becoming swollen and inflamed, and their sufferings were not ended for two or three days.
>
> It took us three consecutive days of such toil to pass all our boats through this miserable lake; when we finally camped on the banks of the river, our goods had all crossed the portage and we were once more ready to proceed.[22]

Fortunately for the *voyageurs*, the return trip in the spring, when the waters were up, was easier, although on the return trip they had to overcome the strong currents of the Illinois and Des Plaines Rivers.

Hubbard had met John Harris Kinzie, then a young man of fifteen, while at Mackinac. Following in his father's footsteps, John Harris was serving an apprenticeship with the American Fur Company. Over his years of passing through the Chicago Portage, Hubbard became close with the Kinzie family, who treated him much like a son. As the American Fur Company grew, it took in more and more of the existing traders, and by 1818 John Kinzie himself was employed by the company.

Although dominant, the American Fur Company was not the only game in town. In 1816, John Crafts came to Chicago as the agent for the Detroit firm of Conant and Mack. He established a successful trading post along the South Branch Chicago River. He was so successful that the American Fur Company hired Jean-Baptiste Beaubien to represent them in Chicago, taking John Kinzie's place, to more effectively compete against Crafts. Beaubien bought a house just south of Fort Dearborn along the lakeshore and developed a successful trading business along the eastern bank of the Chicago River.[23]

The American Fur Company bought out Crafts in 1822 and appointed him to run their Chicago operation, leaving Kinzie and Beaubien now working for Crafts. The men worked amicably together, and Crafts, like Hubbard, became close to the Kinzie family. He courted Maria Indiana Kinzie, the teenage daughter of John and Eleanor, throughout 1824, but Crafts fell ill and died at the Kinzie home in 1825.[24] When the United States shut down the factory system in 1822, the American Fur Company bought the factory at Fort Dearborn, and

Fig. 20. Chicago in 1820. From Henry R. Schoolcraft, *Ethnological Researches, Respecting the Red Man of America: Information Respecting the History, Conditions, and Prospects of the Indian Tribes of the United States* (Philadelphia: Lippincott, Grambo, 1854), pt. 4, 193.

Beaubien set up his trading operation there. At this point, it is possible that the Kinzie family moved into Beaubien's house south of the fort.[25]

In August 1820, Governor Cass arrived in Chicago on the way back from an exploration of the sources of the Mississippi River. Cass had a party of sixteen men in two canoes, and one of the members was Henry R. Schoolcraft, a mineralogist and anthropologist, on whom the sight of Chicago made a strong impression (fig. 20). In Chicago the party decided to split up, with Cass and several others proceeding on horseback to Detroit, while Schoolcraft and the rest followed the Lake Michigan route along its eastern shore back to Mackinac. Schoolcraft described the Chicago River and the Chicago Portage:

> Chicago creek is eighty yards wide, at the garrison, and has a bar at its mouth, which prevents shipping from entering, but is deep within. It is ascended eleven miles in boats, and barges, where there is a portage of seven miles across a prairie, to the river Plein, the main northwestern fork of the Illinois.
>
> The intervening country consists of different strata of marl and clay, presenting great facilities for canal excavation, and the difference in the level of the two streams is so little, that loaded boats of a small class, may pass over the lowest parts of the prairie, during the spring, and autumnal freshets. But at mid-summer, it is necessary to transport them over land, to mount Juliet, a distance of thirty miles. From thence the navigation is good, at all seasons, to St. Louis, a distance of four hundred miles.[26]

And, like others before him, Schoolcraft was taken by the natural beauty of the area and recognized its strategic value as a commercial center for the growing nation:

> The country around Chicago is the most fertile and beautiful that can be imagined. It consists of an intermixture of woods and prairies, diversified with gentle slopes, sometimes attaining the elevation of hills, and irrigated with a number of clear streams and rivers, which throw their waters partly into lake Michigan, and partly into the Mississippi river. As a farming country, it unites the fertile soil, of the finest low land prairies, with an elevation, which exempts it from the influence of stagnant waters, and a summer climate of delightful serenity; while its natural meadows present all the advantages for raising stock, of the most favoured part of the valley of the Mississippi. It is already the seat of several flourishing plantations, and only requires the extinguishment of the Indian title to the lands, to become one of the most attractive fields for the emigrant. To the ordinary advantages of an agricultural market town, it must, hereafter, add that of a depot, for the inland commerce, between the northern and southern sections of the union, and a great thoroughfare for strangers, merchants, and travellers.[27]

Schoolcraft's reference to extinguishing Native American rights to their own land indicates the violence that lay beneath the aesthetic appreciation of the area's natural beauty.

In 1821, Ebenezer Childs went by canoe from Wisconsin to St. Louis. On his return trip, he intended to take the Chicago Portage route from the Illinois River to Lake Michigan. His account of that return trip is a great example of how much the Chicago Portage route could vary in times of low and high waters. Childs arrived at a period of high water and later reported his experience:

> We continued up the Illinois to the junction of the Kankakee and Eau Plains [Des Plaines], and thence up the Eau Plains to where I supposed we had to make a portage to Chicago River; but I could not see any signs of the portage. There had been heavy rains for several days, which had so raised the streams that they overflowed their banks. I concluded that I had gone far enough for the portage. So I left Eau Plains and took a northeast direction. After traveling a few miles, I found the current of the Chicago River. The whole country was inundated; I found not less than two feet of water all the way across the portage. That night I arrived at Chicago, pitched my tent on the bank of the lake, and went to the Fort for provisions. I was not, however, able to obtain any; the commissary informing me that

> the public stores were so reduced, that the garrison were subsisting on half rations, and he knew not when they would get any more. I went to Col. Beaubien, who furnished me with a small supply. I found two traders there from Mackinaw; and as my men were all sick, I exchanged my tent and canoe for a horse, and took passage on board the Mackinaw boat as far as Manitowoc. One of our party had to go by land and ride the horse. There were at this time but two families residing outside of the Fort at Chicago those, of Mr. Kinzie and Col. Beaubien.[28]

Childs had missed the Chicago Portage in its entirety! Such was the ease with which canoes and other boats could pass the portage at high water.

Schoolcraft's lofty sentiments about the region surrounding the Chicago Portage were not shared by all who came through Chicago. William Keating, who accompanied Major Stephen Long on his expedition in 1823, had a decidedly dour view of the place, grousing, "The village presents no cheering prospect, as, notwithstanding its antiquity, it consists of but few huts, inhabited by a miserable race of men, scarcely equal to the Indians from whom they are descended."[29] The soil was unfertile, complained Keating, the wind was cold and damp, there were too many insects, and the landscape was one of "fatiguing monotony."[30] He was duly impressed by the portage itself, however. (For Keating's full account of his impressions of Chicago, see appendix B.)

Another account of the Chicago Portage route, and of early Chicago, comes to us from John H. Fonda. While traveling from St. Louis up the Mississippi River, he made use of the portage route:

> Under [our guide's] direction we paddled along until we came to the Des Plaines river, from which we passed into a large slough or lake, that must have led us into a branch of the Chicago river, for we followed a stream that brought us opposite Fort Dearborn.
>
> At this period, Chicago was merely an Indian agency; it contained about fourteen houses, and not more than 75 or 100 inhabitants at the most. An agent of the American Fur Company named Gordon S. Hubbard, then occupied the Fort. The staple business seemed to be carried on by Indians, and run-away soldiers, who hunted ducks and musk-rats in the marshes. There was a great deal of low land, and mostly destitute of timber. The principal inhabitants were the agent, Mr. Hubbard, a Frenchman by the name of Ouilmette, and John B. Beaubien.[31]

Even as the American Fur Company was consolidating the fur trade, the trade itself was increasingly in jeopardy. The fur trade as practiced by John Kinzie and traders like him depended on a strong Native American and

Métis presence, and that presence was waning. Between 1816 and 1833, the Potawatomi alone ceded to the United States almost eighteen million acres that the Potawatomi had claimed east of the Mississippi River. As Ann Durkin Keating puts it, this "was an almost bloodless conquest of monumental proportions."[32] With each treaty the amount of "Indian Country" decreased, opening these lands to traders who could compete with the established companies without need of a government license.

As its market shrank, the American Fur Company resorted to increasingly questionable practices, including selling illegal whiskey to Native Americans. By the time John Craft died in 1825, the Chicago fur trade was becoming more tenuous. Kinzie and Beaubien did their best to hold the American Fur Company trade together and were able to make a profit in 1826–27. On the basis of that success, they ordered more goods in anticipation of another good trading year, but instead the fur trade for all practical purposes ended in 1828 with a precipitous decline in available furs. The fur trade was dying, as Keating explains, for several reasons: "The development of the lead mines in western Illinois, the invention of the steel trap in 1823, and the cutthroat tactics of the American Fur Company all led to the demise of the fur trade."[33] By 1828 the American Fur Company had begun to close its operations in Chicago. And, as if by way of a coda, John Kinzie had a cerebral stroke and died on January 6, 1828.

The era of the fur trader and the influence of the Métis community in Chicago was coming to an end. The Native Americans and Métis were being displaced and the new Americans were coming in earnest. Unlike the French and British, the Americans had no interest in sharing territory, no tolerance for traditional views of kinship and clan, and no need for the social networks that had sustained the fur trade. To these Americans there was no difference between Native Americans and Métis; both were obstacles to be overcome. Within a few years, most of the Native Americans and Métis were pushed west of the Mississippi. For the few who remained, they did so by deemphasizing their own cultural heritage and adopting the new Americans' ways and values.

7

Chicago, Wisconsin?

Just as there would likely be no Chicago as we know it without the Chicago Portage, so, too, Chicago would not be in Illinois without the Chicago Portage. How that came to be is the story of an ambitious young nephew and his savvy and politically astute uncle who together orchestrated getting Illinois admitted as a US state in 1818 while making sure it included Chicago.

The move for statehood was inextricably bound up with the long-standing idea of creating a canal connecting Lake Michigan and the Illinois River. Ever since Louis Jolliet first saw the Chicago Portage in 1673, he and others had repeatedly remarked on the efficacy of such a canal. Henri de Joutel saw its importance in 1687, as did Thomas Jefferson in 1781. But although the idea was there, the resources for accomplishing such an undertaking were lacking. That started to change in 1816 as the idea of the canal began to inch its way to reality.

Among the various treaties made with the Native Americans following the Battle of Fort Dearborn, the one entered into on August 24, 1816, at St. Louis stands out. As Rufus Blanchard puts it, "Of all the Indian treaties ever made, this will be remembered when all others, with their obligations, are forgotten."[1] In 1804, a treaty had been agreed to between William Henry Harrison, governor of the Indiana Territory, and the chiefs of the united Sauk and Fox Tribes that ceded land to the United States that comprised "roughly the territory between the mouths of the Illinois and Wisconsin Rivers, bounded on the west by the Mississippi and on the east by the Illinois and Fox rivers."[2] This treaty was reaffirmed by a treaty at Portage des Sioux in 1815, but the ownership of the land so ceded was disputed not only between the United States and the Native Americans but among the various tribes themselves. The cession was particularly disputed by the Potawatomi, Ottawa, and Chippewa Tribes who had overlapping ownership claims to the lands. The Treaty of St. Louis signed on August 24, 1816, was intended to settle these disputes.

The treaty was entered into between William Clark, governor of the Missouri Territory; Ninian Edwards, governor of the Illinois Territory; and Auguste Chouteau, who along with Clark and Edwards had negotiated the treaty at Portage des Sioux, on behalf of the United States, and chiefs and warriors of the united tribes of the Potawatomi, Ottawa, and Chippewa. The treaty stated in relevant part:

> Art. 1. The said chiefs and warriors, for themselves and the tribes they represent, agree to relinquish, and hereby do relinquish, to the United States, all their right, claim, and title to all the land contained in the before mentioned cession of the Sacs and Foxes, which lies south of a due west line from the southern extremity of Lake Michigan to the Mississippi river. And they moreover cede to the United States all the land contained within the following bounds, to-wit: beginning on the left bank of the Fox river of Illinois, ten miles above the mouth of said Fox river; thence running so as to cross Sandy Creek, ten miles above its mouth; thence, in a direct line, to a point ten miles north of the west end of the Portage between Chicago Creek [Chicago River], which empties into Lake Michigan, and the river Depleines [Des Plaines River], a fork of the Illinois; thence in a direct line, to a point on Lake Michigan, ten miles northward of the mouth of Chicago Creek; thence along the lake, to a point ten miles southward of the mouth of the said Chicago Creek; thence in a direct line, to a point on the Kankakee, ten miles above its mouth; thence with the said Kankakee and the Illinois river, to the mouth of Fox river, and thence to the beginning: Provided, nevertheless, that the said tribes shall be permitted to hunt and to fish within the limits of the land hereby relinquished and ceded so long as it may continue to be the property of the United States.[3]

The treaty thus established two Indian Boundary Lines north and south of the Chicago Portage, which lay at the center of the corridor. This treaty was the first acquisition of land specifically intended for a canal connecting Lake Michigan and the Illinois River. Governor Edwards later complained that the tribes were not receiving the benefits from this canal that they had been promised and that they had been induced to cede the land including the portage by specific representations that the canal would be "advantageous" to the tribes.[4]

The following year, Acting Secretary of War George Graham wrote to Edwards authorizing the surveying of the boundary lines and noted that if "that tract of land was surveyed and settled, it would very much facilitate the migrations to the Illinois Territory from New England and the State of New York by means of the lake navigation."[5] This point would be repeated when the push began for Illinois statehood. The boundary lines were subsequently surveyed by Captain John Sullivan in 1817 and 1818 and set forth in his map of 1819 showing them to the north and south of Fort Dearborn (fig. 21).

The move to admit Illinois as a state must be seen against the backdrop of the Northwest Ordinance of 1787, which was promulgated to bring governance to the territories obtained from the British through the Treaty of Paris

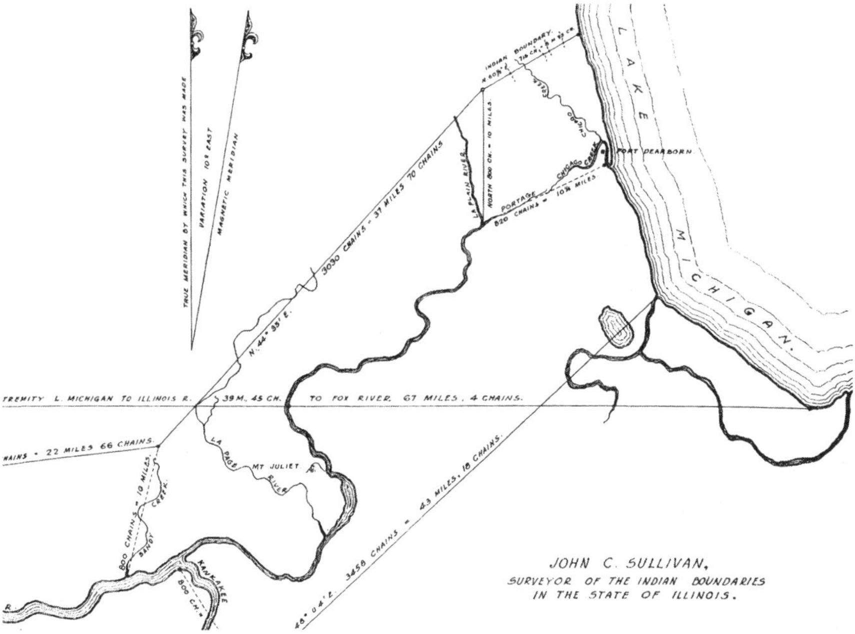

Fig. 21. Detail of a survey by John Sullivan showing Indian boundary lines, 1819. From Robert Knight and Lucius H. Zeuch, *The Location of the Chicago Portage Route of the Seventeenth Century* (Chicago: Chicago Historical Society, 1928), 105.

in 1783. An extraordinary document, the Northwest Ordinance was a precursor of the US Constitution, but we will focus on the process and requirements it set forth for the formation of states out of the Northwest Territory. It was the guiding document for the creation of the states of Ohio (1803), Indiana (1816), Illinois (1818), Michigan (1837), and Wisconsin (1848).

The ordinance of 1787 contemplated that a minimum of three and not more than five states would be created out of the Northwest Territory. There would be three states, a Western (Illinois), Middle (Indiana), and Eastern (Ohio) created below an east-west line as defined in Article V, with the possibility of one or two more states north of that line:

> The boundaries of these three states shall be subject so far to be altered, that if Congress shall here after find it expedient, they shall have authority to form one or two states in that part of the said territory which lies north of an east and west line drawn through the southerly bend or extreme of Lake Michigan.[6]

This language became the subject of intense debate and dispute regarding the establishment of the northern borders of Ohio, Indiana, and Illinois. One issue was where was the "southerly bend or extreme of Lake Michigan"? The other debate was over the meaning of the phrase "in that part of said territory."

The ordinance also established two vertical lines between the lower three states. One was a straight line north to Canada from where the Great Miami River flows into the Ohio River, and the other was along the Wabash River north from where it flows into the Ohio River to "post Vincents," then straight north to Lake Superior. The first line separated Ohio and Indiana, and the second Indiana and Illinois. These lines were never in dispute.[7]

The process for statehood required a population of sixty thousand people within the proposed state boundaries, an application to the US Congress for statehood, the passage of an enabling act by Congress, the drafting of a state constitution, and the subsequent approval by Congress of that constitution. In their movements for statehood, Ohio and Indiana both made cases for establishing their northern borders farther north than that strictly called for by the Northwest Ordinance. Ohio came first and benefited from the uncertainty over the location of the southern extremity of Lake Michigan.

The enabling act passed by Congress for Ohio placed its northern border at the east-west line established by the Northwest Ordinance. However, Ohio's draft constitution raised the eastern end of that line so that it was north of what was then called Miami Bay, now called Maumee Bay, so that Ohio could have access to Lake Erie. It also was clear at the time that Congress passed its enabling act that Ohio did not have the requisite population as established by the Northwest Ordinance. Nevertheless, Congress accepted Ohio's constitution and granted it statehood in 1803. This was the first precedent that the ordinance line was only a starting point in determining the northern boundaries of Ohio, Indiana, and Illinois.

Figure 22 shows the transformation over time of the various territories and states carved out of the Northwest Territory. In 1805, Congress signaled its preference for the four-or-five-state alternative by creating the Michigan Territory, setting its southern boundary at the ordinance line. This action resulted in two conflicting Michigan-Ohio borders, one shown in the upper left corner of the map as the straight east-west ordinance line and one shown in 1805 with the upward angle to the northeast. This confusion eventually led to the Toledo War in 1835 between the state of Ohio and the Michigan Territory that ended with Michigan accepting the angled border in exchange for land in the Upper Peninsula.

With Ohio's northern border now nominally set on its eastern end with the Indiana-Ohio meridian, it was now Indiana's turn to set its northern border. In its enabling act for Indiana statehood, Congress required that Indiana's constitutional convention "shall ratify the borders aforesaid, *otherwise they shall be and remain as now prescribed in the Ordinance*" (emphasis added).[8] That "otherwise" became a tacit acknowledgment by Congress that the ordinance line was not set in stone as the northern border of Ohio, Indiana, and Illinois.

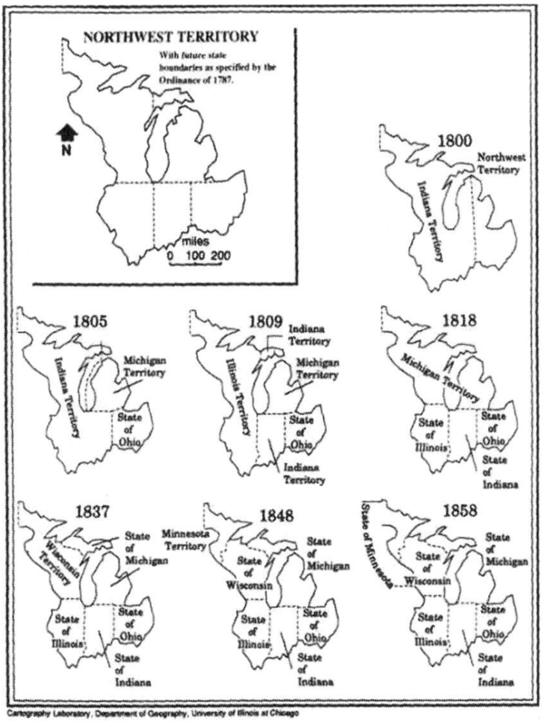

Fig. 22. Evolution of Northwest Territory. Catherine E. Breen, Gerald A. Danzer, Janet A. Lueby, curriculum materials for Illinois Becomes a State: 1818 Compromise, Later Conflict, in *Illinois History Teacher 1995*, vol. 2 (Springfield: Illinois Historic Preservation Agency, 1995), https://www.lib.niu.edu/1995/iht29502cm.html.

Indiana grabbed this opportunity with both hands. In its draft constitution, it set its northern border at a point ten miles north of the southern extreme of Lake Michigan. Moreover, it established, and Congress accepted, the southern extreme of Lake Michigan as being at a northern latitude of 41 degrees, 38 minutes, 58 seconds. With its northern border established, Indiana became a state on December 11, 1816.

Now it was time for Illinois to become a state. In 1809, the Indiana Territory was divided, with the western portion becoming the Illinois Territory with Ninian Edwards as territorial governor and Nathaniel Pope as territorial secretary. Three years later, Illinois advanced to the second grade of territorial government in accordance with the procedures set by the Northwest Ordinance. This step allowed for the election of a legislature, but in a significant advance in representative government, Governor Edwards convinced Congress to allow for the election of delegates without regard to property ownership. The Illinois Territory thereby established the most democratic form of territorial government to be found anywhere in the United States at that time. Under its form, "suffrage was granted to all free white males, twenty-one years of age, who had paid a county or territorial tax, no matter how small, and had resided in the territory one year."[9]

Despite this advance in terms of territorial governance, the fact remained that territorial government was far from "democratic" as we understand that word today. The governor had an absolute veto over any actions taken by the legislature, and for the most part, the actual residents of the territory were not involved or particularly interested in governmental affairs. This situation resulted in a centralized and oligarchical government that lent itself to a few individuals controlling finances and patronage.[10]

The overall political situation in 1817 was one of a dispersed and relatively disinterested populace. To the degree there were political factions, they were primarily groups of men holding or seeking appointive offices, either local or territorial. The general population played little part in electoral politics, which was basically limited to the election of delegates and members of the legislature every two years. People in general did not identify with political parties, and in elections most people were concerned less with broad policy issues and more with what the representatives they elected could obtain for their county.[11]

Given this diffuse and lackadaisical state of affairs, there was hardly widespread agitation in favor of statehood among the population at large. Rather, the case for statehood would come primarily from the efforts of a young man not yet twenty-five years of age.

Governor Edwards appointed Daniel Pope Cook auditor of public accounts for the Illinois Territory in 1816 when Cook was twenty-two years old. About the same time, Cook purchased the only newspaper in the territory, the *Illinois Herald*, and renamed it the *Western Intelligencer*.[12] Cook left Illinois for Washington, DC, in 1817 with the hopes of succeeding his uncle, Nathaniel Pope, as secretary for the Illinois Territory. When that appointment failed, Cook enlisted the aid of John Quincy Adams, who became secretary of state in 1817, to try to secure an appointment as secretary to the Alabama Territory, which Cook believed was soon to apply for statehood. In a candid, if self-serving, appeal to Adams, Cook wrote that being secretary of the Alabama Territory as it strove for statehood would provide Cook "an opportunity for empowerment" that he could not achieve as a clerk in Washington.[13] When that appointment, too, failed to materialize, Cook wrote to Edwards of his plight and his plan to return to the West:

> I could get into the State Department as a clerk, but experience tells me it won't do to engage in close, laborious writing, and it would not satisfy my ambition to be buried in an office—merely as a servant as it were—where the world, perhaps, would never hear of such a being.

> Mr. Adams assures me he will at any time take pleasure in bringing me before the Government when an opportunity offers. There being no situation at present vacant that will suit, I am advised by my own judgment, as well as by his, to return to the West, and remain there until an opportunity presents itself for my advancement.[14]

True to his word, Cook returned to Kaskaskia on November 18, 1817, but instead of waiting for an opportunity to present itself for his advancement, Cook decided to make one for himself.

Two days after returning to Illinois, an editorial appeared in the *Intelligencer* asking rhetorically, "While we are laboring under so many grievances of a territorial, or semi-monarchial government, might not our claims to a state government be justly heard?"[15] Although we don't know for sure that this particular editorial was written by Cook, it promised to present a further discussion of statehood in the paper's next issue.

On November 27, the paper published the first sustained argument for statehood, written by Cook, and signed "A republican." Cook argued that the population of the territory, which he estimated at forty thousand, had reached a point justifying admission, especially given, he claimed, that nine-tenths of that number were Americans who had come to the territory from the original states along the Eastern Seaboard. Given the political maturity of this population, said Cook, the territorial government was anachronistic, particularly the territorial governor's absolute veto power over actions taken by the territorial legislature. Cook argued that the existing form of government failed to encourage participation by talented individuals.[16] Moreover, granting Illinois statehood would benefit the nation as a whole because, freed from the burden of legislating for the local concerns of the territory, Congress could devote attention to national concerns such that "the strength and respectability of the nation would be greatly augmented [by opening] a new field for the enlargement of the human understanding."[17]

This latter, somewhat cryptic, statement was Cook's way of pointing to the issue of slavery that he saw as an underlying issue in Illinois's quest for statehood. The Northwest Ordinance had outlawed slavery in the Northwest Territory. However, it remained possible that a state carved out of the territory could opt for allowing slavery. Cook argued that obtaining statehood and resolving the question of slavery favorably to the antislavery position would encourage migration to Illinois from the free states of the East:

> At present it is doubtful whether slavery will be tolerated when a state government is formed. And many on both sides of the question are remaining in the anxiety of suspense, to know how it will be settled. It is therefore desirable to settle the question at as early a period as possible, for the purpose of giving relief to those who are wanting to emigrate to the territory.[18]

Adding fuel to this fire was the fact that only a few months before Cook's opening salvo for statehood, Missouri had begun circulating petitions asking for admission as a state. It was believed that Missouri would come in as a slave state, and if that happened before Illinois could be admitted, it was feared that the existence of slavery in Missouri would be used as an argument for allowing slavery in Illinois.[19]

Whether driven by Cook's ambition, a desire for more democratic government, to promote migration, or to dissuade slavery, the push for Illinois statehood quickly gathered steam. Just a few days after Cook made his case in the *Intelligencer*, the Illinois territorial legislature met and Governor Edwards laid before it a proposal to conduct a census in preparation for an application for statehood after the legislature's next meeting. This would have been the usual way to proceed, but it wasn't fast enough for Cook, who had been elected a clerk of the house of representatives. With his pushing, the legislature passed a motion "that a committee be appointed to draft a memorial to congress praying for this territory to be admitted into the union, with all the rights and privileges of a state government."[20] The memorial was drafted, passed unanimously by the legislature, and presented to the governor on December 10. The governor approved, and the memorial was sent to Washington.

The pro-statehood people still had to deal with the requirement that the proposed state was supposed to contain a population of sixty thousand. The legislature authorized the taking of a census to begin in April 1818 and to be completed and given to the secretary of the territory in June. Hedging their bets, the legislature passed a supplementary law that said "a great increase of population may be expected between the first day of next June and December following," and that the census was to continue during that period, with additional returns given to the secretary.[21]

The memorial contained two long paragraphs. The first, likely written by Cook, repeated the assertions he had made in the *Intelligencer*. It argued that territorial government was despotic and that as soon as conditions allowed, it should be done away with. The memorial in its first paragraph claimed a population of "not less than forty thousand souls" and stated that most of the population of the territory had come from preexisting states and so was accustomed to self-governance. The second paragraph addressed more practical concerns and asked Congress to give the newly formed state the lead and salt mines that existed there for the purpose of funding state government and internal improvements. It asked that section sixteen of each newly established township be set aside for schools, that the net proceed of land sales made by the state be used for public roads, and that all other "gifts and privileges" that Congress had given to Ohio, Indiana, and Mississippi also be given to Illinois.[22]

The claims of a population of at least forty thousand and vast public support for statehood were simply created out of whole cloth by Cook. On

December 11, Cook argued in the *Intelligencer* that it didn't matter whether a census proved his numbers because the "representatives of the people from each county agree that there are 40,000 inhabitants," and that alone should suffice. Similarly, by sheer assertion alone, and despite the fact there had been no significant discussion of statehood by the territorial population, Cook claimed statehood to be "the first wish of the people." A fairer statement would have been that it was the first wish of Daniel Pope Cook. It had been only three weeks since Cook had returned to Kaskaskia and written his editorial supporting statehood, and already a memorial asking for the same was on its way to Washington.[23]

The memorial arrived in Washington and was delivered to the Illinois Territory's delegate to Congress, Nathaniel Pope, who was also Cook's uncle. When Pope received the memorial in mid-January 1818, he was taken aback because he had played no part whatsoever in the efforts back in Illinois to advance the cause of statehood. Nevertheless, he embraced the cause, and on January 16 Pope presented the petition for statehood to the US House of Representatives. A select committee was formed consisting of Pope, Richard Mentor Johnson of Kentucky, John Canfield Spencer of New York, Ezekiel Whitman from the District of Maine in Massachusetts, and Thomas Claiborne of Tennessee to consider the case for statehood and to formulate an enabling act.

Pope found an ally in Johnson, who was a strong supporter of education and internal improvements and who later became vice president of the United States under Martin Van Buren. Johnson had ties to both Pope and Edwards from the days the two had resided in Kentucky. Johnson had recommended Pope for appointment as territorial secretary in 1809 and had helped Illinois advance to the second stage of territorial government in 1812. He also had supported Edwards in obtaining the popular election of territorial delegates and an expansion of voting rights beyond the provisions of the Northwest Ordinance. Other than Pope, Johnson had a better understanding of the situation in the Illinois Territory than any of the other committee members.[24]

On January 21, Pope wrote a letter to the editors of the *Intelligencer* that his only fear in getting an enabling act passed concerned the issue of population. He noted that the bill he and the committee were drafting required that a census be taken before a state constitutional convention could be called but that he hoped to have that provision struck before final passage. He said that he believed he could get the act passed if it could be shown that the territory had a population of at least thirty-five thousand.[25]

The committee met on January 22, and the next day, just one week after the committee was appointed, reported a bill to the House of Representatives "to enable the people of the Illinois Territory, to form a Constitution and state government, and for the admission of such state into the union, on an equal footing with the original states."[26] The enabling act was modeled on the Indiana enabling act of 1816 and to a lesser extent the Mississippi enabling act of 1817.

In section 2 of the draft enabling act, Pope included a provision that would change both Illinois and US history. Instead of accepting the northern border for Illinois as that set forth in the Northwest Ordinance, Pope proposed "an East and West line drawn through a point ten miles north of the Southern extreme of Lake Michigan." This ten-mile extension was the same extension that had been granted to Indiana, although the geographical impact was different. Indiana obtained forty miles of lakeshore by the extension, whereas Illinois would obtain only four miles of lakeshore but more land, extending west to the Mississippi River. But Pope didn't intend to stop there. In a letter to the *Intelligencer*, Pope wrote, "When the bill is taken up, I will endeavour to procure twenty or thirty miles farther north, and make Lake Michigan part of our eastern boundary. I shall not attempt to explain the importance of such an accession of territory; it is too obvious to every man who looks to the prospective weight and influence of the state of Illinois."[27]

The "obvious importance" of shifting the boundary northward was to include the Chicago Portage and future canal route to the Mississippi River wholly within the state of Illinois. Pope introduced the bill to the full House of Representatives on January 23, where it was read twice and then referred to a Committee of the Whole for further discussion. When the bill came up before the Committee of the Whole on April 4, Pope immediately moved to amend the bill to move the northern border to the line of 42°30' north latitude, about forty-one miles north of the line contained in the bill and fifty-one miles north of the boundary contemplated by the Northwest Ordinance. As recorded:

> The object of this amendment, Mr. P. [Pope] said, was to gain, for the proposed State, a coast on Lake Michigan. This would afford additional security to the perpetuity of the Union, inasmuch as the State would thereby be connected with the States of Indiana, Ohio, Pennsylvania, and New York, through the Lakes. The facility of opening a canal between Lake Michigan and the Illinois river, said Mr. P., is acknowledged by every one who has visited the place. Giving to the proposed State the port of Chicago, (embraced in the proposed limits,) will draw its attention to the opening of the communication between the Illinois river and that place, and the improvement of that harbor.[28]

Given the precedents of Ohio and, especially, Indiana, it was difficult for anyone to argue that Pope's amendment violated the restrictions suggested by the Northwest Ordinance. Pope's argument was that the Northwest Ordinance allowed the boundaries of the three southern states to be extended northward and that Ohio and Indiana proved his point. Remarkably, given the historic impact of Pope's amendment, it "was agreed to without division."[29] Even back in Illinois it garnered little interest. It was mentioned in passing in an April 29 article in the *Intelligencer*, based on an April 6 letter from Pope. Later, after the enabling act finally passed, a May 20 editorial recounted various aspects of the act and thanked Pope for his contributions but failed even to mention the boundary shift.[30]

No sooner had Pope achieved success with the passage of his amendment moving the Illinois boundary northward than the enabling act sputtered to a stop. Congress became distracted by an important issue that directly affected the enabling act and required Pope's considerable political skill to navigate. At issue was the role of the federal government in the building of roads and canals. Although there was consensus that roads and canals were needed, the question was how to fund them. Some said that the federal government could fund roads and canals that solely benefited localities while others said the federal government could fund only roads and canals that benefited the nation generally. Although Pope knew that the canal anticipated by the enabling act would require federal funding if it was to ever become a reality, the broader debate over how to fund internal developments was a minefield that Pope wanted to avoid.

The enabling act as drafted originally had a provision that earmarked 5 percent of the profits from the sale of public lands for internal improvements, two-fifths of these profits to go for roads and canals leading to the state and three-fifths for roads and canals within the state. Because the debate in Congress was focused primarily on whether the federal government should fund improvements within a given state, Pope moved to eliminate this issue from the enabling act. He proposed an amendment that the three-fifths be used instead for education. Pope made this motion immediately following his amendment to move the northern boundary, and, like the former, the latter amendment passed unanimously in the Committee of the Whole. The bill was then reported to the House of Representatives, which approved it on April 6. Only the Senate remained.

The enabling act as passed by the House of Representatives required that Illinois have a population of forty thousand at the time it passed a state constitution. Even more beneficial to the state, under the enabling act, the constitutional convention was to rely on "the enumeration directed to be made by the legislature of the said Territory."[31] In other words, Illinois would be in charge of determining the population of Illinois. This did not sit well with some members of the US Senate, and an effort was made to postpone consideration of the enabling act until an actual census could be performed. But Pope had been busy lobbying on this point, arguing that despite the Northwest Ordinance requirement of sixty thousand, a lesser population was allowable if statehood was in the general interest of the nation. He also pointed out that Ohio had been admitted with a population less than forty thousand and that Mississippi had been admitted with a population of twenty-five thousand whites and twenty thousand blacks, whereas the Illinois number included only whites.[32]

Although Pope's amendment to fund education had carried the day in the House, it found opposition in the Senate, where some senators claimed that the benefit of such education inured only to the state. This view was countered by those who said that providing educational opportunities would encourage migration and benefit the nation generally. The latter view prevailed "by a great majority," wrote Pope, "and has given a character to Illinois that nothing else could have effected."[33]

Although Pope noted that "some jealousy was felt against our gaining so much territory north, say sixty miles," no formal objection was raised in the Senate to the northern boundary.[34] In any event, the Senate suggested some amendments to the enabling act, and it was passed unanimously on April 14. Back in the House, the Senate bill was referred to a committee headed by Pope that on April 15 reported its agreement with the Senate's amendments, and the bill as amended was approved by the House. The bill then went to President James Monroe, who signed it on April 18, 1818. Illinois was a state; and Chicago was in Illinois.

From the time of Cook's first editorial in the *Intelligencer*, it had taken less than five months for Illinois to gain statehood. Having masterfully guided the enabling act through Congress, Pope wrote with justifiable pride:

> We may say with truth, that we will enter upon a state government with better prospects than any state ever did. The best soil in the world, a mild climate, a large state, with the most ample funds to educate every child in the state; however poor, a man may well hope to see his child rise to head of this mighty nation, if he have talents and virtue. Our avenues for navigation are towards the east and the west, the north and the south.[35]

There remained the not inconsiderable tasks of conducting a census, holding a constitutional convention, and having the state constitution ratified by the US Congress, but those would come in due time. For now, Pope's work was done.

For his part, young Daniel Pope Cook had succeeded in creating opportunities for himself. He would go on to serve as the first attorney general for Illinois and then as its second representative in the US House of Representatives. While serving in the House, he helped defeat a proposed proslavery constitutional convention and helped elect John Quincy Adams president in 1824, when the election was thrown to the House of Representatives. Cook married Governor Edwards's daughter, Julia Catherine Edwards, in 1821. Never a well man throughout his young life, Cook died at the age of thirty-three on October 16, 1827. Four years later, Cook County was named in his honor.

Later nineteenth- and early twentieth-century commentators have attributed to Pope a prescience that is perhaps overstated given the actual record.

Pope was a consummate politician and knew how to frame arguments to achieve his end. He also knew how to downplay controversial aspects of his proposals to avoid drawing unhelpful attention. For example, it is interesting that in the draft enabling act he chose to use the less familiar latitude designation for the northern border instead of emphasizing the number of miles he wanted to move the border (it would finally end up being just shy of sixty-one miles north of the southern extremity of Lake Michigan).

According to the congressional record, Pope did argue that moving the border north to allow for a canal connecting Lake Michigan to the Illinois River would "would afford additional security to the perpetuity of the Union, inasmuch as the State would thereby be connected with the States of Indiana, Ohio, Pennsylvania, and New York, through the Lakes."[36] It is also true that Pope himself was antislavery. But others have significantly embellished Pope's arguments beyond anything Pope himself actually said.

Governor Thomas Ford, who served from 1842 to 1846, attributed to Pope a grand vision for moving the Illinois border as being integral to sustaining the union itself. Ford emphasized Illinois's location at the heart of the country's commerce and argued that this centrality made it a linchpin in the slavery question. He asserted that Pope's effort to move the upper boundary of Illinois northward was driven by a desire to ally Illinois more with the northern and eastern states (antislavery) instead of the southern and western ones (proslavery):

> Illinois was certain to be a great State, with any boundaries which that government could give. Its great extent of territory, its unrivalled fertility of soil, and capacity for sustaining a dense population, together with its commanding position, would in course of time give the new State a very controlling influence with her sister States situate upon the western rivers, either in sustaining the federal union as it is, or in dissolving it, and establishing new governments. If left entirely upon the waters of these great rivers, it was plain that, in case of threatened disruption, the interest of the new State would be to join a southern and western confederacy. But if a large portion of it could be made dependent upon the commerce and navigation of the great northern lakes, connected as they are with the eastern States, a rival interest would be created, to check the wish for a western and southern confederacy.
>
> It therefore became the duty of the national government, not only to make Illinois strong, but to raise an interest inclining and binding her to the eastern and northern portions of the Union. This could be done only through an interest in the lakes. At that time the commerce on the lakes was small, but its increase was confidently expected, and indeed it has exceeded all anticipations, and is yet only in its infancy. To accomplish this object effectually, it was not only necessary to give to Illinois the port of Chicago and a route for the canal, but a

> considerable coast on Lake Michigan, with a country back of it sufficiently extensive to contain a population capable of exercising a decided influence upon the councils of the State.[37]

Ford went further in his revisionist history of Pope's arguments, calling on him as an authority in a territorial dispute between Illinois and Wisconsin. Wisconsin Territorial Governor William Doty wanted to establish Wisconsin as a state with a southern border set as described by the Northwest Ordinance, which meant Wisconsin would lay claim to Chicago and the Chicago Portage. Ironically, there was very little popular support for this idea in Wisconsin, but there was some support in northern Illinois to allow the territory created by Pope's northern border to be annexed by Wisconsin.

Ford fought vehemently against this idea. In particular, he refuted Doty's claim that the northern states had to have a southern boundary as described in the Northwest Ordinance by building on Pope's idea that it was permissible for Congress to shift the northern borders of the southern states northward (as it had done with Ohio, Indiana, and Illinois). Ford focused on the language of the Northwest Ordinance that said that Congress could "form one or two States in that part of the said territory which lies north of an east and west line drawn through the southerly bend or extreme of lake Michigan." Ford emphasized the word "in" as meaning the northern states did not have to be created "out of" the northern territory, but rather only within that territory; hence Congress could move northern borders of the southern states northward. Ford's position, although never so particularly stated by Pope, did find support in Congress. By 1846, Doty's attempt to lay claim to Chicago and the Chicago Portage had little popular support among the residents of Wisconsin, and there was strong opposition in Illinois to having any part of Illinois annexed by Wisconsin. Similarly, Congress showed little interest in changing the Illinois border, and so the issue died. Wisconsin accepted the existing border in its constitutional convention of 1848, and Chicago was safely to be forever in Illinois.[38]

Like Ford, historian John Moses also overstates Pope's arguments. According to Moses, Pope argued that without the northern boundary extension, Illinois would be limited to having commercial relations primarily with the South via the Mississippi and Ohio Rivers. Without a direct commercial tie to the North, says Moses, there was a danger that "in the event of an attempted dismemberment of the Union, Illinois would cast her lot with the Southern States." On the other hand, Moses claims that Pope argued that a northern extension of the Illinois border would encourage the building of a canal through the area of the Chicago Portage that would thereby link Illinois "to the states of Indiana, Ohio, Pennsylvania and New York in a bond of common interest well-nigh indissoluble."[39] Again, although it is possible that Pope held these views, there is no evidence to support the claim that he explicitly made such arguments in his quest for Illinois statehood.

Pope biographer William Meese continues the "Pope as visionary" theme when he writes that the "possibilities that were forecast by Mr. Pope actually occurred forty-two years thereafter. The south seceded but Illinois remained in the Union, and to her conservative influence we owe it that the adjoining states remained loyal." Meese continues by speculating that if the boundary had not been moved, the Illinois and Michigan Canal and the Illinois Central Railroad would not have been built and that Illinois would not have been Republican in 1856, and Abraham Lincoln would likely never have become president.[40]

Such assertions about Pope's vision are not supported by the contemporaneous writings and records we have of his efforts on behalf of Illinois statehood. Rather, the facts suggest a politically savvy man on a mission who used his considerable skills to accomplish a remarkable result in an incredibly short amount of time after having been blindsided by Cook's sudden push for statehood. Regardless of what Pope might have envisioned, it is certainly true that his success had far-reaching implications for the whole of United States history.

8

✦

The Portage in Transition

The period following statehood was one of transition for the Chicago Portage, the city of Chicago, and the newly christened state of Illinois. The fur trade was still busy in 1818, but it would soon be winding down. Increasingly, new players emerged on the scene to replace the *voyageurs* and traders. The pioneers and settlers were coming, not for fur but for land, and not to make a quick buck but to establish a home and a future. Farming and agriculture began to spread across northern Illinois, some settlers coming by boat through the Chicago Portage but more and more by horse and wagon over the Portage Trail.

Still, the old days lingered on. The garrison at the second Fort Dearborn left in 1823 under the belief that the threat of Native American violence was over. But in 1827 the Winnebago, frustrated by the increasing encroachment of settlers and perhaps emboldened by the absence of a garrison at Fort Dearborn, carried out several attacks against settlers. This uprising was brought to a quick end largely due to the prompt actions of Governor Lewis Cass, who, after directly confronting the Winnebago over their attacks and summoning military aid from St. Louis, ascended the Illinois River to cross the Chicago Portage to Chicago to personally warn the settlers there of the unrest.

It was July, and Cass's party arrived too late in the day to complete the portage. Fearful of putting a hole in their birchbark canoe, the boatmen anchored the canoe by thrusting their paddles into the mud on either side and settled in for a long night. As Cass's biographer recounted the experience:

> Finding they could not get to shore safely, the party spent the night upon that slimy sheet of water. Eighteen men in a small canoe, in a hot summer night, with the poles stuck into the mud across the canoe to steady it, accompanied with the most intense rain and with the most intense thunder and lightning,—such are the reminiscences which belong to that memorable night. And he who was not there, or has never been in such a place, if such another place there is, has little conception of what a formidable enemy a mosquito can be.[1]

The next day, Cass arrived at Chicago and explained the situation to the settlers. Gurdon Saltonstall Hubbard (whose vivid description of his 1818 encounter with the portage was recounted in chapter 6) was dispatched to gather military assistance from Danville. He was successful, but by the time the makeshift militia made its way to Chicago, the United States had managed such a show of military force that the Winnebago had agreed to peace. Although it was a relatively bloodless affair, the uprising nonetheless raised anxiety throughout Illinois and the territories, which in turn led to the garrison being recalled to Fort Dearborn.[2] This reestablishment of the garrison would prove to be a wise move for the United States because the last of the Native American wars in Chicago was yet to come in just a few years.

Chief Black Hawk and his Sauk, Fox, and Kickapoo followers had never accepted the treaty of 1804 by which the Sauk and Fox chiefs had surrendered their land. The situation finally came to a head in 1832 with the Black Hawk War, instigated as much by the settlers in their aggression against the Native Americans as the other way around. After Black Hawk's forces won a few initial skirmishes, which greatly alarmed the white settlers throughout northern Illinois, the United States advanced an army of more than four thousand troops against Black Hawk and a few hundred warriors. The end was never in doubt, and Black Hawk's warriors were decimated on August 2, 1832, at the Battle of Bad Axe. This outbreak of violence led to the Treaty of 1833, also known as the Treaty of Chicago, in which all remaining Native Americans in Illinois forfeited their lands and, by the end of 1835, were relocated west of the Mississippi River.

The Black Hawk War had mixed results for the area around the Chicago Portage. After the Black Hawk War began in May 1831, the federal government, fearing an attack on Fort Dearborn, decided to send reinforcements to the area. In June, President Andrew Jackson appointed General Winfield Scott to take command of the US war effort, and Scott gathered about 950 troops from along the Eastern Seaboard to head west to Fort Dearborn. Two steamboats were chartered to transport the troops, and in late June the *Sheldon Thompson* left from Buffalo, New York, with General Scott and his staff, six companies of artillery, and two companies of infantry. Shortly thereafter, on July 3, the *Henry Clay* followed, carrying seven companies of infantry.

It was a cursed voyage. The *Henry Clay* was barely under way before the troops began to fall ill. The stricken ship landed on July 7 near Fort Gratiot and the St. Clair River. Frightened soldiers fled the vessel, many of whom were later found dead in the surrounding countryside. By July 9, only 68 men remained alive of the seven companies of infantry that had set sail just days before. The *Sheldon Thompson*, meanwhile, had largely escaped the first days of virulence. But it would not escape unscathed. By the time the ship arrived in Chicago on July 10, 76 troops had gotten sick and 19 had died. In all, of the original 950 men who had left Buffalo, only 350 made it to Chicago; disease and desertion took the rest.[3]

The onboard killer was cholera, a scourge that would haunt and ravage the growing city—indeed, the entire country—for decades to come. The ill-fated timing of Scott's voyage had coincided with the arrival of the disease in the United States as part of a pandemic that would take hundreds of thousands of lives around the globe. In New York, where the disease had arrived from Canada in June, more than 3,500 people died out of a population of about 200,000.

Cholera was a horrible disease, made even more fearsome by the severity and speed of its attack. People who woke up healthy were dead by sunset, besieged with vomiting, diarrhea, and wrenching cramps. Severe dehydration often left the afflicted with skin a deathly bluish-gray. So terrifying was the onslaught of cholera that thousands of people took flight from affected areas, hoping to outrun its reach. Some made it. Others—many—did not. Even worse, they carried the disease with them in their flight, thereby spreading the contagion to smaller towns and outposts, which in turn quickly succumbed.

When Scott's troops arrived at Fort Dearborn, the garrison, swelled in response to the Black Hawk War, numbered about one thousand. The medical officer of the fort would later recount the "frightful havoc" of the disease, which in the end infected one in five and killed more than sixty. General Scott did his best to quarantine the fort, but the illness inevitably spread to the surrounding countryside. Of the troops that had originally set out from Buffalo to assist in the Black Hawk War, few ever made it to their appointed task. Cholera would continue to haunt Chicago for decades until it was finally able to find ways to handle its waste and provide the city with clean drinking water.[4]

On the other hand, the Black Hawk War had an unintended positive effect on Chicago. Prior to the war, most of the migration to Illinois had come in the southern part of the state, in part because of the ongoing fear of violence from the Native American tribes in the northern part of the state. Except for the traders who plied the Chicago Portage, the area around Chicago and northern Illinois was largely unknown to emigrants from the South and East. The soldiers who came to Illinois for the Black Hawk War changed all of that when the survivors returned home with stories of the natural beauty and fecundity of northern Illinois. Like ambassadors, these soldiers helped spur significant new migration to the area.

The glowing reports by the returning soldiers combined with a propitious earlier event that had further enhanced the importance of the Chicago Portage and thereby Chicago itself. The Erie Canal opened in 1825, providing a link to the Eastern Seaboard that benefitted migrants and merchants alike. Goods that had previously been sent to Canada by way of the Great Lakes and the St. Lawrence River now went via the Erie Canal to New York City. Increasingly, the farmers and merchants of Illinois looked to the Great Lakes as a route to the markets of the Northeast.[5] Similarly, the Erie Canal route provided a much easier route heading west than traveling over land.

Increased commerce and migration combined to make the idea of a canal through the Chicago Portage even more obvious and pressing.

Although Chicago itself was growing, the Chicago Portage also during this period gave rise to towns that later became suburbs to the great metropolis. Significant among these in the 1820s and 1830s were the settlements that became Riverside and Lyons. The growth of these settlements pointed to another development in the area around the Chicago Portage. Although it remained a vital waterway, the overland components of the Chicago Portage were growing in significance. There was more and more horse and wagon traffic crossing the area, and the old Native American trails were becoming highways to the west.

In 1826, the Laughton brothers, David and Bernardus (Barney) came to Chicago and settled at Hardscrabble (now Bridgeport) on the South Branch Chicago River. Both men were employed by the American Fur Company, and at least David had been in the area of the Chicago Portage as early as 1822 because he is listed in John Kinzie's account book between February and May of that year. In 1827–28, the brothers moved to the area that is now Lyons and Riverside and established a trading post and a tavern, the latter of which was also their home. David was said to have had three Potawatomi wives, all three of whom were buried at what is now Fairbank Road in Riverside.[6] Barney had an especially close relationship with the Potawatomi Tribe in the area and played a critical role during the Black Hawk War by using this relationship to gather information about a pending attack on a settlement at Hollenbeck's Grove, now Millbrook in Kendall County. His warnings to the settlers prompted them to move to the safety of Fort Dearborn during the conflict.[7] Although their impact on the area of Riverside and Lyons was substantial, their time there was short-lived. The brothers died within eight days of each other in April 1834.

In November 1830, Barney married Sophia Bates, the sister of Elvira Bates Forbes (wife of Stephen Forbes). The Forbes family came to live on land adjacent to that owned by David Laughton. The Forbes family left for a short while because of concerns about Native American uprisings but returned to become leading citizens of the young Riverside. Stephen Forbes bought substantial land holdings in Riverside in 1831–35 and was elected the first sheriff of Cook County in 1832. Some reports say that the Forbeses lived with the Laughtons before the Forbeses built their own home in 1831 just west of the current Riverside train station. There is a stone monument near this location that reads "Site of first home built in Cook County west of Chicago by its first elected sheriff Stephen Van Rensselaer Forbes, 1831—Only voting place of Cook County for its first colonel of the state militia Jean Baptiste Beaubien, June 7, 1834."[8]

There were four important fords, or crossing places, across the Des Plaines River in the vicinity of the Chicago Portage that became increasingly important as the wagon traffic of traders and settlers increased. Just downstream

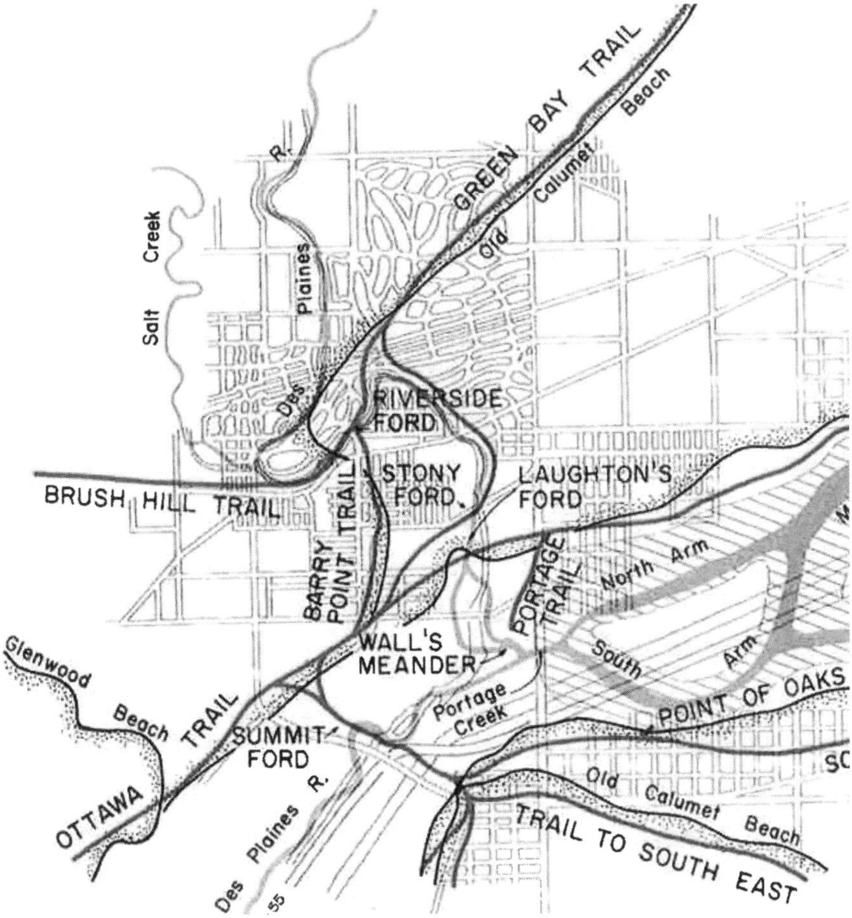

Fig. 23. Native American trails. From William E. Rose and Associates, *Design Study: The Chicago Portage and the Laughton Trading Post Area, "The Waterway West"* (Hinsdale, IL: Wm. E. Rose and Associates, 1975), 11–12.

from the Laughton Tavern, northeast of the Barrypoint Bridge that connects Riverside and Lyons, was the Riverside Ford; continuing downstream, the Stony Ford was approximately 150 feet south of where the current Ogden Avenue bridge crosses the Des Plaines River; next came the Laughton Ford, also known as the Ford of the Des Plaines, located north of the tip of then Prescott Island where the North Portage Trail crossed the Des Plaines River; and finally the Summit Ford, located at current Lawndale Avenue in Lyons where the South Portage Trail crossed the Des Plaines River.[9]

Just as the Native American tribes had used the Chicago Portage for centuries before the arrival of the first Europeans, so, too, the foot trails and fords were well established (fig. 23). The Green Bay Trail had been in long use by

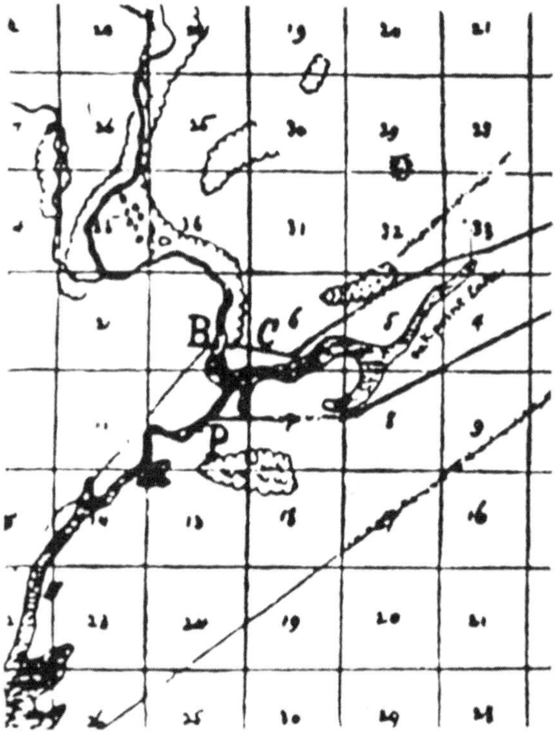

Fig. 24. Detail of map by Justus Post and René Paul, 1823, showing line between designated points *B* and *C* to indicate their proposed location for a canal crossing the Illinois River at the Chicago Portage. From Robert Knight and Lucius H. Zeuch, *The Location of the Chicago Portage Route of the Seventeenth Century* (Chicago: Chicago Historical Society, 1928), 109.

Native Americans and was later also used by traders. It ran near the shore of Lake Michigan and crossed the Chicago River on the sand bar at its mouth. There was an intercepting trail that ran west along the Calumet Beach to Riverside, where it divided. One branch crossed the Des Plaines River at the Riverside Ford and became the Barry Point Trail; the other branch continued along the east side of the river to Stony Ford.[10]

A trail that followed the Calumet and Tolleston Beaches that extended from the southeast around the lower end of Lake Michigan crossed the Summit Ford and then turned north and divided. One branch ran down the Des Plaines River valley and the other ran north toward the Riverside Ford. Just before reaching the Riverside Ford, this trail divided again, one part crossing the Riverside Ford to merge with the Barry Point Road and the other part connecting to the Brush Hill Road that ran through Fullersburg (now

Hinsdale), Downers Grove, and Naperville.[11] The latter trail later became the Southwest Plank Road, which in turn became Ogden Avenue.[12]

Laughton's Ford was the crossing point for the Long Portage Road that ran from Chicago along the north shore of Mud Lake. After crossing the ford, the Portage Road ran southwesterly along the Tolleston Beach ridge until it joined the Ottawa Trail, which ran roughly along the route of the current Joliet Road southwest down the Des Plaines valley.[13]

The Laughton Ford is the ford most closely associated with the Chicago Portage and is directly related to the Laughton Trading Post. Although there is some disagreement about the exact location of the trading post, it was likely located at on the east bank of the Des Plaines River at the Riverside Ford north of the mouth of Portage Creek at the Chicago Portage. In 1823, Justus Post and René Paul were employed to explore the area between Lake Michigan and the Illinois River for the purpose of recommending a route for a proposed canal. They surveyed a number of possibilities, and in their report included a map showing several routes. One of these routes had the canal crossing the Des Plaines River at the "Ford of the Des Plaines," indicating this location by a short line between designated points *B* and *C* (fig. 24). A later report in 1831 by J. M. Bucklin, engineer for the Canal Commissioners, cited the Post and Paul map and referred to this same spot as the "Laughton's Ford." In an 1832 report, United States assistant engineer H. Belin similarly reported conversations with "Mr. Lawton" in 1829 concerning the river levels at "Lawton's trading house."[14]

A. J. Mathewson, an engineer and surveyor working on behalf of the Canal Commissioners, made a map in 1865 in which, based on his numerous surveys of the Chicago River, Mud Lake, and the Des Plaines River, he specifically located the "Lawtons Old Trading House" (fig. 25). This location, although not perhaps exact, places the trading post on the old Tolleston Beach adjacent to the river and on the same line of the Long Portage Road leading to the Laughton Ford.[15]

Mention should be made of the opinion of Philip Vierling, a longtime researcher of the Chicago Portage who for seventeen years (2000–2016) wrote a newsletter called the *Chicago Portage Ledger*. There is a monument stone at the Chicago Portage National Historic Site that claims to be the location of the trading post, based on the conclusion of Robert Knight and Lucius Zeuch, authors of the book *The Location of the Chicago Portage Route of the Seventeenth Century*, published by the Chicago Historical Society in 1928. Knight and Zeuch in turn relied on the Mathewson map. Vierling points out that Knight and Zeuch referred to "an old partially filled-in excavation, that was the cellar of a building" at the location shown by the Mathewson map. Knight and Zeuch suggested the possibility that this ruin was possibly the site of the old trading house. However, an archeological dig sponsored at the site by the Field Museum in 1974 and 1975 determined the foundation of the "cellar" to be concrete, which would have been unusual in a frontier

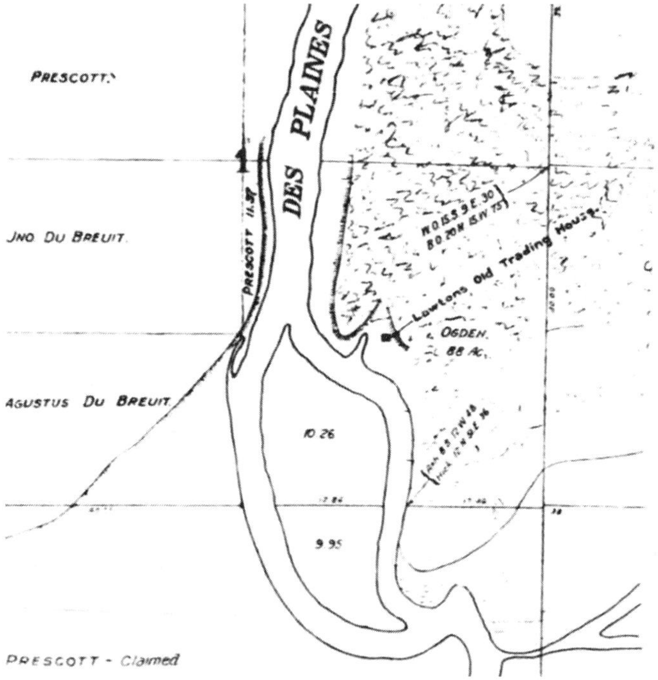

Fig. 25. Detail of map by A. J. Mathewson, 1865, showing Lawtons Old Trading House. From Robert Knight and Lucius H. Zeuch, *The Location of the Chicago Portage Route of the Seventeenth Century* (Chicago: Chicago Historical Society, 1928), 110.

building in 1830, given that hydraulic cement was not found to have been used in the United States until 1818. That fact, coupled with the remains of an old road that Vierling maintains ran from the ruin westward to the location of the Summit Spillway, built in 1893–94 as part of the diversion of the Des Plaines River and that had a core of concrete, led Vierling to conclude that the "cellar" was likely related to the Spillway project. By his calculations made in 2003, Vierling put the trading post about two hundred feet south of the monument.[16] To date, there have been no solid archeological findings that would conclusively settle the exact location of the trading post.

The Laughton Tavern highlights the increased use of overland trails by horses and wagons carrying settlers. Whereas the trading post was located to take advantage of the water traffic passing through the Chicago Portage, the tavern was intended more for travelers using the old Native American trails. Although, like the trading post, the exact location of the Laughton Tavern cannot be fixed with certainty, it was likely on the west bank of the Des Plaines River west of the current Barrypoint Bridge. The tavern became an important meeting and lodging spot for the young Riverside and was used extensively by travelers on their way to Chicago. Juliette Kinzie, in her book *Wau-Bun*, tells of stopping at the tavern with her husband on their way to Fort Dearborn from Fort Winnebago in Wisconsin in March 1831:

> It was almost dark when we reached Lawton's. The Aux Plaines [Des Plaines River] was frozen, and the house was on the other side. By loud shouting, we brought out a man from the building, and he succeeded in cutting the ice, and bringing a canoe over to us; but not until it had become difficult to distinguish objects in the darkness.
>
> A very comfortable house was Lawton's, after we did reach it—carpeted, and with a warm stove—in fact, quite in civilized style. Mr. Weeks, the man who brought us across, was the major-domo, during the temporary absence of Mr. Lawton. Mrs. Lawton was a young woman, and not ill-looking. She complained bitterly of the loneliness of her condition, and having been "brought out there into the woods; which was a thing she had not expected, when she came from the East." We did not ask her with what expectations she had come to a wild, unsettled country; but we tried to comfort her with the assurance that things would grow better in a few years. She said, "She did not mean to wait for that. She should go back to her family in the East, if Mr. Lawton did not invite some of her young friends to come and stay with her, and make it agreeable."[17]

"Mr. Weeks" refers to Cole Weeks (or Weicks), who was a licensed trader.[18] According to Kinzie, Mrs. Lawton must have kept her word about not waiting for her lot to improve because when Kinzie passed by the tavern again a few months later, she found only "a Frenchman and a small number of Indians."[19]

The Laughton Tavern was so well known that the second road determined to be built by the County Commissioners, in June 1832, was to run "from the town of Chicago to the house of B. Laughton, from thence to the house of James Walker on the Du Page River, and so on to the west line of the county."[20] (This road followed the route of the Brush Hill Trail referred to earlier.) In 1834, the first stagecoach route from Chicago to St. Louis ran past Laughton's Tavern, which was its first stop. The line was owned by John D. Winters, and an advertisement that appeared in the *Chicago Democrat*, February 4, 1834, read, "The New Lines of splendid Four Horse Post Coaches in Illinois from Ottawa by way of Holderman's Grove, Walker's Grove and Laughton's to Chicago, once a week, 80 miles, through in one and one half days; fare $5.00 Winters, Mills and Co."[21] The honor of driving the first coach past Laughton's Tavern was given to a young attorney, John D. Canton, who later became the chief justice of the Illinois Supreme Court.[22]

With the shift away from the fur trade to the coming of farmers, settlers, and, in the case of Chicago, land speculators and entrepreneurs, the Chicago

Portage as a water and portage route began to lose importance. But Chicago's defining characteristic as the gateway joining the Atlantic Seaboard and the Gulf of Mexico remained. The Chicago Portage had shown the way, but the needs of the nation had outgrown Mud Lake. It was time to follow the words of Louis Jolliet and "make a canal."

9

The Coming of the Canal

There is a clear, though not unbroken, line from Louis Jolliet's original insight in 1673 that a canal could be cut across the route of the Chicago Portage from the Chicago River to the Des Plaines River and the realization of that insight in the building of the Illinois and Michigan Canal, and, eventually, the Chicago Sanitary and Ship Canal. Jolliet's vision, still remarkable for its prescience, was that a commercial route could thereby be established connecting the St. Lawrence River with the Gulf of Mexico. René-Robert Cavelier de La Salle, too, begrudgingly acknowledged that such a canal could be built, although he deemed the project unworthy, perhaps in part because it did not further his self-interest in developing the Mississippi valley. In 1687, Henri de Joutel reiterated Jolliet's view that a junction between Lake Michigan and the Illinois River could easily be made. But then came a lapse of more than one hundred years during which talk of such a canal was eclipsed by struggles for possession and control of the Chicago Portage and the territory it anchored.

Not until 1795 did the idea of a canal resurface in the Treaty of Greenville when the signatory tribes ceded "one piece of land six miles square, at the mouth of the Chicago River, emptying into the southwest end of lake Michigan," and further guaranteed free travel by the Americans "from the mouth of Chicago, to the commencement of the portage, between that river and the Illinois, and down the Illinois river to the Mississippi."[1] By that treaty, the United States obtained the rights to what would eventually become the route of the Illinois and Michigan Canal.

Thomas Jefferson emphasized in 1781 that the Mississippi River was destined to be "one of the principal channels of future commerce for the country" and that the preferred route to the Mississippi River from Lake Michigan was "via the Chicago Portage."[2] On March 2, 1807, the US Senate passed a resolution asking the Treasury Department to compile a report on how the young nation could address its transportation needs. The task fell to President Jefferson's secretary of the treasury, Albert Gallatin. He submitted his report on "public roads and canals" to the Senate on April 6, 1808. It was a sweeping report concentrating on better communication along the

Eastern Seaboard and of how to access the regions west of the Appalachians. Although he did not specifically recommend a canal at the site of the Chicago Portage, he did note that "the Illinois river, which empties into the Mississippi above St. Louis, rises in a swamp, which, when the waters are high, affords a natural canoe navigation to the sources of Chicago creek, a short stream, which falls into Lake Michigan at its southern extremity."[3]

In 1810, Representative Peter B. Porter of New York set forth a plan to connect the Eastern Seaboard with the western regions. He argued that "the great evil . . . under which the inhabitants of the Western country labor, arises from the want of a market."[4] To solve this evil, he recommended a system of waterways extending from the St. Lawrence and Hudson Rivers to the Gulf of Mexico. He specifically noted:

> At the southwestern extremity of Lake Michigan, the most inconsiderable expense would open a canal between the waters of that lake and the Illinois river, one of the principal branches of the Mississippi. Nature has already made this connexion nearly complete; and it is not uncommon for boats, in the Spring of the year, to pass from the lake into the Illinois, and from thence by the waters of the Illinois and Mississippi to New Orleans, without being taken out of the water.[5]

Despite his impassioned argument, Porter was not able to secure sufficient support for his plan.

Part of the difficulty for the proposed Illinois and Michigan Canal stemmed from the fact that the regions west of the Ohio River were still truly frontiers. The national interest was focused on the Eastern Seaboard and in creating roads and canals to connect with the upper waters of the Ohio, and even in northwestern regions there was no widespread popular support for a canal. Much as with the push for statehood, the fate of the canal would rest in the hands of the press and a few dedicated politicians.

On August 6, 1814, Hezekiah Niles, one of the most influential journalists in America, published a summary of improvements he felt necessary for the nation. He acknowledged that the Illinois Territory was still sparsely populated, but he believed that the population would quickly increase. He drew particular attention to the idea for a canal at the Chicago Portage:

> By the *Illinois* river, it is probable that *Buffalo*, in *New York*, may be united with *New Orleans*, by inland navigation, through lakes *Erie*, *Huron*, and *Michigan*, and down that river into the Mississippi. What a route! How stupendous the idea!—How dwindles the importance of the artificial canals of *Europe*, compared with *this* water communication. If it should ever take place (and it is said the opening may be easily made) the territory will become the seat of an immense commerce; and a market for the commodities of all regions![6]

Niles returned to this theme later in August when he reviewed the inland navigation to be afforded in the West:

> From *Chicago* up Chicago river to a swamp or marsh at the head of the *Illinois*, only *two* miles distant. It is said there already is a passage for canoes through this marsh; and all accounts concur in stating that a communication may be easily made. We, therefore, consider it as done, for it certainly will be done and at a small expence, as soon as it is required by the settlement of the country.[7]

The *Niles' Weekly Register* continued to advocate for the building of the Illinois and Michigan Canal until the project was finally completed.

Although the idea for the Illinois and Michigan Canal had not yet garnered national support, the efforts of leaders such as Gallatin and Porter and support in the press at least kept the idea alive in the broader context of internal improvements. Moreover, the War of 1812 had reminded people that a canal along the route of the Chicago Portage not only was a commercial concern but also had significant military significance. Such a canal would allow military assets to be moved throughout the country free from hostile interference.

President James Madison pointed to the need for a comprehensive plan for such improvements in his State of the Union Address on December 5, 1815. Building on the Greenville Treaty of 1795, the Treaty of St. Louis on August 24, 1816, established the Indian Boundary Lines and thereby obtained the land necessary for the building of the Illinois and Michigan Canal from the Potawatomi, Ottawa, and Chippewa. In September 1816, Secretary of War William H. Crawford sent Major Stephen H. Long to explore the route of a possible Illinois and Michigan Canal.

Long reported his findings on March 4, 1817, to Crawford's successor, acting Secretary of War George Graham. After reviewing the general area of the Chicago Portage, Long concluded:

> A canal uniting the waters of the Illinois with those of Lake Michigan may be considered the first in importance of any in this quarter of the country, and, at the same time, the construction of it would be attended with very little expense compared with the magnitude of the object. The watercourse, which is already opened between the river Desplain and Chicago river, needs but little more excavation to render it sufficiently capacious for all the purposes of a canal. It may be supplied with water at all times of the year by constructing a dam of moderate height across the Desplain, which would give the water of that river a sufficient elevation to supply a canal extending from one river to the other. It would be necessary, also, to construct locks at the extremities of the canal, that communicating with Chicago river

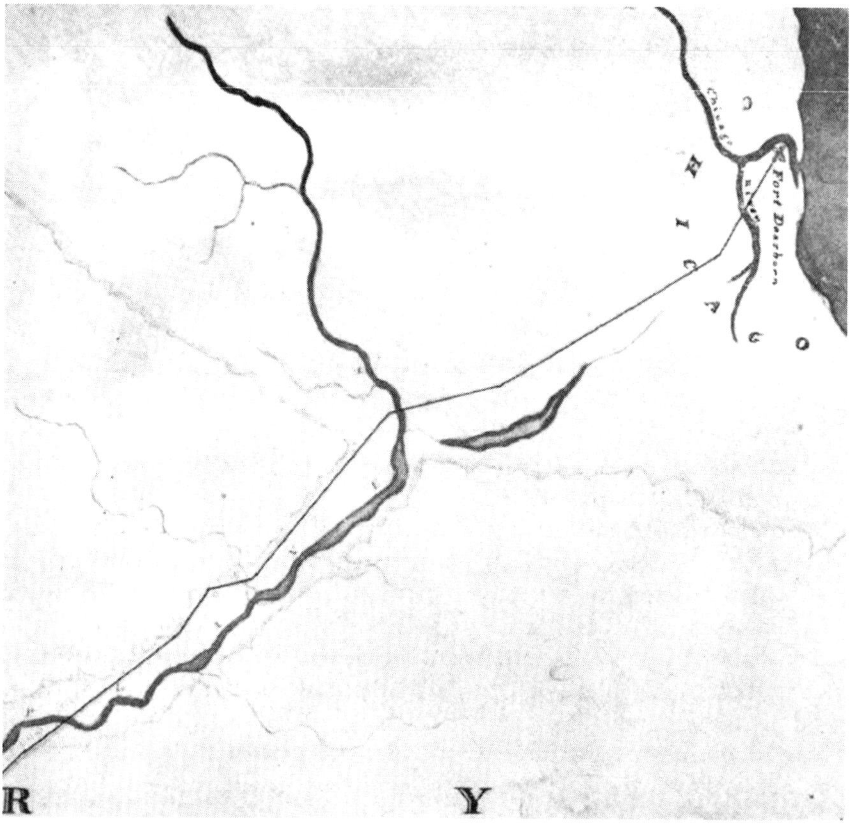

Fig. 26. "Track of S. H. Long, Major of Topographical Engineers, in October 1816" (detail). From Robert Knight and Lucius H. Zeuch, *The Location of the Chicago Portage Route of the Seventeenth Century* (Chicago: Chicago Historical Society, 1928), 103.

> being calculated to elevate about six feet, and that communicating with the Desplain about four feet.[8]

Long included with his report a map showing the track of S. H. Long, Major of Topographical Engineers, in October 1816 (fig. 26). Although there had been many maps made of the Chicago Portage and surrounding area, Long's was the first formal survey made of the region.

Long was accompanied by Richard Graham and Joseph Philips, who were judge and secretary, respectively, of the Illinois Territory.[9] Graham and Philips were tasked with surveying the area and recommending a route for a canal. (See also fig. 21 in chapter 7 for the Indian Boundary Lines map created by Captain John Sullivan, who accompanied the Long expedition.) They submitted their report on April 9, 1819, and in it they were less enthusiastic than Long was about locating the canal along the Chicago Portage route. Although they identified the portage route as one possible location for a canal, they echoed La Salle's earlier disagreement with Jolliet about the limited navigability of the Des Plaines River during periods of low water, stating that it "during half the year, does not contain water enough to float a boat, and so could not become useful as a national highway."[10] Graham and Philips mentioned two other routes south of Chicago as "practicable" for constructing a lake-fed canal cut deep enough across the Valparaiso Moraine to permit the flow from the lake directly to the Des Plaines River farther to the southwest than Long had proposed and would thereby join the Illinois River "at points from which it is constantly navigable."[11] They also mentioned La Salle's preferred St. Joseph–Kankakee–Illinois Rivers route but noted that they had not actually seen that route. Regarding the Chicago Portage route, they concluded:

> The route by the *Chicago*, as followed by the French since the discovery of the Illinois, presents at one season of the year an uninterrupted water communication for boats of six or eight tons burden between the Mississippi and the Michigan lake; at another season, a portage of two miles; at another, a portage of seven miles, from the bend of the *Plein* [Des Plaines River] to the arm of the lake [Chicago River]; at another, a portage of fifty miles, from the mouth of the *Plein* to the lake, over which there is a well-beaten wagon road, and boats and their loads are hauled by oxen and vehicles kept for that purpose by the French settlers at the Chicago.[12]

Luckily for Chicago, the alternate routes suggested by Graham and Philips gathered no support. Perhaps it was the sheer impetus of tradition and long use that propelled the Chicago Portage route as the preferred location for the canal. Regardless, it is difficult to imagine the ramifications for the city of Chicago had the Illinois and Michigan Canal been built elsewhere than the Chicago Portage.

Secretary of War John Calhoun transmitted both the Long report and the Graham and Philips letter to Congress on January 14, 1819, as part of a larger report on a comprehensive plan for roads and canals needed to augment the military defense of the United States (see appendix A). This report had been requested by the US House of Representatives on April 4, 1818. Regarding the western regions, he concluded that a canal from the Illinois river to Lake Michigan would be essential "to carry on military operations in time of war, and the transportation of the munitions of war for the defence of the western portion of our northern frontier."[13]

While Long, Graham, and Philips were doing their studies, Samuel A. Storrow, a judge advocate in the US Army, had been sent in the fall of 1817 by Major General Jacob Jennings Brown, the ranking general officer in the US Army, to examine posts on the western frontier. In a description reminiscent of Joutel's in 1687, Storrow reported:

> The river Chicago (or, in English, Wild Onion river) is deep and about forty yards in width, before it enters the Lake, its two branches unite—the one proceeding from the north, the other from the west, where it takes its rise in the fountain of the De Plein, or Illinois, which flows in an opposite direction. The source of these two rivers illustrates the geographical phenomenon of a reservoir on the very summit of a dividing ridge. In the autumn, they are both without any apparent fountain, but are formed within a mile and a half of each other by some imperceptible undulations of the prairie, which drain it and lead to different directions. But in the spring, the space between the two is a single sheet of water, the common reservoir of both, in the centre of which there is no current towards either of the opposite streams. This circumstance creates the singular fact of the insulation of all the United States excepting Louisiana, making the circumnavigation of them practicable, from the Gulf of St. Lawrence to that of Mexico, with the single hindrance of the Falls of Niagara.
>
> The Chicago forms a third partition of the great country I had passed. The Quisconsin and Fox rivers make a water communication between the Mississippi and Michigan, with the exception of four miles. The Millwackie and *River a la Roche* [Rock River] the same, with half the exception. The Chicago and De Plein make, in the manner I have described, the communication entire. This latter should not escape national attention. The ground between the two is without rocks, and, with little labor, would admit of a permanent connection between the waters of the Illinois and Michigan.[14]

Although there was near-unanimous consensus that a canal connecting Lake Michigan and the Illinois River along the route of the Chicago Portage would have enormous commercial and military advantages, the supporters of such a canal remained thwarted. One obstacle was that at this early time in the nation's history, it was still unclear what the federal government's power was under the Constitution to fund internal improvements within states. President James Monroe believed that Congress did not have such authority. Coupled with this overarching concern, the southern states were indifferent to internal improvements in the West, and the eastern states were opposed to any improvements that might encourage further migration from the Eastern Seaboard. Meanwhile, the general settler population of the West remained relatively disengaged from the entire question.

Despite this disinterest, Illinois politicians recognized the importance of the canal. The same day that the House of Representatives requested that Secretary of War Calhoun prepare a report on roads and canals, Nathaniel Pope amended the draft enabling act to make Illinois a state to extend the state's border northward to encompass the lands within the Indian Boundaries, as described in chapter 7. In 1818, Pope's nephew Daniel Pope Cook resigned his position at the *Intelligencer* to run for Congress and was elected to the House of Representatives, where he was an ardent supporter of a canal. At the first session of the Illinois legislature, Shadrach Bond, the first governor of Illinois, advocated for transportation improvements within the state and in particular noted the importance of a canal, especially given the construction under way on the Erie Canal.[15]

With local interest increasing, at least among elected officials in Illinois, the prospects for a canal were renewed. Meanwhile in Congress, the debate over whether the Constitution allowed the federal government to fund internal improvements reached a head. In opposition to President Monroe, the House of Representatives on March 14, 1818, passed a resolution stating that Congress had the power under the Constitution to appropriate money for "the construction of post roads, military and other roads, of canals, and for the improvement of water courses."[16]

The idea of a canal was aided by continuing support in the press. Thomas Hart Benton wrote an article for the *St. Louis Enquirer* in which he described in detail the route through the Chicago Portage and then advocated for the construction of a canal:

> The communication between the lake and the Illinois is a point which will fix the attention of the merchant and the statesman. They will see in it the gate which is to open the northern seas into the valley of the Mississippi, and which is to connect New York and New Orleans by a water line, which the combined navies of the world cannot cut off. Never did the work of nature require so little from the hand of art to complete so great a design. . . . The French of Canada, and of the valley of the Mississippi, have communicated through this channel since the settlement of the countries. In high water boats of ten or a dozen tons pass without obstruction. In the dry season, they are unloaded, placed on vehicles, and drawn by oxen over a portage of a few miles, and launched into the river or lake, as the course of the voyage may require. Hundreds, nay thousands, of boats have been seen at St. Louis which have made a similar passage. . . . It may be hoped that the government will not limit itself to the barren work of marking the lines about this portage. While the State of New York opens a canal of 300 miles, the federal government should not be appalled at undertaking one of 300 rods. It might be dug in the time that a long-winded member of Congress would make a speech against its constitutionality.[17]

In its second session, the Illinois legislature moved to advance the canal. It requested that the federal government authorize the construction of the canal through public lands, asked the federal government to donate those lands to the state, and requested that 2 percent of all proceeds from the sale of public lands within the state be used to finance the canal.[18] Acting on this request, Representative Cook and, in the Senate, Senator Jesse B. Thomas of Illinois advocated for federal support for the proposed canal as a project of national importance. Although the House had clearly stated that the federal government had the constitutional authority to fund such projects, Cook and Thomas were opposed by some who said that the project would primarily benefit Illinois. Representative John Floyd of Virginia argued that Virginia might as well ask for an appropriation of the public funds "for the purpose of completing canals to the city of Richmond." He went on to say that he would leave the subject of canals "to the energy and ability of those States through which they pass, and for whose benefit they are intended."[19] Cook replied that he was surprised by such opposition given that Illinois was not asking for a "favor" but merely to have a strip of land reserved for the canal.[20] Cook carried the day and the resolution passed. Senator Thomas then took up the fight, and after much debate and slowly making its way through the committee process, the bill became law on March 20, 1822.

It was an important, if partial, victory. The law granted only ninety feet of land on either side of the proposed canal route and offered nothing in the way of funding. Still, it was the first official federal grant of land for the proposed canal. The Illinois legislature responded on February 14, 1823, by establishing a board of commissioners to determine the best route for the canal and to estimate the cost of construction. To this end, Justus Post and René Paul were employed to survey the area. The following year they submitted their report with a map showing five possible routes (fig. 27), all of which ran through the Chicago Portage at the "ford of the Desplaines."[21] Their estimates for the project ranged from $639,542.78 to $716,110.71.[22]

Then ensued years of debate and controversy over how to fund the canal. Various proposals were made by the state, including a short-lived attempt to fund the canal through a corporation—a scheme strongly opposed by Cook, who continued to maintain that the national importance of the canal warranted federal support. Cook found a friendly administration under President John Quincy Adams, and finally, on March 2, 1827, the federal government issued a new land grant providing public land of five miles on either side of the canal route. Cook got to see this success before his death in October 1827. In 1829, a new canal commission was authorized, and land sales began. It was as a result of these sales that the towns of Chicago and Ottawa were first platted.

The land sales failed to produce the necessary revenue, and once again the canal was in crisis. In 1831, a new challenge arose when some opponents began to argue that a railroad line would be preferable to a canal. This argument carried on for years, and at one point even the canal commissioners stated their preference for a railroad. This disagreement led to stalemate, and in 1832, the Illinois legislature abolished the Canal Commission, leaving the state with neither a canal nor a railroad.

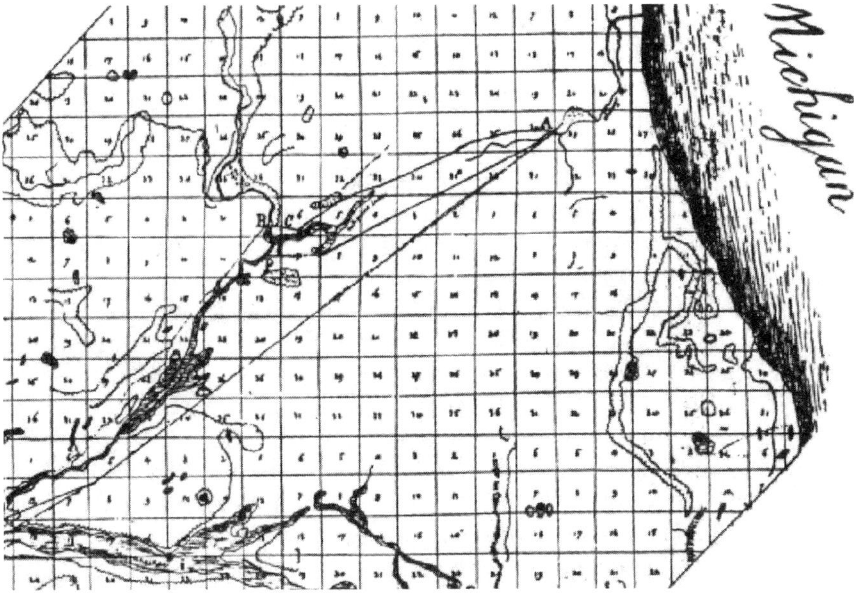

Fig. 27. Detail of map by Justus Post and René Paul, 1823, showing possible routes for a canal between the Illinois River and Lake Michigan, all of them passing through the Chicago Portage. From Robert Knight and Lucius H. Zeuch, *The Location of the Chicago Portage Route of the Seventeenth Century* (Chicago: Chicago Historical Society, 1928), 108.

The canal became a central issue in the elections of 1834, and Joseph Duncan, a strong advocate for the canal, was elected governor. He argued convincingly that a canal had three benefits: (1) it would allow commerce between the two great waterways of the St. Lawrence and Mississippi Rivers; (2) it would improve navigability of the Illinois River; and (3) it would allow farmers to be independent of a railroad monopoly. He even expanded the concept of the canal, arguing for a canal of sufficient size to allow steamboats to pass from Lake Michigan to the Illinois River.[23]

Meanwhile, the press and even popular sentiment had finally rallied around the idea of a canal. Additional support came from the Army Corps of Engineers in 1834 when General Charles Gratiot, chief of the corps, strongly urged the House of Representatives that building the canal was one of the most important public works available to the nation. He rejected the idea of a railroad line, arguing that the canal would provide more reliable, and cheaper, transportation "commensurate with the great thoroughfares it would connect."[24] On June 25, 1834, the Committee on Roads and Canals reported favorably to the House in supporting the canal.

The action in Congress bolstered renewed support for the canal back in Illinois. On February 10, 1835, a third Canal Commission was authorized, and a funding method was finally approved. On July 4, 1836, the long struggle to secure the creation of a canal ended, and construction of the Illinois and Michigan Canal began.

When construction of the canal began, the Chicago Portage for all effective purposes ceased to exist. The land routes associated with the portage continued to be used, but the area of Mud Lake was destined to be platted and sold as the young Chicago began a period of exponential growth. At the time that construction on the canal began in 1836, Chicago's population was 3,820; by the time of the canal's opening in 1848, the city had already grown to 20,023 residents.[25]

The Illinois and Michigan Canal had a major impact not only on the city of Chicago but also on towns along its route.[26] The canal's historical importance was officially recognized in 1964 when it was designated a National Historic Landmark. In 1975, the State of Illinois created the I&M Canal State Trail along the original towpath of the canal. In August 1984, President Ronald Reagan signed a bill authorizing the establishment of the Illinois and Michigan Canal National Heritage Corridor, America's first National Heritage Area. The I&M Canal National Heritage Corridor sparked a national trend, and as of March 2019, there were fifty-five National Heritage Areas, all of which owe their existence to the I&M Canal National Heritage Corridor.[27] The Chicago Portage, itself a National Historic Site, is integral to the I&M Canal National Heritage Corridor.

10

Where Was the Chicago Portage?

Gurdon Saltonstall Hubbard came to Chicago in 1818, and over the next eighteen years, he saw the fur trade expand, transform, and then die away. In 1836, he was one of the three commissioners named to oversee the construction of the Illinois and Michigan Canal. Over the next twelve years of construction before the opening of the canal in 1848, the bustling trade through the Chicago Portage of Hubbard's youth slowly disappeared. With the fur trade gone, the next phase of Chicago's life began—the age of land speculation and industry. The entrepreneur replaced the trader, and within a few short decades, the natural features of the Chicago Portage that had given Chicago its name and spurred its growth were almost eradicated.

So quickly did the natural environment of the portage change that by 1913, when Quaife wrote his account, "despite the historical importance of the Chicago Portage . . . the student will seek in vain for even an adequate description of the physical characteristics of the portage."[1] Even at that time more than a century ago, two factors contributed to the difficulty of determining the exact location of the Chicago Portage as it existed during the early age of exploration through the period of the fur trade. The first factor was the fact that the Chicago Portage was not a static natural feature. As we have seen, the distances and routes of the portage, though contained within somewhat definable boundaries, varied from season to season according to rainfall and the amount and depth of water present in Mud Lake (also variously known as Portage Lake, Oak Point Lake, and *Le Petit Lac*). The second factor was the sheer magnitude of human-made manipulation of the Chicago Portage site during the nineteenth century.

The first factor can be seen through the many differing accounts over time as to how much the physical characteristics of the portage could vary by season. Reading Louis Jolliet and Jacques Marquette's accounts and comparing them with those of René-Robert Cavelier de La Salle or Hubbard, it's difficult to image they were ever in the same place. The extent of the second factor is more difficult to determine given the speed with which changes to the portage site happened over a relatively short period and the multiple sources of those changes.

In his testimony in *United States of America vs. Economy Light and Power Company*, Lyman Cooley, the first chief engineer of the Sanitary District of Chicago, recounted the legacy of human construction that basically obliterated much of the Chicago Portage site, especially Mud Lake. The first was the Illinois and Michigan Canal itself, which cut across the south arm of Mud Lake. Then, in 1852, the Cook County Drainage Commission enlarged the small ditch that at that time connected Mud Lake with the West Fork South Branch Chicago River. From 1852 to 1856, the ditch was enlarged from being four feet wide and three feet deep to being forty feet wide and cut down to the level of Lake Michigan. This dramatic cut caused Mud Lake to become tributary to the Chicago River. Next came the deepening of the Illinois and Michigan Canal in 1866–71, which was the first time the Chicago River's course was reversed to flow westward. At about the same time the "deep cut" was being made on the Illinois and Michigan Canal, three property owners who held substantial portions of the old Mud Lake cut canals through the area to drain the remaining waters to make the land more useful and marketable. The Ogden-Wentworth Ditch and the Nickerson Ditch drained the western portion of Mud Lake. In 1876–77 the City of Chicago built a dam (the Ogden Dam) across Portage Creek at what is now Harlem Avenue. In 1893–94 the Sanitary District of Chicago diverted the course of the Des Plaines River. And lastly came the building of the Chicago Sanitary and Ship Canal, which eventually rendered the Illinois and Michigan Canal obsolete, just as the I&M Canal had rendered the Chicago Portage obsolete.[2]

So complete was the disruption of the Chicago Portage site, which was quickly covered with homes and other buildings in addition to the aforementioned changes, that the true location of the Chicago Portage route of the seventeenth century became a mystery. The Chicago Historical Society, established in 1856, considered solving this mystery a central theme of its founding and purpose. On May 1, 1923, Robert Knight, an engineer, and Lucius Zeuch, a medical doctor, presented their paper, "The Location of the Chicago Portage Route of the Seventeenth Century," before the society. So exhaustive were their research and findings that the society declared that "the age-long quest [of the portage's location] has at last been settled."[3] Knight and Zeuch extended their research over the next few years and published an expanded version of their findings in 1928. The following discussion of the portage's location relies heavily on their work.

Generally speaking, Knight and Zeuch defined the "Chicago Portage Route" as extending from the mouth of the Chicago River at Lake Michigan to the Illinois River at La Salle. They considered the Chicago River, and the Illinois River south of La Salle, as navigable year-round except when ice interfered. The rest of the route was subject to seasonal changes in navigability according to water levels. The seven miles between the West Fork South Branch Chicago River and the Des Plaines River comprised the "Old Chicago Portage" and included Mud Lake, the portage trails or roads, and

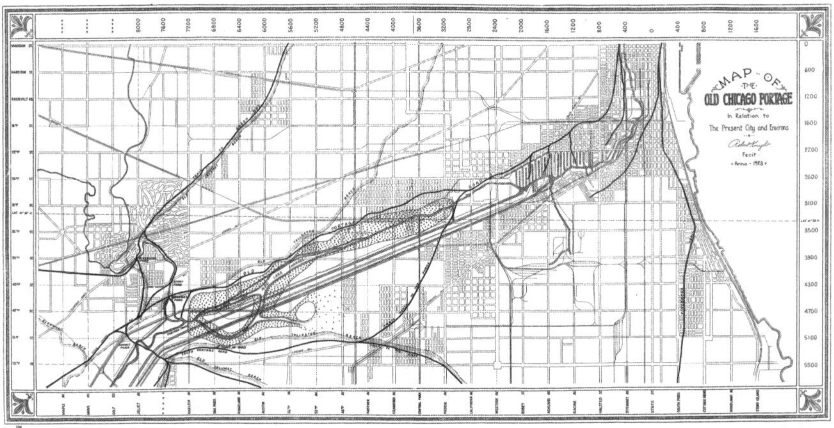

Fig. 28. *Map of the Old Chicago Portage in Relation to the Present City and Environs*, as drawn by Robert Knight, 1928. From Robert Knight and Lucius H. Zeuch, *The Location of the Chicago Portage Route of the Seventeenth Century* (Chicago: Chicago Historical Society, 1928), 129.

Portage Creek. This seven-mile stretch was roughly circumscribed by the old Tolleston Beach and could sometimes be crossed entirely by water, sometimes only by land, and sometimes partially by water and partially by land. In 1928, Knight and Zeuch published their map of the Chicago Portage Route superimposed on the existing city (fig. 28).

In trying to determine the exact route taken by explorers, missionaries, and traders during the seventeenth century, Knight and Zeuch considered four basic parts of the Chicago Portage Route: (1) the route of the continuous waterway at times of very high water from the west end of the West Fork, over the continental divide, across Mud Lake, and through Portage Creek to the Des Plaines River; (2) the route of the portage of "half a league" from the West Fork, over the continental divide, to the entrance of the east end of Mud Lake; (3) the route of the long land portage from the West Fork to the Des Plaines River; and (4) the land route from the West Fork to and across the Des Plaines River and down the Des Plaines River valley to the Illinois River. They also considered a second portage on the south shore of Mud Lake to the Summit Ford.[4]

Knight and Zeuch placed the continental divide at what is now Kedzie Avenue or slightly east at Albany Avenue and Thirty-First Street.[5] Cooley agreed with the latter location, testifying that the "original divide was about 0.1 of a mile, between 0.1 and 0.2 of a mile, east of Kedzie avenue."[6] The crest of the divide was about ten and one-half feet above the level of Lake Michigan, and the area west of the divide that contained Mud Lake was about eight feet above the level of Lake Michigan. The bottom of the Chicago

River, except at the mouth of the river, was at an average depth of twelve feet below the surface of Lake Michigan, and the river surface was level with the surface of Lake Michigan.[7]

Mud Lake lay in an area roughly bounded by Kedzie Avenue on the east, Harlem Avenue on the west, Archer Avenue on the south, and a line parallel to and about one and one-half mile south of Ogden Avenue on the north. Mud Lake was for the most part a swamp or marsh contained in a depression of from two to sixteen feet below the surrounding prairie. The lake varied in width. From its east end at the present line of Albany Avenue and Thirty-first Street extending southwesterly to about the line of present-day Austin Avenue, the lake varied from about one-half to three-quarters of a mile wide. Between Austin and Harlem Avenues, it widened to two and one-half miles and contained an island about one mile long and half a mile wide. The west end of Mud Lake connected with the Des Plaines River through Portage Creek, which was about seven hundred to eight hundred feet long between Mud Lake and the Des Plaines River.

Between the east end of Mud Lake and the head of navigation of the West Fork at South Leavitt Street was the portage of "half a league" referred to by the early explorers. Through extensive use by Native Americans and traders, a shallow ditch was worn through this point. In 1852 this ditch was widened and deepened by the Cook County Drainage Commission, allowing Mud Lake to drain into the Chicago River.

There was a single channel through Mud Lake from Albany Avenue (or Kedzie Avenue, depending on which version of the divide's location you accept) west to the island in Mud Lake (fig. 29). At that point the main channel continued north of the island (the North Arm), while the south channel cut a semicircle around the island (the South Arm) before rejoining the North Arm at Portage Creek. The North Arm was La Salle's little stream that "twined in and out about half a league across the rushes," and under suitable conditions, this was the shorter route. The South Arm, however, was deeper and could still be used for some period after the North Arm became too shallow.

In the testimony previously mentioned by Lyman E. Cooley, we have the clearest account of the various stages of Mud Lake and its relative navigability. The Des Plaines River, too, varied in depth by season, but Mud Lake was much more acutely affected. We can summarize Cooley's findings of the average number of days per year that various conditions existed as follows:

1. For 3.95 days, high water and swift currents, often accompanied by floating ice, made the water route through Mud Lake unusable. At such times there was four to five feet of water going over the continental divide at the east end of Mud Lake.
2. For 48 days, boats drawing less than fifteen inches could travel by water the entire distance from Lake Michigan to the Mississippi River.

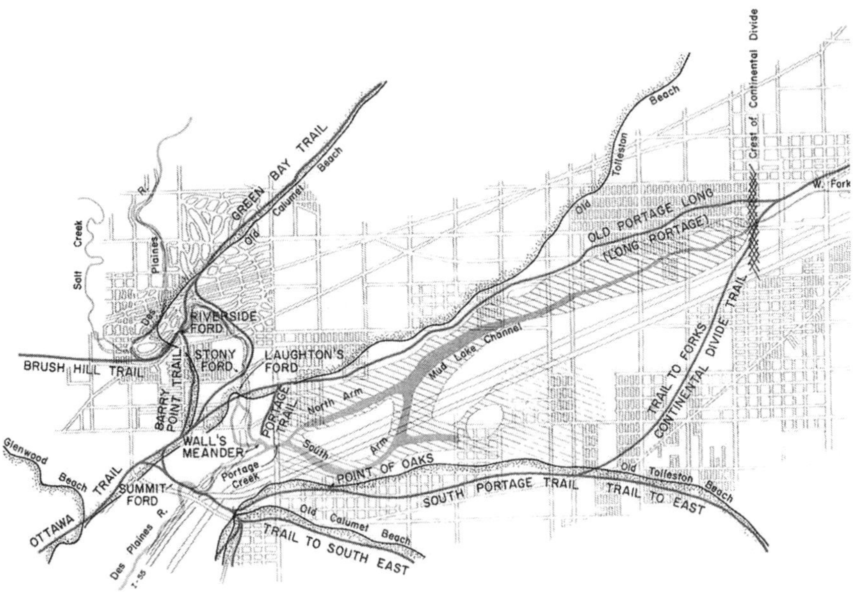

Fig. 29. Map showing Mud Lake. From William E. Rose and Associates, *Design Study: The Chicago Portage and the Laughton Trading Post Area, "The Waterway West"* (Hinsdale, IL: William E. Rose and Associates, 1975), 11–12.

3. For 26 days, the same boats had to portage between Albany Avenue and South Leavitt Street. At such times the water in Mud Lake was level with the crest of the Continental Divide. If there was a ditch through the divide, the water flowing from Mud Lake conformed to its depth.
4. For 44 days, the same boats had to portage one and one-half miles from South Leavitt Street to deep water at Mud Lake. From there they could go by water to the vicinity of Central Avenue and Thirty-Ninth Street, where they either had to follow the South Arm or make a second portage along the Portage Trail on the north bank of Mud Lake to the Des Plaines River. This was the condition of the portage as reported by Major Long.
5. As the dry season advanced, for 103 days the most common route for boats drawing less than fifteen inches was a portage from South Leavitt Street along the Portage Trail on the north bank of Mud Lake to the Des Plaines River. Boats drawing less than eight inches could make a short portage from Central Avenue and Thirty-Ninth Street to deeper water in the South Arm and then to another portage along the south bank of Mud Lake from near Fifty-Fifth Street and Oak Park Avenue to where the Summit Bridge crosses the Des Plaines River.

6. For the remaining 140 days, the water route through Mud Lake was either very shallow or closed by ice. At such times the route was the land portage along the Portage Trail on the north bank of Mud Lake to the Des Plaines River. The Des Plaines River remained navigable for a considerable part of this time to boats of shallow draft, but, depending on the river's depth, the land portage to reach navigable water could vary significantly.[8]

Prior to the diversion of the Des Plaines River in 1893, there was an island about eight hundred feet northwest of the mouth of Portage Creek known as Prescott Island. The island was about one-half of a mile long and one-quarter of a mile wide. The northern end of this island was just below Laughton's Ford. The Des Plaines River flowed southward through two channels east and west of this island before joining again at its southern end.

As mentioned briefly at the beginning of this chapter, the west end of the Chicago Portage went through a number of human-made changes throughout the nineteenth century. Starting around 1865 (the exact date is unclear), William Ogden and John Wentworth, both former mayors of Chicago and both substantial land owners in the Summit area near Mud Lake, dug a ditch that was two hundred feet long and twenty to thirty feet wide, running from Portage Creek north through Mud Lake and then turning east to empty into the West Fork. In the early 1870s, Sparrow Nickerson dug another ditch that extended from Portage Creek through the South Arm of Mud Lake and then north, where it connected to the Ogden-Wentworth Ditch. The purpose of these ditches was to drain the west end of Mud Lake.

An unintended consequence of these ditches was to divert flow from the Des Plaines River eastward in periods of high water, flowing through Mud Lake and into the West Fork. To alleviate this diversion, the city, in 1874 (according to Andreas), or in 1876–77 (according to Knight and Zeuch), built the Ogden Dam across Portage Creek at what is now Harlem Avenue to prevent the Des Plaines River from flowing into Mud Lake.[9] The Ogden Dam also had the effect of lengthening the West Fork more than six miles to the west.[10]

Although the Ogden Dam performed its purpose, it was only partly appreciated by neighboring property owners who liked to harvest ice in the winter for commercial purposes. As a result, these property owners would break through the dam in fall to allow flooding and then rebuild it in the spring to dry out the western end of Mud Lake for agriculture. This circumvention went on for years until the state in 1885 built a concrete version of the Ogden Dam.[11]

As part of the preliminary work for the Sanitary and Ship Canal, the Sanitary District of Chicago decided to divert the Des Plaines River. Work began on August 24, 1892, on a nineteen-mile-long levee to separate the Des Plaines River from the diversion channel both during and after construction.[12]

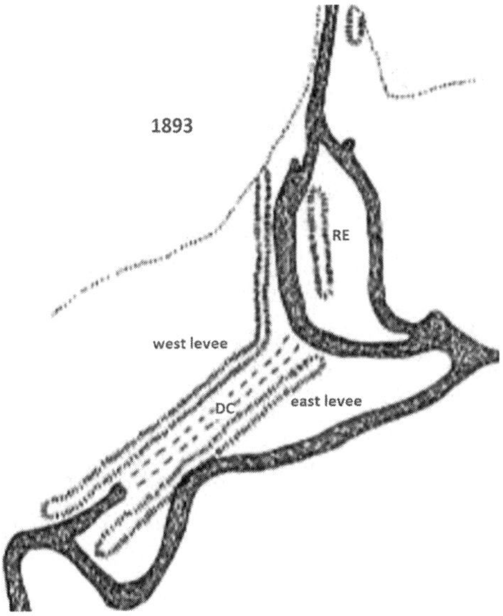

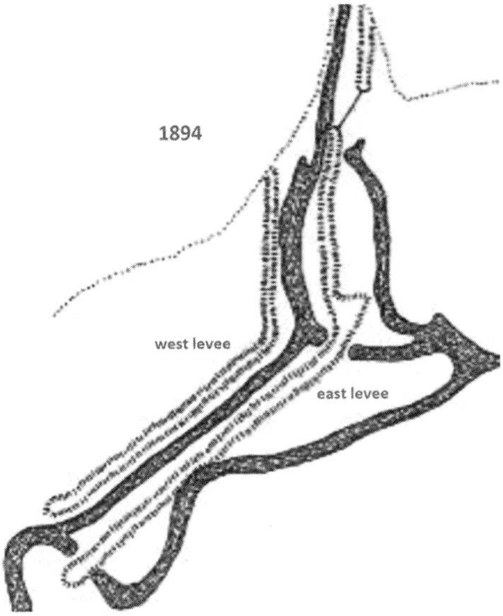

Figs. 30–31. *Top*, diversion levees for rerouting of the Des Plaines River, 1893; *bottom*, route of the river after diversion, 1894. Adapted from Philip E. Vierling, *Engineering Changes to the Des Plaines River* (self-pub., 2010), 3. Courtesy Judith Vierling Close.

As shown in figure 30, by 1893 the various levees, the diversion channel (labeled "DC" in the figure), and an embankment known as the Riverside Embankment (labeled "RE") were in place. The following year, the work was completed and the Des Plaines River assumed its new course (fig. 31).

The diversion levee cut through Prescott's Island and extended from Lyons to Summit. Once the Des Plaines River was diverted, it was prevented from overflowing into Mud Lake. Almost immediately the area began to be developed with buildings and roads. Knight and Zeuch predicted in 1928, "In three or four years at the most all the old landmarks will have been obliterated, and the old Chicago Portage that has been a determining factor in the history of civilization in the Old Northwest for the past two hundred and fifty years will be wiped out of existence."[13] It was exactly this danger that led to efforts to protect the remnants of the Chicago Portage.

A survey done by John Walls, deputy United States surveyor, in 1821 showed the Portage Trail, also called Portage Road, running north of Mud Lake from about the line of present-day Western Avenue westward to just west of Harlem Avenue (fig. 32). There is no documentary evidence showing exactly where the trail extended to the Des Plaines River, possibly because the exact location varied according to the condition of the river. But it is certainly reasonable to conclude that the termination point was on the east bank of the Des Plaines River at the north side of the mouth of Portage Creek. (It is important to distinguish this point, which was where boats would enter the Des Plaines River, from the Laughton Ford to the north, which was a crossing for wagons and such. The embarkation point for boats was too deep to be suitable for fording.)

While conducting his survey, Walls also noted on October 16, 1821, that he ran a line along the east side of the Des Plaines River between two fixed points in the meander that he describes as extending "across Portage Creek or swamp."[14] This is the most exact data we have as to the location of Portage Creek, and Walls's location of Portage Creek is the same as that provided by Sullivan. Knight and Zeuch comment that at the time of the survey, the fur trade was at its height, so Walls was able to observe the actual use of the portage.[15]

At the times when Mud Lake was almost dry and the Des Plaines River itself was too shallow for navigation, a long land portage was required over the Portage Trail. This portage could entail a fifty-mile trek to the mouth of the Des Plaines River at its confluence with the Kankakee River, or even a slog of the entire one hundred miles from the Chicago River to La Salle, the head of navigation for the Illinois River.

About a mile west of Harlem Avenue, at Joliet Avenue and West Forty-Seventh Street in Lyons, Joliet Road begins. This road extends southwest through the present-day cities of Joliet, Channahon, Morris, Seneca, Marseilles, Ottawa, and Utica, following very closely the old portage trail to La Salle. There are conflicting accounts from early in the twentieth century regarding the exact route of the Portage Trail from where it crossed Harlem Avenue to where it connected with Joliet Road.[16] We do, however, have a small-scale map of Illinois and Missouri produced by Henry S. Tanner, a geographer and map publisher, in 1823 "from data obtained from documents found in the public offices of the United Sates and States Governments."[17] The Tanner map is important because it is the only map based on official

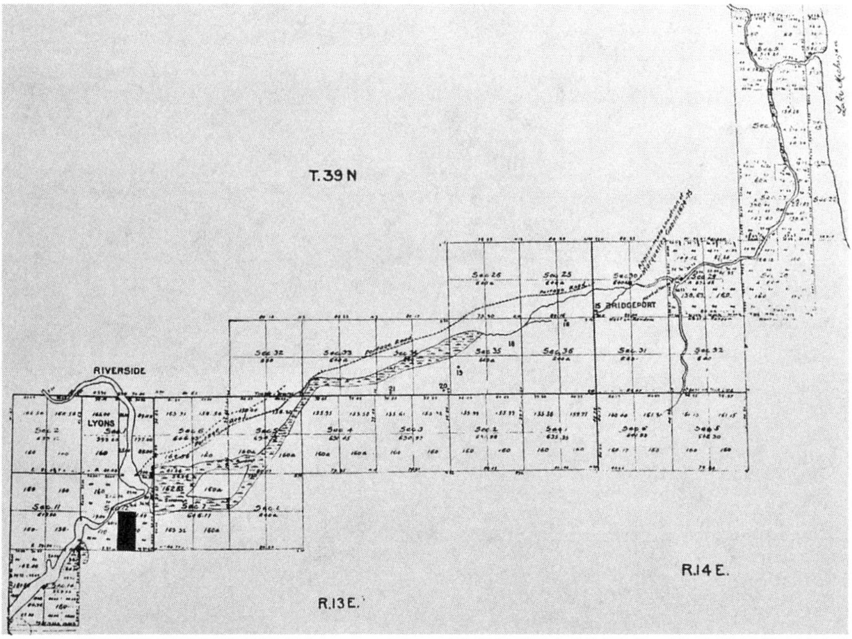

Fig. 32. Survey map by John Walls, 1821. From Robert Knight and Lucius H. Zeuch, *The Location of the Chicago Portage Route of the Seventeenth Century* (Chicago: Chicago Historical Society, 1928), 107.

surveys, including those of Sullivan and Walls, and in particular Tanner mentions that Major Long (a colonel at the time Tanner made his map) had personally assisted in producing the map (fig. 33). The Tanner map shows the north Portage Trail crossing the Des Plaines River at Laughton's Ford and then continuing southwest to the Illinois River. Of note, the map then shows the trail continuing not west along the Illinois River to La Salle but southwest to Fort Clark at present-day Peoria.

There was also a portage along the south side of Mud Lake beginning from about two hundred feet east of the intersection of Oak Park Avenue and Fifty-Second Street, westward to Summit Ford. This South Portage Trail ran along the Continental Divide Trail that came from the east around the southern end of Lake Michigan and followed the ridges of the Calumet and Tolleston Beaches. The South Portage Trail connected with the trail that followed the west bank of the North and South Branches of the Chicago River, to and along the north bank of the West Fork. This trail turned south just east of Kedzie Avenue, passing between the head of the West Fork and Mud Lake on the continental divide. It then continued south to about the vicinity of Archer Avenue, where it turned west along the south shore of Mud Lake to Summit. There it turned north to the Summit Ford across the Des Plaines River.[18]

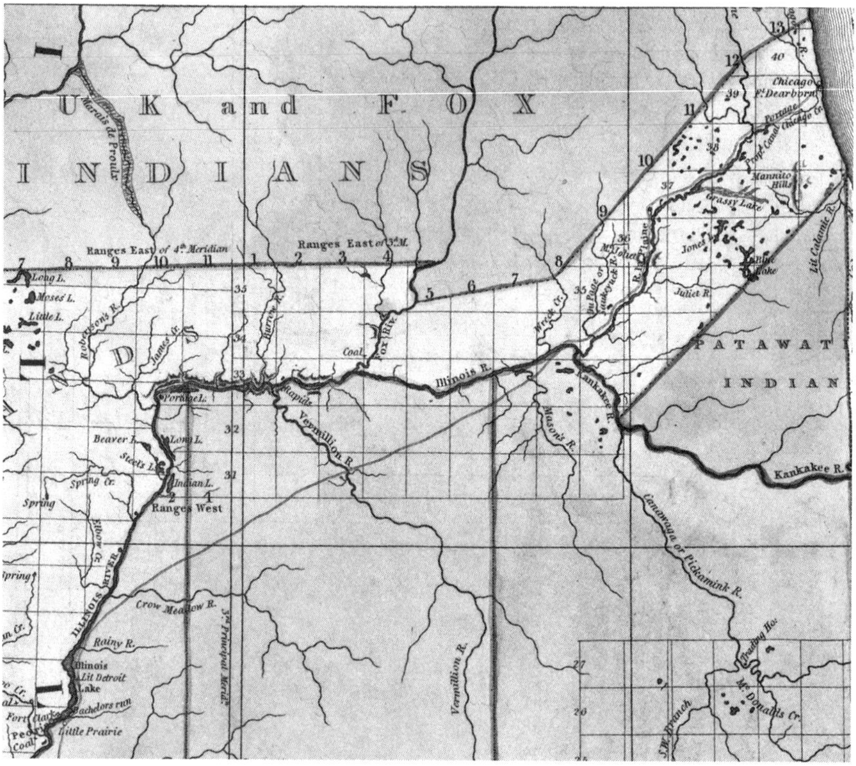

Fig. 33. Detail from map "Illinois and Missouri by H. S. Tanner," 1823. From Henry S. Tanner, *A New American Atlas Containing Maps of the Several States of the North American Union, Projected and drawn on a Uniform Scale from Documents found in the public Offices of the United States and State Governments, and other Original and Authentic Information* (Philadelphia: H. S. Tanner, 1823). Courtesy of David Rumsey Map Collection, https://www.davidrumsey.com.

As chief engineer for the Sanitary District, Cooley investigated various distances along the old portage route. He found that the distance from Lake Michigan, by way of the Chicago River to the continental divide, was 7.5 miles. The distance from the continental divide to the Ogden Dam was 6.3 miles. And the distance of the fifty-mile portage as described by Knight and Zeuch from Lake Michigan to the mouth of the Des Plaines River at its confluence with the Kankakee River was actually 58.3 miles.[19]

To close this description of the location of the Chicago Portage, and of how it was for the most part obliterated by the explosive development of Chicago, we can review the demise of the West Fork. With the coming of the Illinois and Michigan Canal and then the Chicago Sanitary and Ship Canal, the West Fork fell into disuse. It was still there in 1921, when the city began the legal process of filling it in. Congressional hearings were held, at which only a few industrial interests expressed a desire to maintain the West Fork. In January 1923, Congress declared the western portion of the West Fork nonnavigable, which allowed the city to fill it in. Congress declared the eastern portion nonnavigable in 1935, and by the end of 1938 the city had filled it in.[20]

When the Chicago Portage was important to the fur trade, and then later to furthering western expansion, it was a spot worth fighting over. Colonial powers maneuvered to control the portage, and Native Americans were deceived and ultimately displaced and deprived of access to a spot they had used for centuries. Politicians manipulated state boundaries to keep the Chicago Portage firmly in hand, and entrepreneurs schemed to make the most of this singularly valuable location. And then, just like that, it was gone.

11

✦

“A History of Chicanery”

In 1960, Commonwealth Edison (ComEd) opened the first privately financed nuclear power plant in the United States near the city of Morris, Illinois, at the head of the Illinois River. When it came time to name the plant, ComEd reached back in time and picked the name Dresden, which referred to a town no longer in existence. But in the early twentieth century, Dresden Heights was at the center of a scandal that implicated rich entrepreneurs, shady business dealings, corrupt state officials, and politicians on the take. Ironically, it all revolved around the building of a power plant on the Des Plaines River by the Electric Light and Power Company, which eventually became part of ComEd. At stake was who had the right to waterpower generated by the Des Plaines River, private investors, the Sanitary District of Chicago, or the State of Illinois. The scandal resulted in an important legal battle concerning navigable waterways in United States legal history, a battle that lasted for fourteen years and involved the highest courts in both Illinois and the United States. And at the heart of the battle was the Chicago Portage.

The story begins in the spring of 1904 when a young lawyer named Charles Munroe, through a straw purchaser named Harold Griswold, began quietly buying up land at the mouth of the Des Plaines River in Grundy County. When the Sanitary and Ship Canal opened in 1900, the resulting diversion of water from Lake Michigan through the canal and into the Des Plaines River created a new and vigorous flow of water. Munroe focused his attention on a particular stretch of the Des Plaines River where the fall in elevation was significant enough to support a water-powered electrical plant. Munroe originally was joined in his efforts by Raymond Gaylord, but Gaylord's interest in the project was soon taken over by Frank Logan. To add a further wrinkle, at the time the project was conceived, Munroe and Logan were simply business partners, but before all was said and done, they became family when Munroe married Logan's daughter.

In June 1904, the Illinois and Michigan Canal Commission, at that time made up by Clarence Snively and William Sackett, asked Governor Charles Deneen for permission to sell certain lands along the route of the Illinois and Michigan Canal. Deneen approved the request, and the commissioners published in the *Lockport Phoenix Advertiser* newspaper that on August 2, 1904, certain lands would be sold at auction.[1] It was at this so-called auction that things started getting sketchy. Years later it was shown that Snively and Sackett were working in league with Munroe to ensure that the land that was up for sale went to Griswold. Their plan hit a snag when another investor, John Arnold, found out about these plans and sent a representative to Lockport "with $10,000 in his pocket" to bid on the same land. When Arnold's representative arrived, the commissioners adjourned the auction. With Arnold forestalled, Snively and Sackett changed the game by saying the land was no longer for sale and instead worked with Munroe to grant Griswold a twenty-year lease on the property with a right to perpetual renewals. This maneuver allowed them to freeze out Arnold because the land was technically no longer for sale.[2] The result was that the commissioners gave Griswold a perpetual lease over the land at the mouth of the Des Plaines River for $2,200. Later evidence showed that the same two commissioners refused an offer of $75,000 from the Sanitary District of Chicago for the same lease rights.[3]

By the time Griswold had completed his assignment as trustee for Munroe and Logan, the investors had acquired 1,700 acres of land.[4] On November 30, 1906, Munroe and Griswold transferred all their titles and lease rights to the land that included the riverbanks on both sides of the mouth of the Des Plaines River to Economy Light and Power Company (ELP).[5] Griswold later testified that he never met Snively or Sackett, that he "paid nothing" personally for any of the land or lease acquisitions, and that he simply did what he was instructed to do by Munroe and Logan. Indeed, the attorney for ELP admitted that "Mr. Munroe conducted the entire negotiations [with the canal commissioners], and that Mr. Griswold merely took and held title at the convenience of Mr. Munroe."[6]

Sackett later testified that he didn't even know what rights he was granting to Griswold and that he conveyed the rights on the recommendation of the canal commission's attorney, Charles Walker. Sackett said he would never have approved the granting of rights had he known what they were. After a recess in which he met with Snively, Sackett revised his testimony and said that considerable consideration had been given to the grants and that Griswold and Munroe were told that the grants contained in the lease agreement "were beyond our [the commission's] authority, and that they accepted them at their own risk."[7]

For his part, Snively said he didn't remember the details of the August 2, 1904, auction for the sixteen-acre tract that was subsequently leased to Griswold. Snively did claim to remember, however, that the auction was postponed when the commissioners learned that Arnold was interested in placing a bid to purchase the land. Contrary to Arnold's testimony, Snively claimed that Arnold had inspected the land once the auction was postponed and had decided he was no longer interested in purchasing it. Snively said he did not remember why the commissioners decided to lease the land to Griswold instead of going forward with an auction for the sale of the land.

None of these facts were publicly known when they occurred. The situation began to unravel in 1906 when the Sanitary District decided to extend the Chicago Sanitary and Ship Canal as part of a larger statewide effort to create a deep waterway from Lake Michigan to the Gulf of Mexico. The desired extension was blocked by the existence of a dam in Joliet owned by ELP, known as Dam No. 1. The Sanitary District filed suit to condemn Dam No. 1, arguing in part that the people of Chicago had spent $53 million to construct the drainage canal that made Dam No. 1 possible and that ELP was receiving the benefit.[8]

It didn't take long for the rhetoric and maneuvering to get nasty. Robert McCormick, president of the Sanitary District, accused ELP of committing "a fraud upon the people of Chicago."[9] The *Chicago Daily Tribune* reported that both Munroe and Logan were stockholders in ELP with more than $1 million of their own money invested, and McCormick insisted that if Dam No. 1 was condemned, the state could provide enough power to light the city of Chicago at significantly reduced rates.[10] ELP retaliated by trying to get a grand jury impaneled to bring criminal charges against officials of the Sanitary District.[11]

The state won its condemnation suit in March 1907, and the next month Governor Deneen worked out an agreement between the Sanitary District, the Illinois and Michigan Canal Commission, and ELP for the removal of Dam No. 1. As part of this agreement, the Sanitary District was also given the right to develop waterpower along the extension of the Sanitary and Ship Canal. Perhaps not surprisingly, Snively and Sackett opposed removing Dam No. 1 because the Canal Commission received rental revenue from ELP for its use.[12]

Dam No. 1 was only a skirmish. The real battle lay ahead over the dam that ELP was constructing at Dresden Heights. Although there is little doubt that the original intent of the investors was to build a waterpower plant at Dresden Heights, the desire of the Sanitary District to assume control of waterpower along the extension gave ELP another motivation. Isham Randolph, a consulting engineer for the Sanitary District, in a speech before the City Club of Chicago told a story of how an attorney for ELP had made clear to him that ELP was glad either to make money producing power or to receive a windfall in damages from the state if it tried to take over ELP's property at Dresden Heights. Randolph told the attorney that the Sanitary District had estimated potential damages at $500,000, to which the attorney replied "O, lots more than that." Randolph concluded by telling his audience that "much has been said about the innocent purchasers of this property. You see how innocent they are."[13] Echoing Randolph, Lyman Cooley, chief engineer for the Sanitary District and a critical witness for the state, recounted how ELP had tried to "call him off" with job offers.[14]

At that same meeting of the City Club, Representative Morton Hull talked about a bill in the Illinois General Assembly that laid out the issue that would be litigated for the next thirteen years. The bill declared the Des Plaines River a navigable waterway and that therefore no obstruction could be placed in the Des Plaines River without the State of Illinois's consent. That bill eventually passed both the House and Senate and was signed by Governor Deneen.[15] However, the Senate refused to pass a part of the bill known as the "emergency clause" which would have given it immediate effect. Because of that omission, ELP had time to build as much of its dam as possible before the bill went into effect on July 1, 1908. Cooley reported to Governor Deneen that ELP was working with "feverish haste," including working at night, to complete as much construction as possible to maximize any potential damage award. The *Chicago Daily Tribune* accused the Senate of "trickery" and of a "three shell game"—on the one hand pretending to support the idea of a deep waterway while on the other hand refusing to enact a law that would further its progress.[16]

The rest of 1907 became a prelude to the legal battles to come. The Illinois House appointed a committee to investigate the actions of Snively and Sackett made up of three Republicans (John Flannigan, Chester Church, William Gillespie) and two Democrats (Dennis Egan, Campbell Hearn). On its first outing to visit the dam project at Dresden Heights, Snively and Sackett, according to the *Chicago Daily Tribune*, just "happened" to go along.[17] Various efforts were made by legislators friendly to ELP to derail the investigation, and testimony revealed its share of questionable deeds.[18] Samuel Insull, head of ComEd, had contended publicly that ComEd had made no efforts to lobby the legislature concerning the deep waterway or navigability issues, but he had a different story when under oath before the investigative committee.[19] And in some of the last testimony before the committee, Munroe, who was now manager of ELP, admitted that the company had retained the services of Howard Snapp, who became a representative from the eleventh district, to help on the Dam No. 1 condemnation suit. Pressed by attorneys for the committee, Munroe couldn't remember exactly what work Snapp did, but did remember that Snapp never returned any of the retainer and never presented a bill.[20]

The committee concluded its investigation and issued three reports, one by the three Republican members, and one each by the two Democratic members. The majority report found no wrongdoing by Snively or Sackett but that they simply had not foreseen that the rights they transferred to Griswold for $2,200 would ever be worth more than that. The two Democratic members scorned this finding and instead found that both Snively and Sackett had been, at the least, derelict in their duties and should be fired from the commission. Hearn found that the commissioners had been "lax in their duties and . . . woefully unwise" in their actions. Egan's report concluded it "was a bold attempt on the part of the canal commissioners to give to private interests all the rights of the state in perpetuity."[21] The Illinois House adopted the majority report by a voice vote.[22]

Clarence Snively resigned from the canal commission on February 22, 1910.[23] He was the owner and editor of the *Canton Daily Register*, and he remained heavily involved in the Republican Party, including being a delegate to the Republican National Convention in 1912. In August 1921, he was appointed by Governor Lennington Small to be assistant superintendent of fish culture.[24] Snively was then appointed postmaster of Canton, Illinois, by President Warren G. Harding in 1922 and retained that position for the rest of his life; Snively died on September 21, 1937.[25] William Sackett continued to serve as commissioner until July 1913, when Governor Edward Fitzsimmons Dunne replaced him.[26] In May 1917, Governor Frank Lowden appointed Sackett superintendent of waterways, a position he held until his death on December 16, 1924.[27]

On November 6, 1907, Governor Deneen sent a special message to the Illinois General Assembly. He first noted that the legislature had put forward a joint resolution on October 7, 1907, to present to the citizens of Illinois a constitutional amendment that would provide for $20 million in bonds to construct a deep waterway and for "the development of water power incident thereto."[28] He went on to say that the ELP project at Dresden Heights was an obstacle to that development and that the project had not been located farther downstream because the Illinois River was unquestionably a navigable stream and ELP wanted to keep the contention alive that the Des Plaines River was not.[29] He pointed out that ELP was pushing the work at Dresden Heights in an effort to complete it before July, 1, 1908, in the "manifest attempt to secure vested rights inimical to the public interests and fatal to the success of the constitutional amendment." Given this situation, he urged the legislature to pass emergency legislation declaring the Des Plaines River a navigable stream and that if it did not do so, the result would be "protracted litigation" and the possibility of "enormous expenditure in acquiring by condemnation proceedings the Dresden Property."[30] As we have seen, the General Assembly did pass such legislation, but the Senate refused to include the emergency provision. To make matters worse, on the same day that Governor Deneen sent his special message to the legislature, he received an opinion from William Stead, the Illinois attorney general, that went contrary to the action requested by Deneen. Stead's opinion stated that whether or not the Des Plaines River was navigable was a question of fact for a court to decide and that legislation declaring it to be navigable would have no effect.[31]

The Senate's refusal to include the emergency provision and the adverse opinion by Stead left the state little alternative but to go to court. On December 1, 1907, it filed suit in the Circuit Court of Grundy County. The complaint had various counts, but of relevance to the Chicago Portage were those that argued that the Des Plaines River was a navigable stream. The basic argument made in the Grundy County suit would be repeated by the state on appeal to the Illinois Supreme Court and later at the federal level in the district court, circuit court of appeals, and United States Supreme Court.

The state's argument went like this: The Northwest Ordinance of 1787 stated that "the navigable waters leading into the Mississippi and St. Lawrence, and the carrying places between them, shall be common highways and forever free." This law was repeated and ratified by various acts of Congress, including the Enabling Act of 1818 that established Illinois as a state. The Des Plaines River was covered by these various acts, and "the history of the explorations and discoveries of the territory . . . [show that] the Des Plaines River was navigable from a point near where is now situated the City of Chicago . . . to the mouth of the Des Plaines River."[32] The state went on to say that "commerce was carried on over said river and over the Chicago River . . . and connection therewith made by a short portage between the two rivers."[33] Because the Des Plaines River is a navigable stream, argued the state, the dam proposed by ELP was illegal because it would "destroy and interfere with the Des Plaines River as a navigable waterway."[34]

In response, ELP simply denied that the Des Plaines River had ever been a navigable waterway and that even if it had been at one point, it no longer was because of other obstructions along the river such as bridges and dams. Because the Des Plaines River was not navigable at the time of trial, said ELP, the state had no interest in the river and ELP had a right to build its dam.[35]

There was extensive testimony regarding the use of the Chicago Portage route to the Des Plaines River from the seventeenth through nineteenth centuries. Clarence Alvord, then assistant professor at the University of Illinois, was the state's main witness on the historical use of the Chicago Portage route by explorers, missionaries, and traders.[36] The state also called eighty-four-year-old George Reed, who testified to personal recollections of boat navigation on the Des Plaines River in the 1830s.[37] Despite this evidence, Judge John Mack dismissed the state's case on June 25, 1908. Mack rejected the state's argument and found that "though there might have been some slight use of [the Des Plaines River] down stream on rare occasions, [it] would not be deemed and could not be deemed at any time in its history . . . a navigable stream."[38]

The state immediately appealed to the Illinois Supreme Court. In its brief, the state recited extensive evidence of the use of the Des Plaines River, and in particular the use of the Chicago Portage. Reading the back and forth between the state and ELP is like listening to Louis Jolliet and René-Robert Cavelier de La Salle argue about the pros and cons of the Chicago Portage route. The state argued the long and continuous use of the portage by traders while ELP echoed La Salle about how difficult and finicky the portage was depending on the season.[39]

The Illinois Supreme Court noted that "the question that has received the most exhaustive treatment by counsel relates to the navigability of the Des

Plaines River." The evidence on this question alone, said the court, filled more than one thousand pages of the record and several hundred pages in the briefs to the court.[40] The court held that for a stream to be navigable, it must "in its ordinary, natural condition furnish a highway over which commerce is or may be carried on in the customary modes in which such commerce is conducted by water."[41] The state, said the court, "with commendable industry has assembled every fact which has even remote bearing on the question [of navigability]." The court then briefly noted the accounts of Jacques Marquette, Henry Schoolcraft, and Hugh Heward before concluding, somewhat incredibly, "There is not in this entire record a well authenticated instance in which a boat engaged in commerce navigated the waters of the Des Plaines River."[42] Accordingly, the Illinois Supreme Court held, "After the most careful consideration of this question, we are of the opinion that the Des Plaines River in its natural condition is not a navigable stream," and it affirmed the circuit court's dismissal of the state's case on October 5, 1909.[43]

The state subsequently appealed the Illinois Supreme Court's decision to the United States Supreme Court. Once again, the state fell short when the United States Supreme Court held in 1914 that it lacked jurisdiction over the case because no federal questions were presented on appeal.[44] But where the state had failed in the courts of Illinois, a new round began when the United States of America stepped in and filed suit against ELP on December 14, 1909.

The United States took a slightly different tack by arguing that (1) the Des Plaines River was a navigable waterway, (2) under a federal law enacted on March 3, 1899, it was unlawful to obstruct a navigable waterway without prior express approval from the chief of engineers and the secretary of war, and (3) because ELP did not obtain this approval, it had to remove that portion of the dam it had constructed at Dresden Heights.[45] With the issue so squarely presented, ELP had no other recourse than to deny that the Des Plaines River was a navigable waterway and be ready to relitigate that issue in the district court.[46]

If the Illinois Supreme Court thought that the state showed "considerable industry" in presenting evidence regarding the use and navigability of the Des Plaines River, it would have been doubly impressed by the evidence presented by the United States. By the time the trial was over, the abstract of record was 3,186 pages long, and more than fifty maps had been introduced. Clarence Alvord was back as the main witness for the United States on the historical use of the Des Plaines River, but this time his testimony was supplemented by that of Andrew McLaughlin, head of the history department at the University of Chicago, and Reuben Gold Thwaites, secretary and superintendent of the Wisconsin State Historical Society and a lecturer on history at the University of Wisconsin.[47] The view of all was that the Des Plaines River had been a navigable stream from at least the time of Jolliet and Marquette. Alvord summed up his view as follows:

> Giving due weight to all the sources of information that are available, my opinion is that from the latter part of the 17th Century through the first third of the 19th Century, men engaged in the fur trade passed up and down the Chicago and Desplaines rivers in canoes and flatboats very regularly; that the fur trade was pursued by the French as long as they held possession of this country; was developed more fully by the English and later by the Americans. That the most active trade carried on the two rivers falls between the period of 1783 and 1825, or thereabouts; that the traders found a very easy passageway by means of these rivers in the early spring. That during the time of drought such as occurred in the summer or fall, the passage was hard, but even then they forced their boats through the waterway, often being obliged, however, to carry their packages around the shoals and rapids.[48]

In response, ELP called two historians, Judson Lee and Milton Milo Quaife, both of whom taught history at the Lewis Institute.[49] Quaife was the main witness, but the testimony of both men sought to minimize the use of the Des Plaines River by pointing out that at times of low water it was difficult to use and that horses and wagons had increasingly become the preferred mode of travel and commerce.

The district court case was filed in 1909, but a decision was not rendered until November 7, 1917. Judge Kenesaw Mountain Landis pointed out that there was ample evidence that the Des Plaines River had been used "by the customary mode of trade and travel by water" and that the real issue in the case was "as to the extent rather than the fact of such use."[50] He concluded:

> This evidence taken with existence of portage from Chicago River to Desplaines during time mentioned a large collection of historical documents, contemporaneous maps and governmental records and reports, forbids conclusion river was not subjected to such use for trade and travel down to and subsequent to enactments of original legislation referred to. From this, follows river shown by evidence to be navigable water of U.S. when bill filed and at present time.[51]

Landis went on to say that the decision of the Illinois Supreme Court on the issue of navigability was "obviously rendered on record vitally differing in the facts from record here" and that the Illinois court's decision was "not persuasive" because it was "based on the absence of evidence from that record as to such use which evidence is present here."[52]

It was now ELP's turn to appeal, and it did so to the Seventh Circuit Court of Appeals. The litigants covered now familiar ground, the United States arguing that the Des Plaines River was navigable under the 1899 federal law while ELP maintained the opposite. The decision of the appellate court began with a detailed description of the "Chicago-Desplaines-Illinois water route, used from 1673 to 1825 by explorers and in the fur trade," and it specifically included the "Chicago divide" between the Chicago River and the Des Plaines River.[53] Turning to the historical record, the court found that "from the latter part of the seventeenth century through the first third of the nineteenth century men engaged in the fur trade passed up and down the Chicago and Desplaines rivers in canoes and flatboats very regularly."[54] The court noted fourteen specific instances shown in the record and concluded, "No doubt other instances of its use may properly be inferred."[55] The court agreed with the district court that the Des Plaines River might not currently be being used for navigation but held that "we think streams of actual navigable capacity, but not now used for interstate commerce, are within congressional power to preserve for purposes of future transportation, and that the act of 1899 applies to such streams."[56] Given the clear evidence of the navigable capacity of the Des Plaines River between 1673 and 1825, the court held that it was a navigable stream within the act of 1899 and affirmed the district court's decision. Referring to the Illinois Supreme Court decision, the appellate court noted, "The difference in the record in the two cases would not, perhaps, warrant a different conclusion, although the evidence here is somewhat stronger in favor of navigability than in that case." The appellate court concluded that it took "a different view as to the force and effect of the historical accounts of the early use of the river," and so its members asserted that "we should follow our own views."[57]

ELP had one last chance and appealed the Seventh Circuit's decision to the United States Supreme Court. The same arguments were made by the litigants, the same record of evidence was reviewed by the Supreme Court as by the Seventh Circuit Court of Appeals, and the same outcome was reached. The Supreme Court found that the circuit court of appeals had correctly applied the test for navigability of whether a river "in its natural state is used or capable of being used as a highway for commerce over which trade and travel is or may be conducted in the customary modes of trade and travel on water."[58] "Navigability," said the Supreme Court, "in the sense of the law, is not destroyed because the watercourse is interrupted by occasional natural obstructions or portages, nor need the navigation be open at all seasons of the year or at all stages of the water."[59] The court went on to say that a river having actual navigable capacity in its natural state is "within the power of Congress to preserve for purposes of future transportation, even though it be not at present used for such commerce, and be incapable of such use according to present methods, either by reason of changed conditions or because of artificial obstructions."[60] It did not matter, said the court, that the Des Plaines River had fallen into disuse after having been used as a highway of commerce for a century and a half, because even though the Des Plaines River had not been used for navigation for one hundred years, "a hundred years is a brief space in the life of a nation."[61] The court noted that there were likely many other streams in similar condition as the Des Plaines River and that it was always within the power of Congress to restore them to their navigable condition. If such streams were to be abandoned, concluded the court, it was up to Congress, not the court, to do so. With that said, the court affirmed the circuit court's ruling and enjoined ELP from obstructing the Des Plaines River.[62]

The legal battle finally over, there was only the wrapping up to do. In 1927, Insull, on behalf of ComEd, offered to sell the company's rights to the Dresden Heights property and some adjoining sites for $4 million. ComEd ended up getting $975,000.[63] By November 1928, the dam at Dresden Heights was gone and a reporter visiting the site saw only "the wooded island and farm lands, with the rivers flowing smoothly by unhampered."[64] The state succeeded in extending the waterway, and in January 1929 it began work on a lock and dam at Dresden Heights.[65]

And so a story having its origins in 1904 was finally concluded in 1929, a story so sordid that the *Chicago Daily Tribune* referred to it as a "history of chicanery."[66] The battle had at first been waged over the valuable rights to control water-generated power in the Des Plaines River valley but had morphed into an alternative effort to extract reparations from the state for condemning ELP's project at Dresden Heights. That such a dispute should fall finally upon a historical analysis of the Chicago Portage route was extraordinary. Even more remarkable was how the issue at hand—the navigability of the Chicago Portage route—paralleled the old dispute between the views of Jolliet and La Salle on the efficacy of using that route.

Readers of this book would have found the protracted dispute very familiar. Much of what you have read about the history of the Chicago Portage was told in various forms throughout the case. The many instances of use of the portage by explorers, missionaries, and traders; the possible personal motivations of La Salle to disapprove of the Chicago Portage route; the rise and demise of the fur trade; and the subsequent destruction of much of the portage route through land speculation and political power plays—they were all there. By the time the state and federal cases were finally over, their records contained the most extensive historical account of the Chicago Portage ever compiled up until that time.[67]

12

✦

The Past and Future of a National Historic Site

As engineer Robert Knight and doctor Lucius Zeuch pointed out in their book published by the Chicago Historical Society, *The Location of the Chicago Portage Route of the Seventeenth Century*, there wasn't much left of the old Chicago Portage route by 1928. The Des Plaines River had been diverted, the Ogden-Wentworth and Nickerson Ditches had drained much of Mud Lake, the Illinois and Michigan Canal and the Chicago Sanitary and Ship Canal had been cut through the portage route, a railroad track ran along what became the north border of the Chicago Portage Historic Site, and commercial and residential development had taken over much of the land reaching from the old continental divide to the Des Plaines River.[1]

Fortunately, the historical importance of the Chicago Portage was recognized by the Chicago Historical Society at its inception in 1856 and was researched by a succession of members of the society culminating in the May 1, 1923, presentation by Knight and Zeuch on the location of the Chicago Portage and the subsequent publication of their work in 1928. As early as 1920, however, Zeuch and the Chicago Historical Society had been pressing the case for making the Chicago Portage a protected historical site, and their efforts bore fruit when the Forest Preserve District of Cook County approved a resolution on September 20, 1929, accepting a land grant from the Sanitary District of Chicago for just over ninety-five acres "as a Historical Park . . . to properly mark this site as the Portage at the Continental Divide between the waters of the Desplaines and Chicago rivers and for the purpose of parking, beautifying, improving and protecting, restoring and preserving the scenic and historical beauties of the same."[2] It was at this point that the Forest Preserve District prepared the first formal plan for developing the site (fig. 34).

Even at this early date, hopes were high for the historic park. Zeuch wanted a reconstruction of the Laughton Trading Post on the site, and the Chicago Historical Society also wanted a boulder with a bronze plaque placed at the site to commemorate its historical importance. The original plan was to find a cabin similar to the trading post, tear it down, and then reconstruct in on the portage site. The cabin was to be furnished with period items and historical relics, and the grounds themselves restored as closely as possible to the

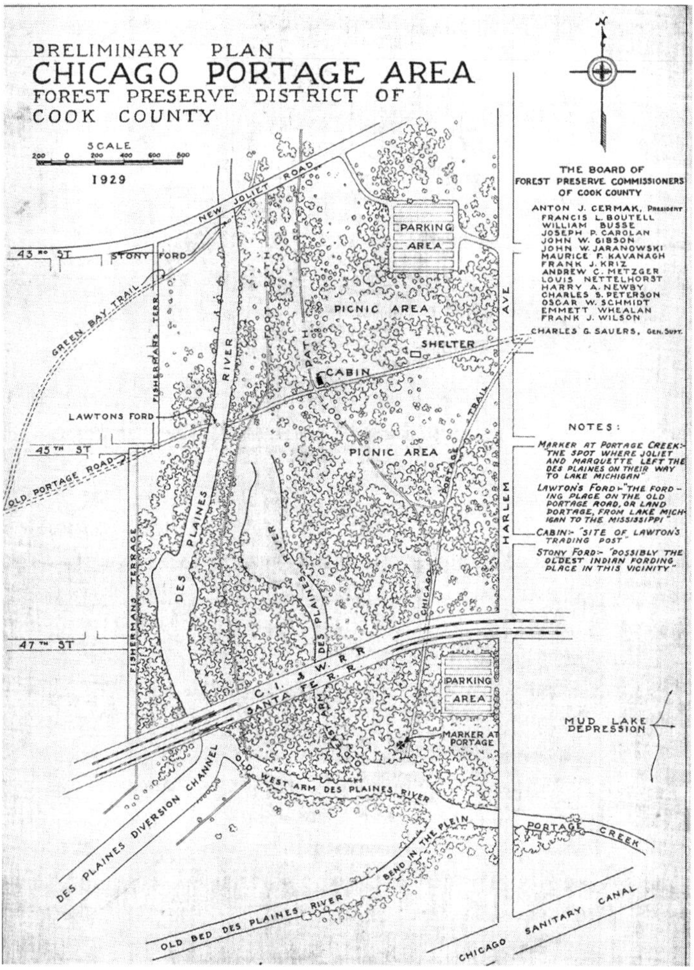

Fig. 34. *Preliminary Plan, Chicago Portage Area*, 1929. Courtesy of Forest Preserve District of Cook County.

conditions that had existed in 1673.[3] By early 1930, the plans for the site also included two parking areas, shelters, and picnic tables.[4] Although the plans for the trading post never materialized, the memorial boulder with a bronze plaque was erected and unveiled on May 16, 1930. It read:

THE CHICAGO PORTAGE, 1673–1836

This marks the west end of the carrying or connecting place uniting the waters of the St. Lawrence River and the Great Lakes with those of the Mississippi River, its tributaries and the Gulf of Mexico. The

> earliest factor in determining Chicago's commercial supremacy. An artery used by the Aborigines in their migrations and later by Joliet, Marquette, La Salle, Tonti and the fur traders of New France. An early strategical point, in the wars incident to the winning of the Northwest for the settlers and discovered by Joliet and Marquette in 1673.
>
> Erected by the Chicago Historical Society in pursuance of a plan to give posterity the facts of Chicago's early history. A.D. 1930

Unfortunately, the original plaque was stolen in 1950. A replacement was put up by the Chicago Historical Society in 1973 in celebration of the three hundredth anniversary of Jolliet's crossing of the portage, but that plaque was also stolen. As of the writing of this book, the boulder is still there, but no plaque. Some minor work on the site was done in the late 1930s by the Works Progress Administration, including a parking area and stone steps leading to the commemorative boulder. In 1936 a separate boulder was placed in Ottawa Trail Woods at the presumed location of the Laughton Trading Post, along with some low stone walls purporting to mark the perimeter of the post. The stone and walls are still there, but the inscription on the stone is now illegible. The inscription originally read, "This is the site of the trading post established and operated by Bernardus and David Laughton, Fur Traders in 1828—Laughton's Ford on the Des Plaines lies directly west." Later archaeological investigations in the 1970s showed that this was not the correct location for the trading post, which is thought to be nearby, and further archaeological investigation is needed to identify the correct location.

The next big step for the Chicago Portage came in 1948 when the Forest Preserve District, under the leadership of General Superintendent Charles G. Sauers, began working with the National Park Service to obtain National Historic Site status. The resulting application, written by National Park Service regional historian Olaf T. Hagen, included a historical narrative written by Paul Angle, the director of the Chicago Historical Society, a monograph on the Laughton Trading Post by G. E. Johnson, a student technician with the Civilian Conservation Corps, and beautiful hand-colored maps prepared by park planner Charles A. Jeffers that relied on the Knight and Zeuch study, more recent aerial photographs, and maps and plats supplied by the Forest Preserve District. (Figure 35 shows an example of one of the maps.)

At the time of the application, the only historical references present at the portage were the commemorative boulders in Portage Woods and Ottawa Trail Woods. As Hagen noted, "the area containing these sites present[s] a desirable natural setting, but their history seems pretty much incidental to recreational developments normal in metropolitan park areas." In fact, said Hagen, "we had to scout around a bit to find the location of the [Laughton] ford and the marked trading post site."[5] Even at this early date, the Forest Preserve District was "negotiating with an able sculptor" to create a work of

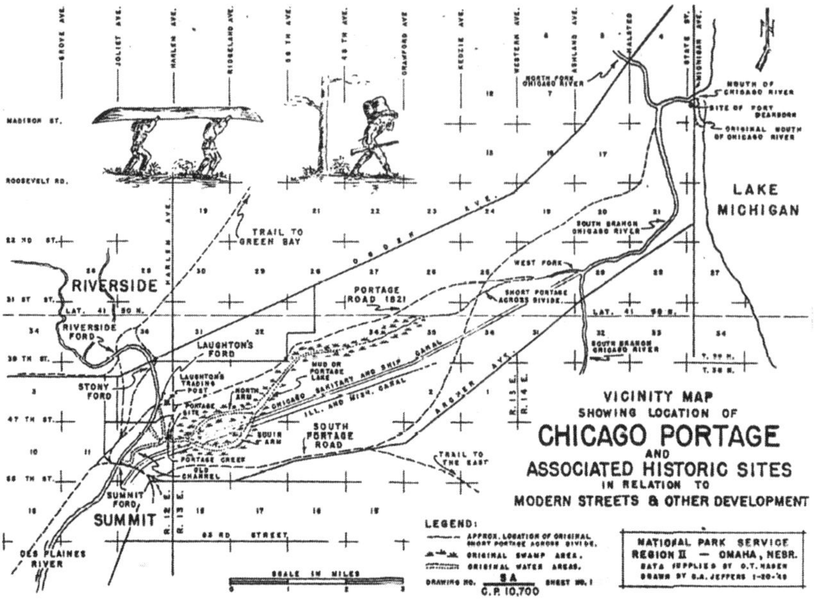

Fig. 35. Map of Chicago Portage by Charles A. Jeffers. From "National Registry of Historic Places Inventory—Nomination Form—Chicago Portage National Historic Site," United States Department of the Interior, received Feb. 22, 1978, approved Nov. 11, 1978. https://npgallery.nps.gov/AssetDetail/NRIS/66000108.

art that would suitably convey the historic importance of the area. The plan for a sculpture would not reach fruition until 1990.

After reviewing the historical significance of the site, Hagen pointed to the significance of the Forest Preserve District as a factor in granting the site historic status, stating that "the perpetuation and interpretation of historic values can be satisfactorily provided by the present administering agency."[6] Hagen then concluded:

> The remnant of the Chicago Portage preserved for public inspection in a unit of the Forest Preserve District of Cook County appears to qualify for favorable consideration under the Historic Sites Act of 1935. The portage was significant in American history; the remains at this site are an important control in establishing the exact location of its route; it is readily accessible, adaptable to development, and should be available for designation. . . . Interpreted through media designed to give [its] historical qualities greater prominence in the present metropolitan park development, it is believed that a unit could be planned which would measure up to the high standards set for historical areas conserved by the National Park Service and be eligible for designation as the Chicago Portage National Historic Site.[7]

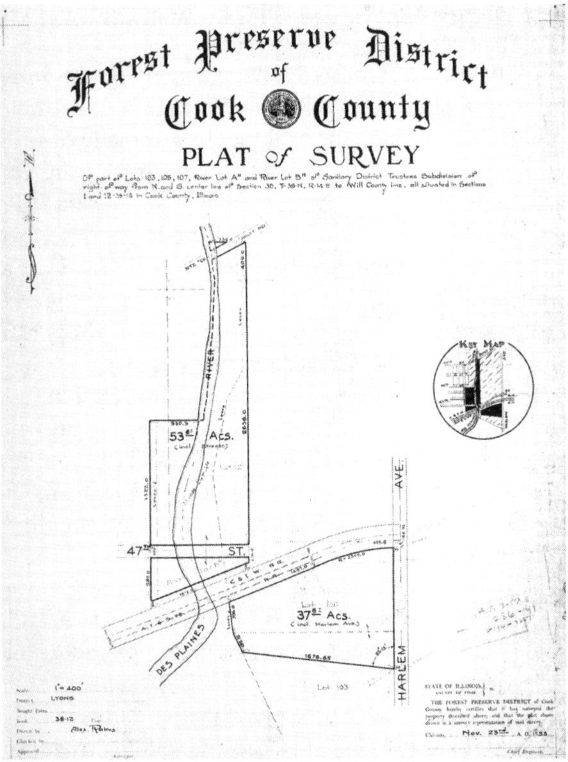

Fig. 36. Forest Preserve District of Cook County plat of survey, certified November 23, 1953, for the site that later became the Chicago Portage National Historic Site. Courtesy of Forest Preserve District of Cook County.

While the Forest Preserve District pursued National Historic Site status from the National Park Service, it was also negotiating with the Sanitary District to purchase the Chicago Portage property. In his letter to the Board of Forest Preserve Commissioners advocating for the purchase, General Superintendent Sauers noted that the Chicago Portage was "of particular historical importance to Chicago because it decided the location of the city," and it was "of national historical significance because of the importance of the portage in the pioneer days of the whole Midwest."[8] The sale of the property was finalized on August 4, 1950, for a purchase price of $125,000. The final parcel that was sold was slightly different from the original land grant from 1929. The earlier grant had included land east of Harlem Avenue and had not included the land where the current commemorative statue now stands at the historic site. The final parcel that was sold to the Forest Preserve District eliminated the land east of Harlem Avenue and included the land on which the statue now sits (fig. 36). The final parcel was smaller at ninety-one acres, and it is this site that became the Chicago Portage National Historic Site we have today.

On January 3, 1952, United States Department of the Interior Secretary Oscar L. Chapman declared the Chicago Portage a National Historic Site, one of only two in Illinois (the other is Lincoln's home in Springfield), and, as of this writing, one of only eighty-nine such sites in the United States. In the order designating the site, the Advisory Board on National Parks, Historic Sites, Buildings, and Monuments recognized the lands described in the order "as possessing national significance because of their relation to the historic portage which determined the location and growth of the Nation's second largest metropolitan center."[9] Pursuant to the order, a cooperative agreement was entered into between the Forest Preserve District and the United States of America, and the Chicago Portage today is considered an "affiliated area" of the National Park Service, one of twenty-five such sites nationwide. As such the Chicago Portage is owned by the Forest Preserve District, but the National Park Service is available to provide technical and financial assistance. To date, the National Park Service has been minimally involved with the Chicago Portage National Historic Site.

After the designation as a National Historic Site, the Chicago Portage fell on hard times. From the 1950s to the 1970s, little was done either to improve the natural conditions of the site or to better promote and develop its historic significance. Instead, the Lake-River Terminal, West Plant, which bordered the Chicago Portage to the south, seriously polluted the remaining waterways. To make matters worse, the area became a de facto dumping ground.[10]

The pollution finally stopped in the early 1970s, although those responsible for defiling the historic site were never held responsible or required to clean up their mess. Instead, it took volunteers and the Forest Preserve District to clean up the worst of the damage that had been done. But even with these efforts, the site itself remained neglected in terms of its development as a National Historic Site.

In 1972, an exploratory archaeological dig was carried out in the Laughton Trading Post under the supervision of Robert Hall of the University of Illinois at Chicago. The dig revealed some artifacts and hinted at the archaeological richness of the area. On June 17, 1974, the Board of Commissioners of the Forest Preserve District passed a resolution emphasizing the archaeological importance of the Chicago Portage and declared the Forest Preserve's "continued interest in and support of such efforts as may be directed toward implementation of all archeological and developmental methods useful in gaining knowledge of the past and imparting this knowledge to the general public through the proposed interpretive center at the Chicago Portage."[11] This resolution set the stage for a formal proposal to fund additional archaeological exploration. The "Background, Purpose, and Objectives for the Archeological Exploration of the Chicago Portage and Laughton's Trading Post in the Forest Preserve District of Cook County" emphasized the importance of conducting the archaeological research "before construction activities occur that may destroy such an investigation forever."[12] The proposal established a budget of $24,797for the work.[13]

The archaeological digs were carried out in the summers of 1974 and 1975. Margaret Kimball Brown supervised the digs using high school students from the summer anthropology course at the Field Museum of Natural History. She was assisted by Forest Preserve District naturalist Ed Lace. The digs took place in the immediate vicinity of the boulder supposedly marking the location of the Laughton Trading Post. Findings included fragments of Late Woodland pottery and artifacts, a few Archaic artifacts, "a large piece of Indian pottery similar to that used in the contact period (1640–1740)," iron—including handmade square nails of the type used circa 1830, glazed pottery and glass from the 1850s, and pieces of clay pipes made in the 1850s. It was determined that "the Indian occupation extends much further north" and that the Laughton Trading Post was likely nearby.[14]

Despite these efforts, the archaeological significance of both the Chicago Portage site and the broader Forest Preserve District holdings remains largely untapped. As of 2014, approximately 1,200 archaeological sites had been recorded in Cook County, and about 550 (nearly 46 percent) of these are located on Forest Preserve District property. Furthermore, less than 20 percent of the Forest Preserve District properties had been systematically surveyed, leaving little doubt that there are hundreds of undiscovered archaeological sites.[15]

The archaeological significance of the Chicago Portage site stems not only from actual archaeological artifacts but also from the landscape of the site itself, a landscape that Paula Bryant, staff archaeologist with the Illinois State Archaeological Survey, calls "a transportation corridor which is a common thread through time."[16] Thus it is not necessarily specific sites that give the Chicago Portage its archaeological importance but rather, Bryant says, "when you look at the sites as activity locations within the context of the larger landscape of the Portage, you are able to begin to see how this section of land has been integral to the livelihood of people since it has been a viable waterway."[17]

In 2014, Illinois State Archaeological Survey archaeologists surveyed a portion of the larger Chicago Portage area as a part of the *Natural and Cultural Resources Master Plan*. Bryant recalls that upon coming back from the field, the survey crew thought they had found a portion of the old Mud Lake.[18] Given the archaeological richness of the Chicago Portage in particular and the Forest Preserve District properties in general, there is still much work to be done to preserve and protect this cultural heritage.

Returning to 1975, the Forest Preserve District established a Chicago Portage Study Committee and commissioned a study by William E. Rose and Associates for the development of facilities highlighting the Chicago Portage's historic features. The study was paid for jointly by the Forest Preserve

Fig. 37. Design for Interpretive Center in proposed Chicago Portage National Historic Site. From William E. Rose and Associates, *Design Study: The Chicago Portage and the Laughton Trading Post Area, "The Waterway West"* (Hinsdale, IL: Wm. E. Rose and Associates, 1975), 34.

District and the Department of the Interior. The study committee included Brown and Lace along with Richard L. Buck, chief landscape architect; Roland F. Eisenbeis, superintendent of conservation; Maureen Goode, historical researcher, Northwestern University; Edward P. Koster, architect; Joseph N. Nevius, landscape architect; Gerald W. O'Connor, superintendent of maintenance; and Marshall Silverstein, administrative assistant.

The resulting *Design Study: The Chicago Portage and Laughton Trading Post Area, "The Waterway West,"* was the most comprehensive plan yet proposed for the National Historic Site. Its salient features included a 6,200-square-foot interpretive center at Ottawa Trail Woods that would include an apartment for a naturalist or caretaker, a separate historian's residence, a reconstruction of the Laughton Trading Post, a large bas-relief interpretive map in the Chicago Portage National Historic Site, a pedestrian bridge connecting Ottawa Trail Woods and Portage Woods, restored waterways, and an extensive trail system. The study also emphasized the archaeological importance of the area.

The *Design Study* estimated that the proposed complex would draw 600,000 visitors a year, with the Interpretive Center and the reconstructed Laughton Trading Post being the focus of the Ottawa Trail Woods component. The Interpretive Center was to "utilize an architectural flavor reminiscent of the nineteenth century" and be constructed of native limestone, wood siding,

Fig. 38. Design for Laughton Trading Post reconstruction in proposed Chicago Portage National Historic Site. From William E. Rose and Associates, *Design Study: The Chicago Portage and the Laughton Trading Post Area, "The Waterway West"* (Hinsdale, IL: Wm. E. Rose and Associates, 1975), 37.

and wood-shake shingles (fig. 37). It was to be the "visual and functional focal point of all activities within the proposed development," where visitors would view exhibits, obtain literature, and learn about the trail system and other points of interest.[19]

The reconstruction of the Laughton Trading Post was proposed to take place after additional archaeological digs had identified its correct location (fig. 38). It was intended to re-create as closely as possible the original trading post and be furnished accordingly, including a large table on which to display furs, tools, trade items, dry goods, and "bottles reminiscent of the tavern aspect."[20] It was also intended to house exhibits of artifacts found in the associated archaeological digs.

In the nearby Portage Woods, the plan called for a 35-by-25-foot bas-relief map to show the physical relationship between the Des Plaines River Valley and Lake Michigan, including various geological and historical features (fig. 39). Convex in shape, the giant map was to be depressed within a large paved surface to provide easy viewing by up to several classes of thirty students at a time and was to include a "stage" area for a teacher or interpreter.[21]

The plan called for a pedestrian overpass connecting Ottawa Trail Woods and Portage Woods, along with an extensive trail system to interconnect various points of interest that would serve as "interpretive nodes." The plan specifically highlighted Stony Ford, Laughton's Ford, Ottawa Trail, Green

Fig. 39. Design for a curved bas-relief map of the Chicago Portage Area in the proposed Chicago Portage National Historic Site. From William E. Rose and Associates, *Design Study: The Chicago Portage and the Laughton Trading Post Area, "The Waterway West"* (Hinsdale, IL: Wm. E. Rose and Associates, 1975), 11–12.

Bay Trail, Long Portage Road, and one of the last Potawatomi villages in the area as among these interpretive nodes and called for archaeological explorations to specifically locate these sites (fig. 40).[22]

In addition to the constructed features proposed by the plan, new plantings and landscaping were called for to restore the area to its natural state. Of special significance, the plan proposed to restore the Des Plaines River channel as it was prior to being diverted in 1893 (fig. 41). This plan was to include two sections. The first section, in Ottawa Trail Woods, would extend the Katherine Mitchell Lagoon, which sits just west of the claimed site of the Laughton Trading Post. The lagoon was to be deepened and its shoreline stabilized, and a control inlet installed at its northern end to allow Des Plaines River water to flow into it during dry seasons. The second section, in Portage Woods, involved widening and deepening the part of the waterway that meandered through the historic area and establishing a control weir at its southeast corner to maintain a constant level of water at an elevation between 584 and 585 feet.[23]

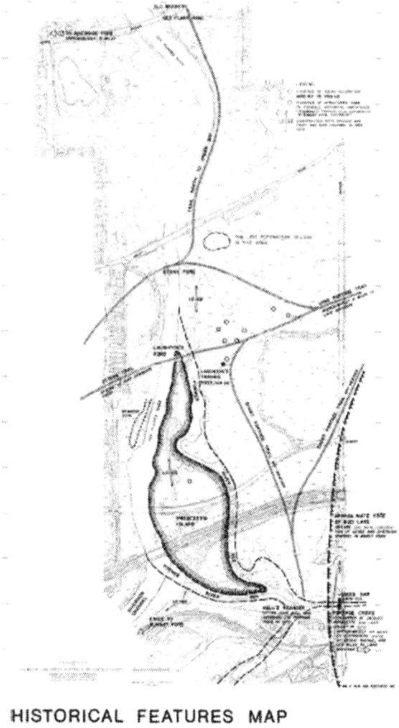

Fig. 40. Map of historical features to be highlighted via "interpretive nodes" in the proposed Chicago Portage National Historic Site. From William E. Rose and Associates, *Design Study: The Chicago Portage and the Laughton Trading Post Area, "The Waterway West"* (Hinsdale, IL: Wm. E. Rose and Associates, 1975), 16.

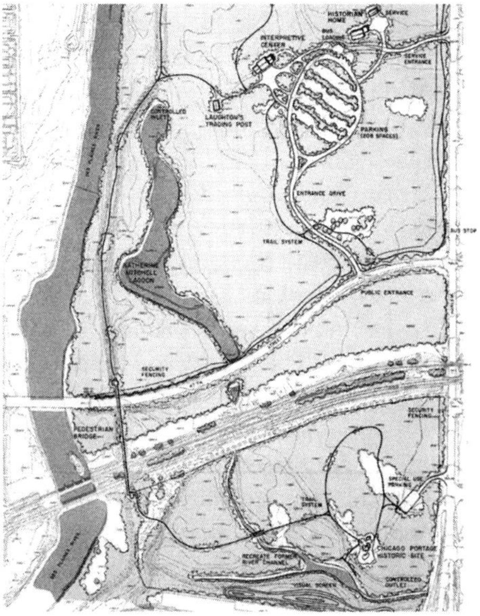

Fig. 41. Map of restored waterways in proposed Chicago Portage National Historic Site. From William E. Rose and Associates, *Design Study: The Chicago Portage and the Laughton Trading Post Area, "The Waterway West"* (Hinsdale, IL: Wm. E. Rose and Associates, 1975), 32.

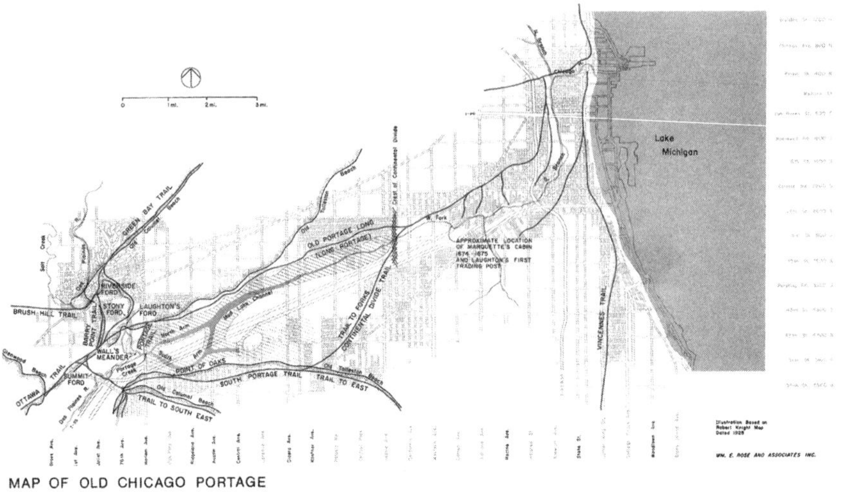

Fig. 42. *Design Study* revision of Knight and Zeuch's Chicago Portage map. From William E. Rose and Associates, *Design Study: The Chicago Portage and the Laughton Trading Post Area, "The Waterway West"* (Hinsdale, IL: Wm. E. Rose and Associates, 1975), 11.

The total cost for the proposed plan was $1,593.675 Unfortunately, it remained only a plan, and none of proposed work was ever accomplished. Once again, the Chicago Portage National Historic Site fell dormant except for the work of dedicated volunteers and Forest Preserve District personnel who did their best to maintain and promote the site. The *Design Study* was useful, however, as part of an application to have the Chicago Portage National Historic Site placed on the National Register of Historic Places, and that application was approved on November 15, 1978.[24] The *Design Study* also is notable because it reproduced and revised the Knight and Zeuch map of the portage (fig. 42).

In September 1981, a National Park Service report entitled *Illinois & Michigan Canal Corridor: A Concept Plan* proposed a conceptual plan for protecting and enhancing the Illinois and Michigan Canal corridor.[25] The report opened with Louis Jolliet's comment that a canal could be cut along the route of the Chicago Portage, and then emphasized the Chicago Portage site as the first of twenty primary historic sites that deserved protection along the corridor.[26] The report concluded that the Chicago Portage site was:

> A good site for interpretation because it is publicly owned (Cook County Forest Preserve District) and a plan for its interpretation has already been prepared. It figures prominently in the history of early exploration and of the I&M Canal. Located just over the Chicago border, it also would be a good place to introduce people from Chicago to the corridor.[27]

The report, along with broad-based support across the region, led to the federal government creating the Illinois and Michigan Canal National Heritage Corridor on August 24, 1984. As mentioned in chapter 9, the Illinois and Michigan Canal National Heritage Corridor also was the first National Heritage Area and helped spark a national trend.[28] Also in 1984, the Illinois General Assembly created the Illinois and Michigan Canal National Heritage Corridor Civic Center Authority to promote the historic, recreational, and economic development of the Illinois and Michigan Canal National Heritage Corridor in Cook County.

In 1989, the Illinois and Michigan Canal National Heritage Corridor Civic Center Authority, chaired by Stanley A. Johnson, prepared its *Application for State Financial Support for the Chicago Portage Historical Site Interpretive Center*, seeking state funding support under the Metropolitan Civic Center Support Act.[29] The *Application* was amended and resubmitted on July 30, 1990, and envisioned a three-phase development of the Chicago Portage National Historic Site. Working with Johnson were Charles Gregorsen, principal project architect, and Joseph Nevius, project construction manager with the Forest Preserve District.

Phase 1 had already begun in 1983, when the Forest Preserve District commissioned Ferdinand G. Rebechini to create a commemorative sculpture that would portray "the feeling of struggle of the portage and the travels of the people."[30] The sculpture was designed by Rebechini and his wife June Lois Rebechini, (née Decker) and depicts Marquette pointing the way and Jolliet and a Native American pulling the canoe across the portage (fig. 43). The sculpture itself cost $68,000 and initial fabrication took about six months. The massive sculpture was then delivered in pieces on two flat-bed trucks to the site in spring 1989. Problems arose with the concrete base on which the sculpture was to stand, and that led to the pieces being left at the site until spring 1990. The final fabrication of welding the various pieces together was completed by Ferdinand, his son Glenn Rebechini, and Gordon Manary and the sculpture was erected on April 25-26, 1990.

Marquette stands about seventeen-feet tall above the base and the overall length of the sculpture is twenty-five feet. The statue weighs about 7000 pounds and is constructed of Corten steel, which oxidizes to a rich patina creating a surface that does not require maintenance. The original design included a moat between the outer wall and the base of the sculpture, but upon completion it was discovered that the Forest Preserve District was not allowed to have artificial water retention devices on its properties, so the moat was filled with dirt and landscaped.[31] The sculpture is shown here (fig. 44) with Ferdinand G. Rebechini at the time of its installation.

Phase 2 was the focus of the *Application* and called for the construction of a major interpretive facility and visitor center in Ottawa Trail Woods north of Forty-Seventh Street (fig. 45). The center was to include 4,200 square feet of exhibit space, an auditorium with a capacity of 130 people, an information

Fig. 43. Commemorative Corten steel sculpture by Ferdinand G. Rebechini at Chicago Portage National Historic Site. Photograph courtesy Joe Balynas, Canal Corridor Association.

Fig. 44. Ferdinand G. Rebechini with the commemorative sculpture, April 1990. Photograph courtesy of Glenn Rebechini/Rebechini Studios, Inc.

Fig. 45. Artist's rendering of proposed interpretive center. From Illinois and Michigan Canal National Heritage Corridor Civic Center Authority, *Application for State Financial Support for the Chicago Portage Historical Site Interpretive Center* (Willow Springs, IL: Illinois and Michigan Canal National Heritage Corridor Civic Center Authority, 1990), 341.

Fig. 46. Artist's rendering of the proposed interpretive center interior. From Illinois and Michigan Canal National Heritage Corridor Civic Center Authority, *Application for State Financial Support for the Chicago Portage Historical Site Interpretive Center* (Willow Springs, IL: Illinois and Michigan Canal National Heritage Corridor Civic Center Authority, 1990), 342.

desk and shop for the sale of educational and site-related materials, a library and classroom, staff offices, and a laboratory and workshop (fig. 46). Because the *Application* proposed the use of volunteer docents, the interpretive center also included a lunchroom, lockers, restrooms, and shower facilities.[32] The projected cost for phase 2 was $3,333,000 and was to be paid for by a $2,500,750 grant from the Illinois Metropolitan Civic Center Support Program and about $883,000 from the Forest Preserve District in the form of $350,000 in cash and a transfer of nine acres of land within the site to the Illinois and Michigan Canal National Heritage Corridor Civic Center Authority at a value of $483,250.[33] Arthur L. Janura, the general superintendent of the Forest Preserve District, wrote in a letter to Johnson that the proposed development had been a longtime goal for the Forest Preserve District and that the center would be "one of the premier educational and recreational attractions in the I&M Canal Heritage Corridor."[34]

Phase 3 of the *Application*'s proposed plan included reconstructing Laughton's Trading Post, building a historian's residence and maintenance facilities, constructing an extensive trail system, and widening and deepening the Katherine Mitchell Lagoon in Ottawa Trail Woods. The projected cost for phase 3 was $2,051,600, to be paid for by the Forest Preserve District and grants procured from private foundations.

All three phases included accompanying drives, parking facilities, lighting, fencing, signage, and landscaping.[35] The *Application* also included an extensive discussion of the vast range of interpretive, educational, and archaeological opportunities at the site.[36]

At a total cost of $5,952,600, the *Application*'s proposed development was intended to be "the largest interpretive and visitor information center in the Illinois & Michigan Canal National Heritage Corridor and the closest to Chicago."[37] Whereas the earlier proposal in 1975 had estimated that the facility would attract 600,000 visitors annually, the 1990 proposal estimated that number at one million.[38]

Unfortunately, this plan, like the earlier 1975 plan, went nowhere except for the erecting of the memorial statue. Between 1990 and 1999, however, the idea for building an interpretive center remained alive within the Forest Preserve District. In 1999, the United States Army Corps of Engineers completed the *Chicago Portage Literature Overview and Assessment*, which the Forest Preserve District saw as an "important step" toward the development of an interpretive center.[39] The Army Corps report was to provide the Forest Preserve District with a "user friendly" inventory of cultural features, an overview of past archaeological work, a history of land use and human occupation, an assessment of potential significance of cultural features, an assessment of probable impacts of proposed development, and an estimate of work necessary for compliance with the National Historic Preservation Act.[40] The Army Corps report concluded, contrary to generally accepted historical views of the Chicago Portage, that the site's primary importance was not its use by Jolliet and

Marquette and other early French explorers; rather, it was "significant because of its association with prehistoric archaeological sites and features and early nineteenth century American fur trade and settlement."[41] Because the focus of the report was on the archaeology of the site and because no archaeological artifacts associated with the early French explorers had been found at the site, the report argued that, from an archaeological perspective, the site's "significance comes from its association with other historic and prehistoric events."[42]

In 1999, a volunteer group was formed that has played an important role in the Chicago Portage ever since. Gary Mechanic, the general manager of the Illinois and Michigan Canal National Heritage Corridor Civic Center Authority, presented a proposal to Christine Radogno, who at that time was the state senator for the area that included the Chicago Portage. In his proposal, Mechanic asked for state funding to establish the Friends of the Chicago Portage and to create a history curriculum for elementary school children based on the Chicago Portage.

The goals of the Friends of the Chicago Portage were to promote historic interpretation, ecological restoration, and recreational access to the Chicago Portage National Historic Site, to conduct tours and events to increase public awareness of the site, and to conduct workdays to restore native species and enhance the site's natural areas. The school curriculum was to rely on primary sources to tell the story of the Chicago Portage from its geological beginnings up to current times.

Mechanic was successful in obtaining funding for both the Friends of the Chicago Portage ($25,000) and the development of the curriculum ($150,000). At its start, the Friends of the Chicago Portage numbered about twenty-five volunteers, largely from the ranks of volunteers for the Illinois and Michigan Canal National Heritage Corridor Civic Center Authority, but that number grew to at one point to include 120 dues-paying members. Beginning in 2000, the Friends of the Chicago Portage conducted workdays on the last Saturday of the month to clear invasive plants and clean up litter and debris at the site. The organization was joined in these efforts by the Forest Preserve District and the Friends of the Forest Preserve District. The Friends of the Chicago Portage also began giving guided tours on the first Saturday of the month, a service its members still provide during the summer months. On January 3, 2002, the Friends of the Chicago Portage celebrated the fiftieth anniversary of the portage's designation as a National Historic Site with a cake and candles, representing the group's dedication to the site. Since its inception, the Friends of the Chicago Portage has been a strong advocate for the National Historic Site and has succeeded in getting interpretive signage and making important improvements to the trail system. The Friends of the Chicago Portage also created and maintains a website promoting the historical significance of the Chicago Portage.[43]

When asked why he has devoted so much time and energy to the site, Mechanic explains that he thinks it is important "to preserve the roots of our history and teach them not just to visitors but to our children."[44] This ideal fueled the Swamp to City curriculum, which was developed by the Chicago Metro History Education Center. From its inception in 2001, hundreds of teachers have used the curriculum to educate students on the history and significance of the Chicago Portage.[45]

One of the key figures in the Friends of the Chicago Portage was Philip E. Vierling, a retired teacher who first visited the Chicago Portage in 1959. In his retirement years, Vierling made the Chicago Portage his personal project. In the late 1960s and early 1970s, Vierling cut trails through Portage Woods and wrote and published the first self-guided public historical tour guide for Portage Woods and Ottawa Trail Woods.[46] He documented the plant life at the site and named one of the burr oak trees the Hubbard Oak because it was thought to have been growing there when Gurdon Saltonstall Hubbard first camped in Portage Woods in 1818. Beginning in 2000 and until his death in 2016, Vierling did extensive research on the Chicago Portage and self-published it in his *Chicago Portage Ledger*, which in the end numbered fifty-six issues covering a wide range of topics related to the portage. Throughout his time at the portage, Vierling fought against the pollution that almost ruined the site, and he was a strong advocate for developing the site in a manner befitting its historical purpose. The Friends of the Chicago Portage rightly calls Vierling "the first Friend of the Chicago Portage."[47]

After the 1999 Army Corps report, little was done in furtherance of the grand plans conceived for developing the Chicago Portage site. Care for the site fell once again to volunteers, especially the Friends of the Chicago Portage, and the Forest Preserve District. Still, the obvious importance of the connection between the Chicago Portage National Historic Site and the Illinois and Michigan Canal National Heritage Corridor remained. In 2005, the *I&M Canal National Heritage Corridor Interpretive Plan* concluded that "one site that cries out for additional interpretation is the Chicago Portage National Historic Site."[48] The *Interpretive Plan* took issue with the Army Corps report's assertion that evidence of early French presence at the site was "ephemeral at best" and concluded that "whatever the case, the site is still important as an archaeological/historic site."[49] The *Interpretive Plan* went on to argue that the Chicago Portage site "can and should serve as a gateway to the rest of the [Illinois and Michigan Canal National Heritage] corridor."[50]

Still, no further significant action occurred until 2013, when the Forest Preserve District commissioned Hitchcock Design Group to create a schematic plan for the Chicago Portage site. The Hitchcock plan recommended a new shelter, improved interpretive signage, and improvements to the site and trail. This plan was followed in 2015 by a *Gateway Master Plan* prepared by the Lakota Group that emphasized the importance of the Chicago Portage site as a gateway to encourage public use of forest preserves. Then, in 2016, following the lead of the Hitchcock plan, the Forest Preserve District installed a new interpretive pavilion incorporating new interpretive signage, storytelling graphics, and an illustrated portage timeline alongside the portage sculpture. As part of that effort, a group of young volunteers with the Friends of the Forest Preserves did extensive landscape work at the site to beautify the grounds. This work was funded by Phillip Dowd, who also funded the digitizing of Vierling's *Chicago Portage Ledger*.

The studies from 2013 to 2016 set the stage for the latest iteration of the Forest Preserve District's vision for the future of the Chicago Portage National Historic Site. In December 2018, the Forest Preserve District hired Design Workshop to prepare the *Chicago Portage National Historic Site Master Plan*. Design Workshop consulted directly with the Friends of the Chicago Portage, the Friends of the Forest Preserves, the Metropolitan Water Reclamation District, the Canal Corridor Authority, and the Civic Center Authority to create the plan. In addition, public meetings were held to gather input from the broader community. The prior studies and plans from 1975 and 1989–90 were consulted, as were the more recent plans and implementations from 2013–16.

The *Master Plan* represents a sea change from earlier plans that emphasized structures such as an interpretive center and the reconstruction of Laughton's Trading Post. Instead, the *Master Plan* emphasizes accessibility and information. As Kindy Kruller, senior planner with the Forest Preserve District, put it, the plan takes "a pragmatic approach that incorporates ideas from all of the previous plans."[51] The *Master Plan* started with the following goals: (1) improving public awareness of the portage and connectivity to the site, (2) enhancing accessibility within the site and to adjacent areas, (3) encouraging a greater and deeper understanding of the portage story, (4) improving site facilities, and (5) clarifying operational and management systems for the site.[52] In furtherance of these goals, the *Master Plan* recommends infrastructure improvements such as improved sidewalks, roadways, turn lanes, regional bicycle trails, and wayfinding signage to make it easier for visitors to get to the site. To highlight the site's historic status as a waterway, the *Master Plan* also recommends adding the site to the Des Plaines River paddling trail and creating a canoe landing at the site. And because there are other ways to visit a historic site than physically being there, the *Master Plan* also emphasizes the need to improve and consolidate the site's presence on the internet.[53]

As with earlier studies, the *Master Plan* recommends significantly improving the trail system throughout Portage Woods and Ottawa Trail Woods. In connection with these improvements, the *Master Plan* places a strong emphasis on finding ways to enhance visitors' experience at the site, such as using digital media and including the portage monument in the Chicago Park District's Statue Stories program, which is a self-guided tour of Chicago as told through statues throughout the city. The plan also recommends creating a nature play area to help children learn more about the portage by interacting with their natural surroundings.[54]

Although the *Master Plan* is clearly the product of a more modern perspective that emphasizes connectivity, regional access, and the use of improved technology to tell the story of the Chicago Portage, it does still retain a dream from earlier studies—an interpretive center. Just south of the Portage Woods portion of the site lies a parcel of land owned by the Metropolitan Water Reclamation District. This land is currently unusable due to pollution in the soil but could be remediated for recreational use. This parcel is especially appealing for an interpretive center because it is contiguous to Portage Woods. This location would eliminate the problem of having such a center in Ottawa Trail Woods, which is cut off from Portage Woods by Forty-Seventh Street. The *Master Plan* concludes that "a permanent facility, such as an interpretive center or visitor center, is a worthwhile goal for any National Historic Site that regularly receives a large number of visitors."[55] Having said that, and based on the experience of past plans failing due to lack of funding, the plan recognizes "the requisite funding, staffing, operations, and maintenance impacts that having a permanent center creates."[56]

The last recommendation of the *Master Plan* directly addresses the question of funding. It urges the creation of a list of organizations and individuals who might provide possible funding assistance. It stresses the need for organizations already devoted to the Chicago Portage site to coordinate their efforts to maximize the site's presence both physically and on the internet, and it specifically declares a need to reengage the National Park District as a participating partner in the Chicago Portage site.[57]

Although more modest in scope than the 1975 and 1989–90 plans, the *Master Plan* focuses on realistic steps that can be taken at relatively little cost to significantly increase the historic site's presence in the public mind. It strives to find ways to educate the public about the site, make it easier to get to and, once there, easier to get around and understand the various points of historic interest and value. It seeks ways to make the site a place for families with children to visit and appreciate. And it provides discrete projects that are attainable without large amounts of funding, while keeping alive the decades-old desire for an interpretive center worthy of the site's national historic status.

It remains an open question whether the grander goals of the *Master Plan* and the other possibilities being explored by the Forest Preserve District will ever come to fruition, or, as with previous plans, find themselves on a shelf awaiting the next study. Part of the problem with the Chicago Portage National Historic Site has always been that although it is owned by the Forest Preserve District, it is unique among the district's many holdings. The site's significance is not necessarily its natural endowments, especially given how it has been mangled over the decades, but its historic importance. The Forest Preserve District isn't equipped, in terms of either personnel or resources, to fully develop, staff, and maintain the kind of facilities that the site deserves.

As such, the site's future will be determined not only by individuals, groups, and organizations already devoted to the site but also by the broader community. In the end, it will be up to current and future generations to determine whether they will provide the resources needed to preserve and promote the site and to properly tell the extraordinary story of the Chicago Portage.

Epilogue

✦

The Past Embedded

The early history of Chicago still lives in place-names reminiscent of the story you have just read—DuSable Park and Harbor, Hubbard Street, Kinzie Street, LaSalle Street, Vincennes Avenue, Wolcott Avenue, Clark Street, Ogden Avenue, and of course Joliet Avenue and Road, and Marquette Avenue. Some of the spellings might have changed over time, but these places, streets, and avenues all hark back to the time of the Chicago Portage, the fur trade, and Fort Dearborn. Rogers Avenue follows the old northern Indian Boundary Line. We still follow some of the old Native American trails when we drive on Milwaukee Avenue in Chicago, Green Bay Road on the North Shore, Deerpath Avenue in Lake Forest, Ridge Avenue in Evanston, Joliet Avenue and Road in the near-west suburbs, and Archer Avenue, Clark Street, North Michigan Avenue, Grand Avenue, Elston Avenue, and Vincennes Avenue in Chicago. Ogden Avenue was the old stagecoach route and Plank Road to Chicago. Interstate 55 traces through the Des Plaines River Valley where ages ago the Chicago Outlet cut through the Valparaiso Moraine, setting the geological stage for the Chicago Portage and its progeny, the Illinois and Michigan Canal, the Chicago Sanitary Ship Canal, and the Illinois Waterway. "Waukegan" is a Potawatomi word meaning "little fort," and "Ouilmette" is still with us as Wilmette. The entire Chicagoland area is a quilt of Native American and early European settlements stitched together with trails and waterways used since prehistory.

In *Requiem for a Nun*, William Faulkner wrote, "The past is never dead. It's not even past." And so in Chicago we still follow the old highways even if they are unacknowledged, and we use names that evoke our earliest history even if it is not remembered. So much of our early history, and prehistory, now exists only in the abstract, referred to by the occasional plaque or statue. We can stand at the site of Fort Dearborn, if by that we mean standing atop layers of landfill and concrete that cover where that site used to be. But for the most part the old landscape is gone. We have changed the course of rivers, cut canals through the ancient waterways, rebuilt and extended the western shoreline of Lake Michigan where Jolliet and so many others once hugged close to avoid the tempest of the broader lake. We have changed much of what once was, and yet one place remains, at least in part, as it was.

At the Chicago Portage, an old remnant of Portage Creek is still there. So, too, perhaps a bit of Mud Lake remains. You can stand, literally stand, where the Laughton brothers traded their wares and still see the bedrock fords of Riverside, Laughton, and Stony. At the Chicago Portage you can tread the same land where once walked the likes of Marquette, La Salle, and Tonty, and where Hubbard and his men sat around a campfire "ridding themselves of the blood suckers." You can leaf through the pages of this book and find name after name, event after event, historical drama after drama—all still alive in the memory of the forests at Portage Woods and Ottawa Trail Woods and in the still-standing Hubbard Oak from Hubbard's time at the portage.

We have seen that the area that became the Chicago Portage was already a place of habitation in prehistory, as evidenced by the archaeological findings at the Laughton site. It was a place of commerce and trade by Native Americans long before the French found their way there in the seventeenth century. From that point on, it was a fateful place—Jolliet immediately saw its importance as a trade route linking the Gulf of Mexico with the Atlantic Ocean. It truly became the "key to the continent" and was a focal point of contention among French, British, and new Americans alike, all seeing its pivotal importance for the opening of the West and as the critical transportation connection between the natural resources of the frontier and the eastern marketplace.

Chicago owes its existence to the Chicago Portage, as do the towns that developed there during the fur trade. And when the portage gave way to the Illinois and Michigan Canal, a whole new string of canal communities sprang up along its waterway, towns that remain tied to it through the ongoing efforts associated with the Illinois and Michigan Canal National Heritage Corridor.

The success of the Chicago Portage as a natural bridge between the Mississippi and St. Lawrence watershed basins led to its demise when Jolliet's vision of a canal became a reality with the building of the Illinois and Michigan Canal. But even though the Chicago Portage site is now hemmed in on all sides by the development it spawned, it remains a serene and verdant vestige of an earlier time when travel was by foot or boat, the "great river" remained a fable told by Native Americans to French explorers dreaming of empire, and Chicago referred not to a metropolis but to a marshy bridge between two sleepy rivers. What lays in store for the Chicago Portage National Historic Site is uncertain, but what is certain is that the Chicago Portage made Chicago and helped make America.

ACKNOWLEDGMENTS

I have been generously assisted in this work by many skilled scientists, historians, research librarians, archivists, and curators. Thank you to Glenn Longacre with the National Archives in Chicago; Lisa Schoblasky, Andrew Risley, and Patrick Morris at the Newberry Library; Lesley Martin, Ellen Keith, Michael Featherstone, Katie Levi, and Gabrielle Christianson at the Chicago History Museum; Tracy Pierceall, Beckie Dyer, and DeeAnn Watt at the Illinois State Museum; Sarah Dysken at the Harold Washington Library Center, Chicago Public Library; Alesha Cerny, with the National Park Service, and George Franchois, director at the United States Department of the Interior Library. Thank you to Kyle Moore at the Wayne County Register of Deeds for his help in locating the Point de Sable bills of sale on file there, and to Paul Dialing for his reporting and insights on the demise of Jean Lalime. Charles Markman reviewed the chapter on prehistoric Chicago and provided much-appreciated comments and suggestions, and Patrick J. Jung provided guidance on the notoriously complicated history of Jean Nicolet's travels. Thank you to Paula Bryant of the Illinois State Archaeological Survey for background and references on Chicago area archaeology. Duane Esarey with the Illinois State Museum provided perspective on the use of the Chicago Portage by Native Americans, and David Dolak provided background and references on the geological history of the Chicago River and Des Plaines River. Thank you to Pamela Sielski with the Forest Preserve District of Cook County for background on the Army Corps of Engineers portage study and for providing access to the Forest Preserve District's archives, and to Garret Wais for help with gathering documents. Thank you to Kindy Kruller and Christine Slattery with the Forest Preserve District of Cook County for background on the 2018 *Master Plan* for the portage site. Gary Mechanic provided information only he could provide about the founding and invaluable work of the Friends of the Chicago Portage, and thank you to John Langer and Jeff Carter with the Friends of the Chicago Portage for the informative talks about the portage's past and present. Thank you to Amy Barbeau with the Prairie du Rocher Chamber of Commerce and Nicholas Poke with the Northwestern Alumni Association for help in locating interviewees for the book, to Glenn Rebechini for information on the commemorative sculpture at the Chicago Portage National Historic Site, and to Margaret Kimball Brown for information on archaeological digs at the portage site. Thank you to the editorial team at Northwestern University Press, Parneshia Jones, Patrick Samuel, Maia Rigas, and Lori Meek Schuldt for their expertise in turning my manuscript into a book. And, lastly, a special thank you to my wife, Jill Mateo, for her wise counsel, encouragement, and patience during the research and writing of this book.

Appendix A

✦

Communication of John C. Calhoun with Excerpts from Reports of Stephen Long, R. Graham, and Joseph Philips

CANAL TO CONNECT THE ILLINOIS RIVER WITH LAKE MICHIGAN.

Communicated to the House of Representatives, on December 28, 1819.
Sir: In compliance with a resolution of the House of Representatives of the 15th instant, directing the Secretary of War "to lay before that House the several topographical reports that have been made to the War Department, in pursuance of instructions to that effect, respecting the practicability of uniting, by a canal, the waters of the Illinois river and those of Lake Michigan, and such other information as he may be in possession of on that subject," I have the honor to transmit an extract of Major Long's report, and a copy of a report made by R. Graham and Joseph Philips, Esqs., which comprehend all the information on the subject in this Department. I have the honor to be, very respectfully, sir, your most obedient servant, J. C. CALHOUN.

Hon. HENRY Clay, Speaker of the
House of Representatives U. S.

Extract from a report of Major Stephen H. Long to George Graham, Esq., acting Secretary of War, dated Washington, March 4, 1817.

The Illinois is formed by the union of three considerable rivers—the Desplain [Des Plaines River], the Despage [DuPage River], and the Kankakee; the last of which is nearly double the size of either of the two former. The Illinois is about three hundred miles in length, and is of variable width, from seventy yards to one mile. It has a very moderate current, and a depth of water sufficient to render it navigable, at all times, for boats of considerable burden, about two hundred and thirty miles from its mouth. At the mouth of the

Vermilion there are rapids, perceivable only in the lower stages of winter. Farther up, the water is not generally so deep as it is below the Vermilion.

The valley of the Illinois varies in its width from three to ten miles; is generally flat and marshy; and, for the most part, subject to inundation when the river has no more than a medial height. In some parts of it, however, prairies and bottoms of considerable extent are to be met with, elevated much above high water mark. In ascending the river, the bluffs gradually decrease in height, being about one hundred and fifty feet high at the mouth, and about one hundred feet at the head of the river. Imbedded in the bluffs are strata of limestone, slate, and coal, which occasionally make their appearance along the surface of the declivities.

The river Desplain is a small stream rising in the low lands bordering upon the west side of Lake Michigan, and has its general course in a southwesterly direction. The valley of this river has an average width of about one mile, and is terminated on both sides by regular banks, nearly parallel to each other, extending along the river about thirty miles from the head of the Illinois. In ascending this river, also, the banks or bluffs gradually decrease in height, being, as before mentioned, about one hundred feet high at the mouth, and only twenty or twenty-five at the distance of thirty miles higher up the river, where, instead of maintaining their parallel direction, they form nearly right angles with the course of the river—that on the right taking an easterly, and that on the left a north westerly course; but, being gradually inflected from these courses, they form an extensive curve, encircling a large tract of flat prairie, in no part elevated more than twelve or 14 feet above the common level of the water in this vicinity. The river, throughout the above-mentioned distance, has four or five short rapids or ripples that make their appearance only in times of low water. In every other part it has the appearance of being a chain of stagnant pools and small lakes, affording a sufficient depth of water for boats of moderate draught.

In the flat prairie above mentioned is a small lake, about five miles in length, and from six to thirty or forty yards in width, communicating both with the river Desplain and Chicago river by means of a kind of canal, which has been made partly by the current of the water, and partly by the French and Indians, for the purpose of getting their boats across in that direction in time of high water. The distance from the river Desplain to Chicago river, by this watercourse, is about nine miles; through the greater part of which there is more or less water, so that the portage is seldom more than three miles in the driest season; but, in a wet season, boats pass and repass with facility between the two rivers.

Proposed canals and roads.

A canal uniting the waters of the Illinois with those of Lake Michigan may be considered the first in importance of any in this quarter of the country, and, at the same time, the construction of it would be attended with very little expense compared with the magnitude of the object. The watercourse, which is already opened between the river Desplain and Chicago river, needs but little more excavation to render it sufficiently capacious for all the purposes of a canal. It may be supplied with water at all times of the year by constructing a dam of moderate height across the Desplain, which would give the water of that river a sufficient elevation to supply a canal extending from one river to the other. It would be necessary, also, to construct locks at the extremities of the canal, that communicating with Chicago river being calculated to elevate about six feet, and that communicating with the Desplain about four feet.

To render the Desplain and the Illinois navigable for small boats and flats requiring but a small draught of water, nothing more is necessary than the construction of sluices in a few places where there are ripples of a sufficient width to admit the boats to pass through them. This may be effected by clearing away the loose stones from the bottom, and forming banks, riveted with stone two or three feet high, on each side of the sluice. Thus, a water communication between the Illinois and Lake Michigan may be kept open at all times sufficient to answer all the purposes for which a canal will be wanted for many years to come. . . .

Kaskaskia, April 4, 1819.

Sir: In addition to the notes of Mr. Sullivan, the surveyor, which describe the face of the country over which the lines were run, we beg leave to suggest some views which occurred to us on the subject of communications between the river Illinois and the Michigan lake.

By reference to the map herewith forwarded, it will be seen that the little river *Plein* [Des Plaines River], coming from the northwest, approaches within ten miles and a quarter of Lake Michigan, and then, bending to the southwest, unites with the *Theakiki* [Kankakee River] at the distance of about fifty miles, and forms the river Illinois.

The country between the lake and the *Plein*, at this point of approach, is a prairie (natural meadow) without trees, covered with grass, and, to the eye, a perfect level. From the bank of the *Plein*, standing on the ground, the trees are distinctly seen, with the naked eye, at Fort Dearborn, on the shore of the lake; from Fort Dearborn they are, in like manner, seen on the bank of the *Plein*. Standing on any intermediate point between the lake and the river, the judgment is at a loss to say to which side the ground declines, and whether the level of the *Plein* or the lake is the highest. It was, however, determined, from certain data, that the level of the river was two feet, or thereabouts, above the level of the lake. From this view, it would seem that the cutting of a canal in this place, between the *Plein* and the lake, would be a work of neither skill, difficulty, nor expense. Small, however, as the labor would be, under this view, it is still diminished, upon a close examination, and by finding that an arm of the lake, called *Chicago* [Chicago River], puts out in the direction of the *Plein*, and that an arm of the *Plein*, also called *Chicago* [Portage Creek and Mud Lake], puts out in the direction of the lake. They approach within two miles of each other; so that, in common water, there is only dry ground to that extent between them. The character of these two arms is essentially different: that of the lake [Mud Lake] being about sixty feet wide, and from ten to forty feet deep; that of the river [Chicago River] being, in high water, from four to six feet deep, and, in places, a mile wide, and in low water either dry or reduced to a gutter. Between the heads of these two arms [i.e., between the Chicago River and Mud Lake] is also a gutter, which is dry in the dry seasons of summer and fall, and full of water in the spring; and, when thus filled with water, the boats, of six or eight tons, engaged in the Mackinaw and Mississippi trade, run through, backwards and forwards, so as to make no portage between Mackinaw and the Mississippi. This gutter, judging from the appearance of others now forming, was, at first, a path worn out by the feet of those who carried things across the portage, and afterwards deepened by the attrition of the waters, until formed into a little canal. The wind alone gives the water a current in this little canal, and its direction depends upon the course of the wind. Objects have been seen to float out of it, from the same point, to the river and to the lake.

It is incontestably true that an east wind will drive the water of the lake through this gutter into the *Plein*, and that water from Lake Michigan has been discharged by this outlet into the Mississippi, and thence into the Gulf of Mexico. It is equally incontestable that the waters of the *Plein* have been driven, by the same channel, into the lake; and these phenomena may now be witnessed at any time when the waters are high and the wind blows hard. It follows, therefore, that, to finish the canal begun by nature in this place, would require, as we have already Said, but little of skill, time, or expense. On opening the canal, however, two difficulties would be experienced:

1st. The *Plein* would be found to be above the level of the canal; its water, of course, would be diverted from its natural channel, and pass by the canal into the lake.

2nd. Supposing that evil remedied by a lock to lift vessels into the *Plein*; yet the *Plein*, during half the year, does not contain water enough to float a boat, and so could not become useful as a national highway.

To remedy this defect of water in the *Plein*, two projects suggest themselves: 1st. To sink the bed of the *Plein* below the level of the canal, and thus increase the depth of the *Plein*, as well by feeding it out of the lake as by collecting its water into a narrower channel. 2nd. To make the canal unite with the *Plein* lower down in its course. A few miles lower would be sufficient to give the water of the lake a descent into the river, as the *Plein* has a sensible descent in this place, insomuch that the people of Chicago call it

"The Rapids," having no other word to distinguish moving water from that which stands still. Of the *Plein*, below its point of approach to the lake, we would remark that it has hardly the attributes of a river, being, in most places, without current and without banks, lying as a sheet of water in the prairie, sometimes a mile wide, and so shallow that the tall grass appears almost everywhere above its surface. Having said thus much of the facility of communication by the *Chicago*, we would now remark that several other routes are perfectly practicable. 1st. From a point in the lake south of *Chicago*, to enter the *Plein* below Mount *Juliet*, at or near what is called Lake *Despagc*, but which is only a dilatation of the waters of the *Plein*. This route would lie over level prairie, through a multitude of small lakes or ponds, which have neither name nor place in any map. 2nd. By a canal leaving the lake near its south end, and uniting with the *Theakiki* just above its confluence with the *Plein*. Both of these canals would be fed from the lake; would require few or no locks; would go over ground of the same sort; would be fifty or sixty miles long, and would join the waters of the Illinois at points from which it is constantly navigable. A third route was spoken of, but not seen by us. It would lie between the *Theakiki* and the St. Joseph's of the lake. Information says that it has been practised by French traders. You will perceive, sir, that we have not spoken of the nature of the soil through which these several routes would pass. It not being our business to search for, and report upon the practicability of water communications, our observations were limited to what fell under the eye while engaged in another duty; and, in making this report to you, it is our object to excite inquiry, not to furnish plans of practicable projects. We shall, therefore, only say, on this point, that the country in general, and the bed of the *Plein*, exhibited much loose stone and pebble and firm ground.

To conclude: the route by the *Chicago*, as followed by the French since the discovery of the Illinois, presents at one season of the year an uninterrupted water communication for boats of six or eight tons burden between the Mississippi and the Michigan lake; at another season, a portage of two miles; at another, a portage of seven miles, from the bend of the *Plein* to the arm of the lake; at another, a portage of fifty miles, from the mouth of the *Plein* to the lake, over which there is a well-beaten wagon road, and boats and their loads are hauled by oxen and vehicles kept for that purpose by the French settlers at the Chicago. Respectfully, your obedient servants,

R. Graham, Joseph Philips
The Hon. J. C. Calhoun, Secretary of War, Washington.

Source: *American State Papers, Documents, Legislative and Executive, of the Congress of the United States, From the First Session of the Eleventh to the Second Session of the Seventeenth Congress, inclusive: Commencing May 22, 1809, and Ending March 3, 1823: Miscellaneous* (Washington, DC: Gales and Seaton, 1834), 2:555–57.

Appendix B

✦

Report of William Keating on the Chicago Portage (1823)

We were much disappointed in the appearance of Chicago and its vicinity. We found in it nothing to justify the great eulogium lavished upon this place by a late traveller [Henry Schoolcraft], who observes that "it is the most fertile and beautiful that can be imagined." "As a farming country," says he, "it unites the fertile soil of the finest lowland prairies with an elevation which exempts it from the influence of stagnant waters, and a summer climate of delightful serenity." The best comment upon this description of the climate and soil is the fact that, with the most active vigilance on the part of the officers, it was impossible for the garrison, consisting of from seventy to ninety men, to subsist themselves upon the grain raised in the country, although much of their time was devoted to agricultural pursuits. The difficulties which the agriculturist meets with here are numerous; they arise from the shallowness of the soil, from its humidity, and from its exposure to the cold and damp winds which blow from the lake with great force during most part of the year; the grain is frequently destroyed by swarms of insects; there are also a number of destructive birds of which it was impossible for the garrison to avoid the baneful influence, except by keeping, as was practised at Fort Dearborn, a party of soldiers constantly engaged at shooting at the crows and blackbirds that depredated upon the corn planted by them. But, even with all these exertions, the maize seldom has time to ripen, owing to the shortness and coldness of the season. The provisions for the garrison were for the most part conveyed from Mackinaw in a schooner, and sometimes they were brought from St. Louis, a distance of three hundred and eighty-six miles up the Illinois and Des Plaines rivers. The appearance of the country near Chicago offers but few features upon which the eye of the traveller can dwell with pleasure. There is too much uniformity in the scenery; the extensive water prospect is a waste uncheckered by islands, unenlivened by the spreading canvass, and the fatiguing monotony of which is increased by the equally undiversified prospect of the land scenery, which affords no relief to the sight, as it consists merely of a plain in which but few patches of thin and scrubby woods are observed scattered here and there.

The village presents no cheering prospect, as, notwithstanding its antiquity, it consists of but few huts, inhabited by a miserable race of men, scarcely equal to the Indians from whom they are descended. Their log or bark houses are low, filthy and disgusting, displaying not the least trace of comfort. Chicago is perhaps one of the oldest settlements in the Indian country; its name, derived from the Potawatomi language, signifies either a skunk, or a wild onion; and either of these significations has been occasionally given for it. A fort is said to have formerly existed there. Mention is made of the place as having been visited in 1671 by Perot, who found "Chicagou" to be the residence of a powerful chief of the Miamis. The number of trails centering all at this spot, and their apparent antiquity, indicate that this was probably for a long while the site of a large Indian village. As a place of business, it offers no inducement to the settler; for the whole annual amount of the trade on the lake did not exceed the cargo of five or six schooners even at the time when the garrison received its supplies from Mackinaw. It is not impossible that at some distant day, when the banks of the Illinois shall have been covered with a dense population, and when the low prairies which extend between that river and Fort Wayne, shall have acquired a population proportionate to the produce which they can yield, that Chicago may become one of the points in the direct line of communication between the northern lakes and the Mississippi; but even the intercourse which will be carried on through this communication, will we think at all times be a limited one; the dangers attending the navigation of the lake, and the scarcity of harbours along the shore, must ever prove a serious obstacle to the increase of the commercial importance of Chicago. The extent of the sand banks which are formed on the eastern and southern shore, by the prevailing north and northwesterly winds, will likewise prevent any important works from being undertaken to improve the post of Chicago.

The south fork of Chicago river takes its rise, about six miles from the fort, in a swamp which communicates also with the Des Plaines, one of the head branches of the Illinois. Having been informed that this route was frequently travelled by traders, and that it had been used by one of the officers of the garrison, who returned with provisions from St. Louis a few days before our arrival at the fort, we determined to ascend the Chicago river in order to observe this interesting division of waters. We accordingly left the fort on the 7th of June, in a boat which, after having ascended the river about four miles, we exchanged for a narrow pirogue that drew less water; the stream we were ascending was very narrow, rapid, and crooked, presenting a great fall; it continued so for about three miles, when we reached a sort of swamp designated by the Canadian voyagers under the name of *le petit lac* [the little lake]. Our course through this swamp, which extended for three miles, was very much impeded by the high grass, weeds, &c. through which our pirogue passed with difficulty. Observing that our progress through the fen was very slow, and the day being considerably advanced, we landed on the north bank, and continued our course along the edge of the swamp for about three miles, until we reached the place where the old portage road meets the current, which was here very distinct towards the south. We were delighted at beholding for the first time, a feature so interesting in itself, but which we had afterwards an opportunity of observing frequently on the route; viz. the division of waters starting from the same source, and running in two different directions, so as to become the feeders of streams that discharge themselves into the ocean at immense distances apart. Although at the time we visited it, there was scarcely water enough to permit our pirogue to pass, we could not doubt, that in the spring of the year the route must be a very eligible one. Lieut. Hopson, who accompanied us to the Des Plaines, told us that he had travelled it with ease, in a boat loaded with lead and flour. The distance from the fort to the intersection of the Portage road and Des Plaines, is supposed to be about twelve or thirteen miles; the elevation of the feeding lake above Chicago river was estimated at five or six feet; and, it is probable that the descent to the Des Plaines is less considerable. The Portage road is about eleven miles long; the usual distance travelled by land seldom however exceeds from four to nine miles; in very dry seasons it has been said to amount to thirty miles, as the portage then extends to Mount Juliet, near the confluence of the Kankakee. When we consider the facts above stated, we are irresistibly led to the conclusion, that an elevation of the lakes of a few feet, (not exceeding ten or twelve,) above their present level, would cause them to discharge their waters, partly at least, into the Gulf of Mexico; that such a discharge has at one time existed, every one conversant with the nature of the country must admit; and it is equally apparent that an expenditure, trifling in comparison to the importance of the object, would again render Lake Michigan a tributary of the Mexican gulf.

Source: William Keating, *Narrative of an Expedition to the Source of St. Peter's River, Lake Winnipeek, Lake of the Woods, etc., etc., Performed in the Year 1823, by order of the Hon. John C. Calhoun, Secretary of War, under the command of Stephen R. Long, Major U.S.T.E.*, 2 vols. in 1 (Philadelphia: H. C. Carey & I. Lea, 1824), 1:162–67.

Appendix C

✦

Designation for Chicago Portage National Historic Site

Chicago Portage National Historic Site Designation As a National Historic Site (January 3, 1952, 17 F.R. 236)

Whereas, the Congress of the United States has declared it to be a national policy to preserve for the public use historic sites, buildings and objects of national significance for the inspiration and benefit of the people of the United States; and

Whereas, the Advisory Board on National Parks, Historic Sites, Buildings, and Monuments has recognized the lands hereinafter described as possessing national significance because of their relation to the historic portage which determined the location and growth of the Nation's second largest metropolitan center; and

Whereas, a cooperative agreement has been entered into by the Forest Preserve District of Cook County, Illinois, and the United States of America, providing for the designation, preservation, and use of the remains of the Chicago Portage as a national historic site;

Now, therefore, I, Oscar L. Chapman, Secretary of the Interior, by virtue and of pursuant to the authority contained in section 2 of the act of August 21, 1935 (49 Stat. 666; 16 U.S.C., 1946 ed., sec. 462), do hereby designate the following described lands, together with all historic structures thereon and appurtenances connected therewith, to be a national site, having the name "Chicago Portage National Historic Site":

All those tracts or parcels of land known as the Chicago Portage Area, consisting of the actual portage point at the west end of the Chicago Portage, existing west and abandoned east channel of the Des Plaines River, the westerly end of Portage Creek, and the Laughton and Stony Fords across the west channel of the Des Plaines River, all located within the Forest Preserve District of Cook County and more particularly described as follows:

Lots One Hundred and Three (103) and One Hundred and Five (105) including the sixty (60) foot road common to both, of Sanitary District Trustees Subdivision of Right of Way, from North and South Center line of Section

30, Township 39 North, Range 14 East of the Third Principal Meridian to Will County Line, except that part of said Lot One Hundred and Five (105) lying Northwesterly of a line beginning at a point in the east line of said lot which is sixty-six and ninety-two hundredths (66.92) feet South of the Northwest corner thereof; thence Southwesterly on a line curved to the left, convex to the north, having a radius of two thousand three hundred (2300) feet, to its point of tangency to a line which is sixty-seven (67) feet, Southwesterly of, normally distant from, and parallel to the Northwesterly line of said lot; thence Southwesterly in a line sixty-seven (67) feet Southeasterly of, normally distant from and parallel to said Northwesterly line to the Westerly line of said lot; and except that part of Lot One Hundred and Three (103) lying South of a line beginning in at a point in the east line of said lot which is one thousand, three hundred and eight, and fifty-seven hundredths (1308.57) feet South of the Northeast corner of said Lot One Hundred and Five (105); thence Northwesterly in a line making an angle of eighty-three degrees and thirteen minutes (83°13') with the East line of said Lot One Hundred and Three (103) measured from North to West, one thousand, six hundred and seventy-six and sixty-five hundredths (1,676.65) feet, more or less, to the Southwesterly line of said lot; containing thirty-seven and six tenths (37.6) NATIONAL HISTORIC SITES17 acres, more or less, subject to the dedication of the easterly portion thereof for Harlem Ave.

Also Lot One Hundred and Seven (107), River Lot AR, and River Lot BR of said Subdivision except those parts of Lot One Hundred Seven (107) and River Lot BR lying south of a line parallel to and fifty (50) feet Northwesterly of, measured at right angles, the Northerly Right of Way Line of the Chicago and Illinois Western Railroad as it existed on September 9, 1931, containing fifty-three and six tenths (53.6) acres, more or less, subject to the dedication of parts thereof for 47th Street and US Highway Route 66:

All situated in Sections One (1) and (12) Township 38 North, Range 12 east of the Third Principal Meridian in the County of Cook and State of Illinois.

The administration, protection, and development of this national historic site shall be exercised in accordance with the provisions of the above-mentioned cooperative agreement and the act of August 21, 1935.

Warning is expressly given to all unauthorized persons not to appropriate, injure, destroy, deface, or remove any feature of this historic site.

In witness whereof, I have hereunto set my hand and caused the official seal of the Department of the Interior to be affixed at the City of Washington, this 3d day of January 1952.

[SEAL] OSCAR L. CHAPMAN,
Secretary of the Interior.

Source: National Park Service, US Department of the Interior, *Proclamations and Orders Relating to the National Park Service*, vol. 2, *January 1, 1945 to January 20, 2001* (Washington, DC: National Park Service, 2004), 16–17.

Appendix D

✦

Chronology

14,500–10,200 BP	Lake Michigan Lobe of Woodfordian subphase of Wisconsinian glaciation extends over Illinois, including the Chicago area, and creates the Valparaiso Moraine; Chicago Outlet formed
12,000–10,000 BCE	Paleo-Indian habitation of northeastern Illinois, including Chicago area
8000–600 BCE	Archaic period of habitation; Prairie Peninsula extends to Chicago area
3000–600 BCE	Late Archaic period of habitation
600–200 BCE	Early Woodland period of habitation
500 BCE–0 CE	Three-part Chicago River system of Main Stem, North Branch, South Branch established; Des Plaines River begins flowing westward; Mud Lake and Chicago Portage formed
200 BCE–400 CE	Middle Woodland period of habitation; Havana Hopewell culture develops in Illinois region; likely first regular use of Chicago Portage by Native Americans as trade route
400–1000	Late Woodland period of habitation
900–1500	Mississippian culture develops; possible use of Chicago Portage as trade route by Mississippian peoples; Cahokia flourishes around 1200 but is abandoned around 1300
1500–1600	Pre-European contact use of Chicago Portage by Native Americans
1550s	Demand for beaver fur in Europe ignites the fur trade
1600–1650	Iroquois and Huron battle for control of fur trade in St. Lawrence River region; Iroquois drive Huron from the region; Iroquois then carry attacks westward, including into the Chicago region
1634	Jean Nicolet explores Lake Michigan, reaching Green Bay
1655–1660	Iroquois attack Illinois and Miami Tribes at Chicago, driving them west of the Mississippi River

1650–66	Iroquois and French battle for control of fur trade, reaching peace in 1666
1671	Jacques Marquette founds St. Ignace Mission
1673	Louis Jolliet expedition reaches Mississippi River; Kaskaskia villagers show Jolliet and Marquette Chicago Portage route from Illinois River, via Des Plaines River, to Chicago River and Lake Michigan
1674	Jolliet's journal and map lost in canoe accident; Jolliet gives oral account to Claude Dablon, who transcribes that Jolliet said it would be possible to build a canal at Chicago Portage; Marquette, Pierre Porteret, and Jacques Largilliers begin return trip to Kaskaskia, spending winter at Chicago Portage
1675	Marquette dies on return trip from Kaskaskia
1677	Claude Allouez crosses Chicago Portage
1680	Iroquois attack Starved Rock, driving out Henri de Tonty and his five men; Tonty's group crosses Chicago Portage on retreat to Mackinac, arriving there in 1681
1682	La Salle expedition camps at Chicago Portage and then crosses it on the way to Mississippi River; expedition reaches Gulf of Mexico and La Salle lays claim to "Louisiana"
1682–83	La Salle sends men to build "fort" at Chicago; in June 1683, La Salle writes letter from "portage de Checagou"; in late 1683, La Salle writes detailed description of the portage and takes issue with Jolliet regarding its efficacy as a trade route
1684	Olivier Morel de La Durantaye enlarges fort at Chicago Portage
1685	Jesuits build fortified structure on Chicago River
1687–88	Henri de Joutel at Fort St. Louis and Chicago Portage; Joutel writes detailed description of area and Chicago Portage
1690–1730	Fur trade through Chicago Portage greatly reduced due to conflicts between the French and Native American tribes; in 1696, Louis XIV issues edict prohibiting trade with western territories
1696	François Pinet establishes Mission of the Guardian Angel at Chicago
1698	Jean François Buisson de St.-Cosme describes his crossing of Chicago Portage
1763	British take control of Chicago Portage
1765–83	Control of Chicago Portage contested during American Revolution

1783	Treaty of Paris makes Chicago Portage an American possession
1784–88	Jean Baptiste Point de Sable moves to Chicago and establishes farm and trading business, beginning first sustained European settlement at Chicago; he remains there until 1800
1795	Treaty of Greenville includes ceding of Chicago Portage by Native Americans to United States
1803	First Fort Dearborn constructed
1804	John Kinzie moves to Chicago
1812	Battle of Fort Dearborn; first Fort Dearborn burned down
1816	Second Fort Dearborn constructed; Indian Boundary Lines created; Major Stephen H. Long explores possible route for Illinois and Michigan Canal
1818	Illinois becomes a US state, with northern border raised to include Chicago Portage; Gurdon Saltonstall Hubbard makes first trip to Chicago Portage
1821	John Walls surveys portage area for General Land Office of the United States
1824	Justus Post and René Paul survey portage area to determine best route for Illinois and Michigan Canal
1828–34	Laughton Trading Post and tavern do business in vicinity of Chicago Portage
1830	Riverside and Lyons are population centers in Cook County
1832	Black Hawk War; first cholera outbreak in Chicago
1833	Town of Chicago organized
1834	Last group of Potawatomi leave Chicago
1835	By end of year, all Native Americans in Illinois relocated west of Mississippi River
1836–48	Construction of Illinois and Michigan Canal
1837	City of Chicago incorporated
1856	Chicago Historical Society founded
1887–1922	Planning and construction of Chicago Sanitary and Ship Canal
1892–94	Diversion of Des Plaines River at Chicago Portage
1893	Sanitary District of Chicago purchases land that later becomes Chicago Portage National Historic Site
1907–21	Economy Light and Power litigation
1923	Robert Knight and Lucius Zeuch present paper on location of Chicago Portage
1929	Sanitary District of Chicago gives land grant to Forest Preserve District of Cook County to create a historical park commemorating Chicago Portage

1930	Commemorative boulder placed at Chicago Portage
1950	Forest Preserve District of Cook County purchases Chicago Portage site from Sanitary District of Chicago
1952	United States Department of Interior establishes Chicago Portage National Historic Site
1975	*Design Study: The Chicago Portage and Laughton Trading Post Area, "The Waterway West"* published
1978	Chicago Portage National Historic Site placed on National Register of Historic Places
1984	Illinois and Michigan Canal National Heritage Corridor established as America's first National Heritage Area
1989–90	Illinois and Michigan Canal National Heritage Corridor Civic Center Authority prepares application for developing Chicago Portage National Historic Site
1990	Commemorative sculpture erected at Chicago Portage National Historic Site
1999	US Army Corps of Engineers prepares *Chicago Portage Literature Overview and Assessment*; Friends of the Chicago Portage founded
2005	*I&M Canal National Heritage Corridor Interpretive Plan* published
2013	Hitchcock Design Group creates schematic plan for Chicago Portage National Historic Site
2015	Lakota Group prepares *Gateway Master Plan*
2016	Improvements made at Chicago National Historic Site, including landscape work and installation of new interpretive pavilion
2018	Design Group prepares *Chicago Portage National Historic Site Master Plan* for Forest Preserve District of Cook County

NOTES

Introduction

1. Archer Butler Hulbert, *Portage Paths: The Keys to the Continent* (Cleveland: Arthur H. Clark, 1903), 165.

2. Justin Winsor, "Joliet, Marquette, and La Salle: Historical Sources and Attendant Cartography," in Winsor, ed., *Narrative and Critical History of America*, vol. 4, *French Explorations and Settlements in North America and Those of the Portuguese, Dutch, and Swedes, 1500–1700* (New York: Houghton, Mifflin, 1884), 224n1.

3. Some canoes were up to 35 feet long and 6 feet wide and were sometimes equipped with paddles or the occasional sail. These boats were handled by eight men and could carry upwards of four tons. The pirogue was a kind of wide dugout canoe, as if a dugout had been cut in half and a wide centerpiece installed. The bateau was slightly larger than a pirogue, around 30 feet in length and 8 feet wide, with a flat bottom and a pointed bow and stern. The larger boats of the fur trade were the Mackinaw and Durham boats. The former was 40 to 50 feet long and 12 feet wide, with a flat bottom, and the latter were 60 feet long and 8 feet wide with a capacity of up to fifteen tons. Testimony of Reuben Gold Thwaites in *Abstract of Proofs, United States of America vs. Economy Light and Power Company*, United States District Court for the Northern District of Illinois, Eastern Division, In Chancery, no. 29776, 3 vols. (Chicago: Gunthorp-Warren Printing Co., 1912), 1:498–99.

Chapter 1

1. *BP* is used by geologists and archaeologists to refer to the number of radiocarbon years prior to January 1, 1950. Therefore, by comparison, the year 2000 BP would equate to the year 50 BCE, or "before the Common Era." BP is used in this chapter to be consistent with the accompanying footnotes and illustrations that use the same term or the similar term "radiocarbon years." In some illustrations you will also see the abbreviation "ka," which means "kilo annum," or one thousand years. It likewise refers to years before the present, so, for example, "14.5 ka" means the same as 14,500 BP. In subsequent chapters the more common BCE and CE ("of the Common Era") are used.

2. H. B. Willman, *Summary of the Geology of the Chicago Area*, Illinois Geological Survey Circular 460 (Urbana: State of Illinois Department of Registration and Education, 1971), 54; Jerry Sullivan, *Chicago Wilderness: An Atlas of Biodiversity* (Chicago: Chicago Region Biodiversity Council, 1999), 6.

3. Sullivan, *Chicago Wilderness*, 6 (one-quarter mile thick); Willman, *Summary of Geology*, 54 (three thousand to five thousand feet thick).

4. Sullivan, *Chicago Wilderness*, 8–9.

5. Willman, *Summary of Geology*, 54.

6. William C. Alden, "Description of the Chicago District," *Geologic Atlas of the United States*, folio 81 (Reston, VA: US Geological Survey, 1902), 1.

7. James Walter Goldthwait, *Physical Features of the Des Plaines Valley*, Illinois State Geological Survey Bulletin 11 (Urbana: University of Illinois, 1909), 2.

8. Michael J. Chrzastowski and Todd A. Thompson, "Late Wisconsinan and Holocene Geologic History of the Illinois-Indiana Coast of Lake Michigan," *Journal of Great Lakes Research* 20, no. 1 (January 1994): 16.

9. There is disagreement as to whether the Glenwood phase gave way directly to the Two Creeks phase or whether there was an intermediate drop to 620 feet above sea level known as the Calumet I phase. Under the latter scenario, there was an initial Calumet phase, a drop to the Two Creeks levels, and then a recurrence of the Calumet levels at Calumet II. For this view, see J. Harlen Bretz, "The Double Calumet Stage of Lake Chicago," *Journal of Geology* 67, no. 1 (November 1959): 681–84. The view presented here derives from more recent research. See, e.g., Chrzastowski and Thompson, "Late Wisconsinan and Holocene," 16; Allan Schneider and Ardith Hansel, "Evidence for Post-Two Creeks Age of the Type Calumet Shoreline of Glacial Lake Chicago," in *Late Quaternary History of the Lake Michigan Basin*, ed. Allan Schneider and Gordon Fraser (Boulder, CO: Geological Society of America, 1990), 1–8.

10. Willman, *Summary of Geology*, 57.

11. J. Harlan Bretz, *Geology of the Chicago Region: Part II—The Pleistocene*, Illinois State Geological Survey Bulletin 65, pt. 2 (Urbana: State of Illinois Department of Registration and Education, 1955), 120. Some earlier geologists surmised that Lake Algonquin also included waters from the basin of Lake Superior, but Bretz cites later research that remaining glacial ice in the Superior basin made this unlikely

12. Bretz, *Geology of Chicago Region*, 121.

13. Bretz, *Geology of Chicago Region*, 121.

14. Bretz, *Geology of Chicago Region*, 121.

15. Willman, *Summary of Geology*, 58, puts the low water level of Lake Chippewa at 230 feet; Chrzastowski and Thompson, "Late Wisconsinan and Holocene," 18, put it at 260 feet.

16. Chrzastowski and Thompson, "Late Wisconsinan and Holocene," 18.

17. Willman, *Summary of Geology*, 58.

18. Willman, *Summary of Geology*, 58.

19. Chrzastowski and Thompson, "Late Wisconsinan and Holocene," 15.

20. Michael J. Chrzastowski, *The Chicago River—a Legacy of Glacial and Coastal Processes* (Champaign: Illinois Geological Survey, 2009), 11.

21. Chrzastowski, *Chicago River*, 12.

22. Chrzastowski, *Chicago River*, 13.

23. Chrzastowski, *Chicago River*, 14.

24. Chrzastowski, *Chicago River*, 14.

25. Chrzastowski, *Chicago River*, 14.

26. Chrzastowski, *Chicago River*, 16.

27. Chrzastowski, *Chicago River*, 16.

28. Chrzastowski, *Chicago River*, 16.

29. Willman, *Summary of Geology*, 59.

30. Goldthwait, *Physical Features of Des Plaines Valley*, 56–57.
31. Goldthwait, *Physical Features of Des Plaines Valley*, 56–57. Goldthwait cites L. E. Cooley, consulting engineer of the Internal Improvement Commission, as being of this opinion.

Chapter 2

1. Timothy Pauketat, *A Tour Guide to the Prehistory and Native Cultures of Southwestern Illinois and the Greater St. Louis Area* (Springfield: Illinois Historic Preservation Agency, 1993), 5–6; Charles Markman, *Chicago before History* (Springfield: Illinois Historic Preservation Agency, 1991), 9.
2. Markman, *Chicago before History*, 46–47; Brad Koldehoff, *Paleoindian and Archaic Settlement and Lithic Procurement in the Illinois Uplands*, Illinois State Archaeological Survey Technical Report148 (Urbana: University of Illinois, 2013), 1.
3. Markman, *Chicago before History*, 48–49.
4. Markman, *Chicago before History*, 45. See also Joel Greenberg, *A Natural History of the Chicago Region* (Chicago: University of Chicago Press, 2002), 12, for the significance of fire in determining the complicated vegetation patterns of the Chicago area; and James A. Brown, "The Prairie Peninsula: An Interaction Area in the Eastern United States" (PhD diss., University of Chicago, 1965), for extensive coverage of the nature and influence of the Prairie Peninsula.
5. Pauketat, *Tour Guide to Prehistory*, 7.
6. Markman, *Chicago before History*, 53.
7. Pauketat, *Tour Guide to Prehistory*, 7. In addition to nuts, squash and the seeds of wild plants and sunflowers were food sources during the late Archaic period.
8. Markman, *Chicago before History*, 53–54.
9. Markman, *Chicago before History*, 55.
10. Markman, *Chicago before History*, 9, 61; Pauketat, *Tour Guide to Prehistory*, 7.
11. The Havana Hopewell tradition had "a continuous range from northern Illinois across northwestern Indiana and into southwestern Michigan." James A. Brown, "The Northeastern Extension of the Havana Tradition," in *Hopewellian Studies*, ed. Joseph Caldwell and Robert Hall, Illinois State Museum Scientific Papers 12.4 (Springfield: Illinois State Museum, 1964), 110.
12. Steven Sarich, "Deconstructing the Hopewell Interaction Sphere," *Nebraska Anthropologist* 25 (2010): 42–43, http://digitalcommons.unl.edu/nebanthro/59.
13. Markman, *Chicago before History*, 65.
14. Markman, *Chicago before History*, 10.
15. Markman, *Chicago before History*, 71.
16. Markman, *Chicago before History*, 71.
17. Thomas Emerson, "Some Perspectives on Cahokia and the Northern Mississippian Expansion," in *Cahokia and the Hinterlands*, ed. Thomas Emerson and R. Barry Lewis (Urbana: University of Illinois Press, 1991), 222.
18. John E. Kelly, "Cahokia and Its Role as a Gateway Center in Interregional Trade," in Emerson and Lewis, *Cahokia and the Hinterlands*, 75.
19. Timothy Pauketat, *Ancient Cahokia and the Mississippians* (Cambridge: Cambridge University Press, 2004), 3; Markman, *Chicago before History*, 73.

20. Markman, *Chicago before History*, 73.
21. Pauketat, *Ancient Cahokia*, 79.
22. Kelly, "Cahokia and its Role," 64. See also Pauketat, *Ancient Cahokia*, 120.
23. Kelly, "Cahokia and its Role," 65.
24. Pauketat, *Ancient Cahokia*, 35–36.
25. Kelly, "Cahokia and its Role," 67–71.
26. Duane Esarey, director, Illinois State Museum—Dickson Mounds, telephone conversation with the author, June 22, 2019.
27. Recent evidence suggests the possibility that the area was then inhabited by members of the Illinois Confederation. A. J. White, Samuel E. Munoz, Sissel Schroeder, and Lora R. Stevens, "After Cahokia: Indigenous Repopulation and Depopulation of the Horseshoe Lake Watershed, AD 1400–1900," *American Antiquity* 85, no. 2 (2020): 263–78, doi:10.1017/aaq.2019.103.
28. William Strong, *The Indian Tribes of the Chicago Region with Special Reference to the Illinois and the Potowatomi* (Chicago: Field Museum of Natural History, 1938), 6. "Father Marquette, as well as Father Hennepin, give in their journals the signification that the Illinois Indians gave to their name. The former in his narrative journal observes: 'To say Illinois is, in their language, to say 'the men,' as if other Indians compared to them were mere beasts.' 'The word Illi-nois," says Father Hennepin, 'signifies a man of full age in the vigor of his strength. This word Illinois comes, as has already been observed, from Illini, which in that language signifies a perfect and accomplished man.' " Hiram Beckwith, *The Illinois and Indiana Indians* (Chicago: Fergus Printing Co., 1884), 100–101.
29. Frank Grover, *Our Indian Predecessors: The First Evanstonians* (Evanston, IL: Evanston Historical Society, 1901), 7.
30. Grover, *Our Indian Predecessors*, 10. "[The Illinois'] favorite and most populous villages were upon the Illinois and its two principal branches, the Desplaines and the Kankakee." Beckwith, *Illinois and Indiana Indians*, 102.

Chapter 3

1. Eric Jay Dolin, *Fur, Fortune, and Empire: The Epic History of the Fur Trade in America* (New York: W. W. Norton, 2010), 9–10.
2. Harold Innis, *The Fur Trade in Canada: An Introduction to Canadian Economic History* (New Haven, CT: Yale University Press, 1930), 5.
3. Dolin, *Fur, Fortune, and Empire*, 9.
4. Nicholas Perrot, "Memoir of the Manners, Customs, and Religions of the Savages of North America," in *The Indian Tribes of the Upper Mississippi Valley and Region of the Great Lakes*, ed. Emma Helen Blair (Cleveland: Arthur H. Clarke, 1911), 1:154–57n122. See also Wayne C. Temple, *Indian Villages of the Illinois Country: Historic Tribes*, Scientific Papers 2.2, rev. ed. (1966; reprint, Springfield: Illinois State Museum, 1987), 57.
5. Innis, *Fur Trade in Canada*, 34.
6. Louise Phelps Kellogg, *Early Narratives of the Northwest, 1634–1699* (New York: Charles Scribner's Sons, 1917), 4–5.
7. Louise Phelps Kellogg, *The French Regime in Wisconsin and the Northwest* (Madison: State Historical Society of Wisconsin, 1925), 82. Although it is widely accepted by historians that Nicolet went no farther than Green Bay, Robert Hall argued that Nicolet instead had traveled "south along the Lake Michigan shore"

as far as the Calumet region. Robert Hall, "Rethinking Jean Nicolet's Route to the Ho-Chunks in 1634," in *Theory, Method, and Practice in Modern Archaeology*, ed. Robert Jeske and Douglas Charles (Westport, CT: Praeger, 2003), 246. Elsewhere, Hall asserted that Nicolet had traveled through the Chicago Portage on this trip. Robert Hall, "Relating the Big Fish and the Big Stone: Reconsidering the Archaeological Identity and Habitat of the Winnebago in 1634," in *Oneota Archaeology, Past, Present, and Future*, ed. William Green (Iowa City: University of Iowa Press, 1995), 21. Hall's claims have not been generally accepted and were reviewed and rejected in Patrick J. Jung, *The Misunderstood Mission of Jean Nicolet: Uncovering the Story of the 1634 Journey* (Madison: Wisconsin Historical Society Press, 2018); and Nancy O. Lurie and Patrick J. Jung, *The Nicolet Corrigenda: New France Revisited* (Arlington Heights, IL: Waveland Press, 2009), 63–69, 117–21. The current work accepts the later and widely accepted view that the limit of Nicolet's travels was at Green Bay and that Jolliet and Marquette were the first Europeans for which we have historical evidence of having been at the site of the Chicago Portage.

8. Kellogg, *Early Narratives*, 152. Allouez gives an account of an Iroquois attack "at the foot of the Lake of the Ilinioues, which is called Machihiganing." Kellogg takes this as a reference to Chicago at the foot of Lake Michigan. Kellogg, *Early Narratives*, 152n2.

9. Kellogg, *Early Narratives*, 223–28.

10. Francis Borgia Steck, *The Jolliet-Marquette Expedition, 1673* (Glendale, CA: Arthur H. Clark, 1928), 146 (recommending of Jolliet), 228 (instructing Marquette).

11. Steck, *Jolliet-Marquette Expedition*, 146.

12. Jacques Monet, "Marquette, Jacques," in *Dictionary of Canadian Biography*, vol. 1, *1000–1700* (University of Toronto/Université Laval, 2003), http://www.biographi.ca/en/bio/marquette_jacques_1E.html.

13. Jean Delanglez, *Life and Voyages of Louis Jolliet (1645–1700)* (Chicago: Institute of Jesuit History, 1948), 31.

14. Steck, *Jolliet-Marquette Expedition*, 149.

15. Kellogg, *French Regime*, 193; Alfred Andreas, *History of Chicago from the Earliest Period to the Present Time*, 3 vols. (Chicago: Alfred T. Andreas, 1884), 1:42–43.

16. Kellogg, *French Regime*, 193; Steck, *Jolliet-Marquette Expedition*, 150.

17. Delanglez, *Life and Voyages of Jolliet*, 103–5.

18. Michael McCafferty notes that the possibility that Porteret took part in Jolliet's expedition "is not supported by contemporary sources," citing a letter written by Pierre Cholenec in 1675. Michael McCafferty, "A Fresh Look at the Place Name Chicago," *Journal of the Illinois State Historical Society (1998–)* 96, no.2 (Summer 2003): 127–28n12.

19. Steck, *Jolliet-Marquette Expedition*, 151.

20. Jacques Marquette, "Of the first Voyage made by Father Marquette toward new Mexico, and How the idea thereof was conceived," in Reuben Thwaites, ed., *The Jesuit Relations and Allied Documents*, vol. 59, *Travels and Explorations of the Jesuit Missionaries in New France, 1610–1791: Lower Canada, Illinois, Ottawas, 1673–1677* (Cleveland: Burrows Brothers, 1900), 107.

21. Marquette, "Of the first Voyage," in Thwaites, *Jesuit Relations*, 59:107.

22. "As we coasted along rocks frightful for their height and length, we saw two monsters painted on one of these rocks, which startled us at first, and on which the boldest Indian dare not gaze long. They are as large as a calf, with horns on the head like a deer, a fearful look, red eyes, bearded like a tiger, the face somewhat like a man's, the body covered with scales, and the tail so long that it twice makes the turn of the body, passing over the head and down between the legs, and ending at last in a fish's tail. Green, red, and a kind of black, are the colors employed. On the whole, these two monsters are so well painted, that we could not believe any Indian to have been the designer, as good painters in France would find it hard to do as well; besides this, they are so high upon the rock that it is hard to get conveniently at them to paint them." "Narrative of Father Marquette," in John Gilmary Shea, *Discovery and Exploration of the Mississippi Valley* (Clinton Hall, NY: Redfield, 1852), 39.

23. Steck, *Jolliet-Marquette Expedition*, 163.

24. Steck, *Jolliet-Marquette Expedition*, 163.

25. Marquette, "Of the first Voyage," in Thwaites, *Jesuit Relations*, 59:161.

26. Delanglez, *Life and Voyages of Jolliet*, 123.

27. Delanglez, *Life and Voyages of Jolliet*, 127–28.

28. Steck, *Jolliet-Marquette Expedition*, 167–68.

29. Steck, *Jolliet-Marquette Expedition*, 168.

30. Steck, *Jolliet-Marquette Expedition*, 168. See also Edward Neill, "Discovery along the Great Lakes," in Winsor, *Narrative and Critical History of America*, 4:179n2.

31. Delanglez points out that the handwriting on the map does not resemble Jolliet's, that style of the map is unlike any of the other maps known to have been drawn by Jolliet, and that there is no known example of Jolliet ever signing his name with one "l" the way it appears on the map. Jean Delanglez, "The Jolliet Lost Map of the Mississippi," *Mid-America: An Historical Review*, n.s., 17, no. 2 (April 1946): 69. The original French title, shown in a banner across the map, is "Nouvelle decouverte de plusieurs nations dans la Nouvelle France en l'année 1673 et 1674." Control Number 2001620471, Library of Congress, Geography and Map Division, Louisiana: European Explorations and the Louisiana Purchase, https://www.loc.gov/resource/g3300.ct000655.

32. A translation of the "Relation," including variants found in the four extant copies, can be found in Steck, *Jolliet-Marquette Expedition*, 173–80.

33. Claude Dablon, "Relation of the discovery of many countries situated to the south of New France, made in 1673," in Reuben Thwaites, ed., *The Jesuit Relations and Allied Documents*, vol. 58, *Travels and Explorations of the Jesuit Missionaries in New France, 1610–1791: Ottawas, Lower Canada, Iroqouois, 1672–1674* (Cleveland: Burrows Brothers, 1899), 105.

34. Melchisédech Thevenot, *Recueil de voyages de Mr. Thevenot* (Paris: Étienne Michallet, 1681).

35. Steck, *Jolliet-Marquette Expedition*, 266.

36. Shea, *Discovery and Exploration of the Mississippi Valley*; "Account of the second voyage and the death of Father Jacques Marquette," in Thwaites, *Jesuit Relations*, 59: 184–211.

37. Steck, *Jolliet-Marquette Expedition*, 262–310.

38. Steck, *Jolliet-Marquette Expedition*, 306–10. See also Francis Steck, "What Became of Jolliet's Journal," *Americas* 5, no. 2 (1948): 173–80.

39. Delanglez, *Life and Voyages of Jolliet*, 91–99. See also Jean Delanglez, "The 'Recit des voyages et des decouvertes du Pere Jacques Marquette' Part 1," *Mid-America: An Historical Review*, n.s., 17, no. 3 (July 1946): 173–94.

40. Kellogg, *French Regime*, 200n29.

41. Unlike the uncertainty of authorship of the *Récit* of the expedition, there is no question that Marquette's journal of this second voyage was authored by him. It is in his handwriting and is kept in diary form with dated entries. In his journal of this trip, Marquette wrote that he "departed with Pierre Porteret and Jacque [blank space left in manuscript], on the 25th of October, 1674, about noon." Marquette, "Unfinished Journal of Father Jacques Marquette, addressed to the Reverend Father Claude Dablon, superior of the Missions," in Thwaites, *Jesuit Relations*, 59:165. Both Steck and Delanglez agree that it was Jacques Largilliers who accompanied Marquette. See Steck, *Jolliet-Marquette Expedition*, 150; Delanglez, *Life and Voyages of Jolliet*, 129.

42. Marquette, "Unfinished Journal," in Thwaites, *Jesuit Relations*, 59:181.

43. Marquette's journal, found in Thwaites, *Jesuit Relations*, 59:165–83, ends on April 6, 1675. The remaining account of the voyage, including Marquette's death, is told by Dablon in "Account of the second voyage," in Thwaites, *Jesuit Relations*, 59:184–211.

44. "Account of the second voyage," in Thwaites, *Jesuit Relations*, 59:201–5. At 201n46 the *Relations* gives the date of Marquette's death as May 19, but that is incorrect. The correct date is May 18.

45. "Narrative of Father Allouez," in Shea, *Discovery and Exploration of the Mississippi Valley*, 73.

46. "Narrative of Father Allouez," 77. The mention of Allouez's 1678 trip is an addendum by Dablon.

47. Milo Milton Quaife, *Chicago and the Old Northwest, 1673–1835* (Chicago: University of Chicago Press, 1913), 30–31.

48. *Chicago and the Old Northwest*, 31–32.

49. *Chicago and the Old Northwest*, 33. See also the account by Tonty in Kellogg, *Early Narratives*, 294; and the account in Pierre Margry, *Découvertes et établissements des français dans l'ouest et dans le sud de L'Amérique septentrionale (1614–1754)*, 3 vols. (Paris: Imprimerie D. Jouaust, 1877), 1:512.

50. Francis Parkman, *La Salle and the Discovery of the Great West* (Boston: Little, Brown, 1902), 295.

51. Account by Tonty in Kellogg, *Early Narratives*, 296.

52. Edward G. Mason, *Chapters from Illinois History* (Chicago: Herbert S. Stone, 1901), 125.

53. Account by Tonty in Kellogg, *Early Narratives*, 296–97.

54. Kellogg, *Early Narratives*, 310.

55. Mason, *Chapters from Illinois History*, 134.

56. Kellogg, *French Regime*, 223.

57. Mason, *Chapters from Illinois History*, 156. But Quaife claims the fort was named after Louis XIV; see Milo Milton Quaife, *Checagou: From Indian Wigwam to Modern City, 1673–1835* (Chicago: University of Chicago Press, 1933), 20.

58. Quaife, *Chicago and the Old Northwest*, 35.

59. Bessie Louise Pierce, *A History of Chicago: The Beginning of a City, 1673–1848* (Chicago: University of Chicago Press, 1937), 9, 9n29.

60. Quaife, *Checagou*, 20–21.

61. Mason, *Chapters from Illinois History*, 144–45.

62. Mason, *Chapters from Illinois History*, 150–51.

63. Mason, *Chapters from Illinois History*, 152–53; *Report concerning Canadian Archives for the Year 1905* (Ottawa: S. E. Dawson, Printer to the King's Most Excellent Majesty, 1906), 1:lx–lxi.

64. Roland Chardon, "The Linear League in North America," *Annals of the Association of American Geographers* 70, no. 2 (June 1980): 135–36: "The league of 2,000 *toises* was known by other names, including *lieue de Paris, lieue Parisienne*, and *petite lieue de France*. It also became the official *lieue de poste* (postal league) of France in the latter 1600s and was the official league in all North American French colonies during the 1700s. . . . This league's modern equivalent is 3,898.1 m." The French league is a source of confusion in historical documents. See, e.g., Joseph J. Thompson, "The Time and a Place for a Monument to Marquette," *Illinois Catholic Historical Review* 4, no. 2 (October 1921): 126: "At different times and under different circumstances France has had a linear measure which made a league at one time 2.42 miles; at another time 2.764, and at still another time 3.52 miles. Near about the time that Marquette made this journey the posting league of the French was 3.52 miles, so that full two leagues would mean about seven miles." To confuse matters more, Knight and Zeuch assume a league to equal 3 miles; see Robert Knight and Lucius H. Zeuch, *The Location of the Chicago Portage Route of the Seventeenth Century* (Chicago: Chicago Historical Society, 1928), 24. The latter may have confused a land league with a marine league, which at times in France did equal 3 miles, according to Chardon, "Linear League," 136.

65. Quaife, *Chicago and the Old Northwest*, 5–6. See also Margry, *Découvertes*, 2:82.

66. For an excellent discussion of the origins of "Chicago" as a place-name, see McCafferty, "Fresh Look." For an earlier attempt to decipher "Chicago," see John F. Steward, "Chicago—Origin of the Name of the City and the Old Portages," *Transactions of the Illinois State Historical Society for the Year 1904* (Springfield: Phillips Bros., State Printers, 1904), 460–66.

67. Margry, *Découvertes*, 2:166–67; translation by Clarence Alvord in *Abstract of Proofs*, 1:34–35.

68. Margry, *Découvertes* 2:168; translation by Alvord, *Abstract of Proofs*, 1:35.

69. Alvord testimony in *Abstract of Proofs*, 1:41–42.

70. *Abstract of Proofs*, 1:156.

71. Kellogg, *French Regime*, 228.

72. Mason, *Chapters from Illinois History*, 159–60.

73. Mason, *Chapters from Illinois History*, 162–63.

74. Kellogg, *Early Narratives*, 307; Mason, *Chapters from Illinois History*, 163.

75. Mason, *Chapters from Illinois History*, 163–64.

76. Joutel recounts that Allouez was very concerned about the possible return of La Salle to Fort St. Louis in 1687 because of fear that these efforts to derail La Salle's efforts might come to light. Margry, *Découvertes*, 3:500.

77. Mason, *Chapters from Illinois History*, 164.

78. Milton Quaife, "Was There a French Fort in Chicago?" *Publications of the Illinois State Historical Library, Illinois State Historical Society*, no. 17 (1912): 115–21.

79. Quaife, *Checagou*, 20–21.

80. Chicago Historical Society, *Chicago Historical Society Annual Report: 1905* (Chicago: Chicago Historical Society, 1905), 339.

81. Chicago Historical Society, *Annual Report: 1905*, 339. But see Kellogg, *French Regime*, 271n3, where Kellogg suggests this reference could be to the re-establishment of Fort Checagou in or around 1701 by Tonty and La Forest.

82. Margry, *Découvertes*, 3:509.

83. *American State Papers, Documents, Legislative and Executive, of the Congress of the United States, From the First Session of the First to the Third Session of the Thirteenth Congress, inclusive: Commencing March 3, 1789, and Ending March 3, 1815: Indian Affairs* (Washington, DC: Gales and Seaton, 1832), 1:562. Quaife dismisses this latter point as a mere assertion of power by the United States and argues that Little Turtle, a Miami chieftain, disputed the existence of such a fort.

84. Mason, *Chapters from Illinois History*, 177–78.

85. Margry, *Découvertes*, 3:510.

86. Parkman, *La Salle and the Discovery of the Great West*, 464.

87. Margry, *Découvertes*, 3:485–86; translation by Alvord, *Abstract of Proofs*, 1:45–46.

88. Margry, *Découvertes*, 3:511.

89. Kellogg, *French Regime*, 250.

90. Kellogg, *French Regime*, 257.

91. Kellogg, *Early Narratives*, 346–47.

92. Quaife, *Checagou*, 25.

93. Kellogg, *Early Narratives*, 347.

94. Kellogg, *Early Narratives*, 348.

95. Father Gravier to Father Jacques de Lamberville, February 16, 1701, in Reuben Thwaites, ed., *The Jesuit Relations and Allied Documents*, vol. 65, *Travels and Explorations of the Jesuit Missionaries in New France, 1610–1791: Lower Canada, Mississippi Valley, 1696–1702* (Cleveland: Burrows Brothers, 1900), 101.

96. Kellogg, *French Regime*, 267.

Chapter 4

1. Kellogg, *French Regime*, 271.

2. Jean Bochart de Champigny to Louis XIV in M. de Champigny, "Licenses to Trade Are Revoked," *Collections and Researches Made by the Michigan Pioneer and Historical Society* 33 (1904): 75.

3. M. de Champigny, "Licenses to Trade Are Revoked," 75.

4. Milo Quaife, introduction to Quaife, ed., *The Western Country in the Seventeenth Century* (Chicago: Lakeside Press, 1947), xxvii.

5. Quaife, *Western Country*, 87–88.
6. Kellogg, *French Regime*, 272.
7. Joseph Kellogg quoted in Timothy Hopkins, *The Kelloggs in the Old World and the New* (San Francisco: Sunset Press, 1903), 1:59–61.
8. Hopkins, *Kelloggs*, 61.
9. Quaife, *Chicago and the Old Northwest*, 59–61.
10. Quaife, *Chicago and the Old Northwest*, 65.
11. As translated in Louise Phelps Kellogg, ed., *Journal of a Voyage to North America* (Chicago: Caxton Club, 1928), 2:153.
12. Kellogg, *Journal of a Voyage to North America*, 2:169–70.
13. "Representation of the Lords Commissioners for Trade and Plantations to the King upon the State of His Majesties Colonies & Plantations on the Continent of North America, dated September the 8th 1721," *Documents Relative to the Colonial History of the State of New-York*, ed. E. B. O'Callaghan, vol. 5 (Albany, NY: Weed, Parsons, 1855), 621–22.
14. Pierce, *History of Chicago*, 11.
15. Joseph Kirkland, *The Story of Chicago* (Chicago: Dibble Publishing, 1892), 47.
16. Pierce, *History of Chicago*, 11.
17. Henry Hamilton to Frederick Haldimand, October 14, 1778, H. W. Beckwith, ed., *Collections of the Illinois State Historical Library*, vol. 1 (Springfield, IL: H. W. Rokker, 1903), 357.
18. Beckwith, *Collections*, 433.
19. Beckwith, *Collections*, 436–37.
20. Capt. Dederick Brehm to Gen. Haldimand, May 8, 1779, in "The Haldimand Papers," *Collections and Researches Made by the Michigan Pioneer and Historical Society* 19 (1892; reprint, 1911): 405.
21. Capt. Dederick Brehm to Gen. Haldimand, May 12, 1779, in "The Haldimand Papers," *Collections and Researches Made by the Michigan Pioneer and Historical Society* 19 (1892; reprint, 1911): 410.
22. Quaife, *Chicago and the Old Northwest*, 90–91.
23. Mason, *Chapters from Illinois History*, 289–90.
24. Quaife, *Chicago and the Old Northwest*, 94–95.
25. For a fuller description of the actions taken by the Spanish and of the consequences of the attack on St. Louis, see James Alton James, "The Significance of the Attack on St. Louis, 1780," *Proceedings of the Mississippi Valley Historical Association for the Year 1908–09* (Cedar Rapids, IA: Torch Press, 1910), 2:199–217.
26. Letter to Captain Langlade, cited and translated by Alvord, *Abstract of Proofs*, 1:74–75.
27. Quaife, *Chicago and the Old Northwest*, 97.
28. Lt. Gov. Patrick Sinclair to Lt. Col. Mason Bolton, June 4, 1780, "The Haldimand Papers," *Collections and Researches Made by the Michigan Pioneer and Historical Society* 19 (1892; reprint, 1911): 529–30.
29. Lt. Gov. Patrick Sinclair to Gen. Frederick Haldimand, June 21, 1780, *Report of the Pioneer Society of the State of Michigan together with Reports of County Pioneer Societies* 9 (1886; 2nd ed., 1908): 558.
30. Quaife, *Chicago and the Old Northwest*, 97.

31. Letter from Guillaume La Mothe, unaddressed, April 24, 1782, in "The Haldimand Papers," *Collections and Researches Made by the Pioneer Society of the State of Michigan* 10 (1886; 2nd ed., 1908): 569–70.

32. Henry Hurlbut, *Chicago Antiquities: Comprising Original Items and Relations, Letters, Extracts, and Notes, Pertaining to Early Chicago* (Chicago: Fergus Printing Co., 1881), 59.

33. Emily J. Blasingham, "Indians of the Chicago Area," in *Chicago Area Archaeology*, Illinois Archaeological Survey Bulletin 3, rev. ed., ed. Elaine A. Bluhm (Urbana: University of Illinois, 1983), 167–68 and 168n32.

34. Guillaume La Mothe to Joseph Chew, July 19, 1794, "Indian Affairs," *Collections and Researches Made by the Michigan Pioneer and Historical Society* 20 (1892; reprint, 1912): 365.

35. Pierce, *History of Chicago*, 14; *American State Papers, Indian Affairs*, 1: 562. The treaty listed the signatory tribes as the "Wyandots, Delawares, Shawanese, Ottawas, Chippewas, Pattawatamies, Miamies, Eel Rivers, Weas, Kickapoos, Piankeshaws, and Kaskaskias."

36. *American State Papers, Indian Affairs*, 1:562.

37. Quaife, *Chicago and the Old Northwest*, 127.

38. See Blasingham, "Indians of the Chicago Area," 163, which suggests that the Miami might have been in the Chicago vicinity ca. 1650, but there is no conclusive evidence of a permanent settlement.

39. Quaife, *Checagou*, 29–30.

40. Quaife, *Chicago and the Old Northwest*, 137–38.

41. John Reynolds, *The Pioneer History of Illinois* (Chicago: Fergus Printing Co., 1887), 168. But see John F. Swenson, "La Compt, Madam," in *A Compendium of the Early History of Chicago to the Year 1835 when the Indians Left*, ed. Ulrich Danckers and Jane Meredith (River Forest, IL: Early Chicago, 2000), 227–28, wherein Swenson argues that Reynolds has conflated two different women into his account of "Madame La Compt." In any event, even Reynolds says that his account is based solely on his own memory.

42. Reynolds, *Pioneer History of Illinois*, 169.

43. For Hubbard's letter to Rufus Blanchard relating this story, see Rufus Blanchard, *Discovery and Conquests of the North-West, with the History of Chicago* (Wheaton, IL: R. Blanchard, 1881), 757–58.

44. Blanchard, *Discovery and Conquests of the North-West*, 758.

45. Quaife, *Checagou*, 30–31.

46. Ulrich Danckers, "French Chicago during the 18th Century," in Danckers and Meredith, *Compendium of Early Chicago*, 384.

47. There are many variants of the spelling of Point de Sable's name, among them Point du Sable, Pointe du Sable, Point de Saible, De Saible, De Sable, Du Sable, Point Sable, Point au Sable, and more recently, DuSable. Swenson argues that "Point de Sable was his chosen legal name; he was never called Du Sable during his lifetime." John F. Swenson, "Jean Baptiste Point de Sable—The Founder of Modern Chicago," in Danckers and Meredith, *Compendium of Early Chicago*, 388. Contemporaneous spellings included "Point Sable" (by Durand; Swenson, "Jean Baptiste Point de Sable," 390, 391; and on the bill of sale of Point de Sable's Chicago home), and "Point au Sable" (used in a ledger entry by Thomas Smith; Quaife, Checagou, 38; and by Lt. Thomas Bennett; *Report of Pioneer Society*,

393, 395). "Point de Sable" was used by then Lt. Governor Patrick Sinclair, who was personally familiar with Point de Sable because Point de Sable managed Sinclair's Michigan estate. *Report of Pioneer Society*, 600, 605.

48. The earliest account of Point de Sable's origin is that of Juliette Kinzie, who says he was born in "St. Domingo" [Haiti]. Juliette Kinzie, *Wau-Bun: The Early Day in the Northwest* (Philadelphia: J. B. Lippincott, 1873), 150. This account, which was told to Juliette by her mother-in-law, Eleanor Kinzie (wife of John Kinzie), has been repeated by numerous authors with sometimes fanciful embellishments. See, e.g., references cited in Timothy Baumann, "The Du Sable Grave Project in St. Charles, Missouri," *Missouri Archaeologist* 66 (December 2005): 59–66, for claim that Point de Sable was the son of a French seaman and an African mother and was educated in France. *Wau-Bun*, generally, is viewed today as a slanted account intended to make John Kinzie and his family the heroes and founders of Chicago while downplaying the roles of other contemporaneous figures. Nehemiah Matson says that Point de Sable was a slave from Kentucky brought to Illinois by his master from Virginia. Nehemiah Matson, *French and Indians of Illinois River* (Princeton, IL: Republican Job Printing Establishment, 1874), 187. Quaife theorizes that Point de Sable was born in Canada of a slave mother and a father of the Dandonneau family. Quaife, *Checagou*, 31–36. Lastly, Ann Durkin Keating suggests Point de Sable was the son, "Jean," of a slave mother held by Jacques Brunet dit Bourbonnais and his wife Elisabeth Dehayes. The couple successfully petitioned the French colonial government in 1741 to free Jean and his sister Catherine. Ann Durkin Keating, *Rising Up from Indian Country* (Chicago: University of Chicago Press, 2012), 30n17.

49. Swenson, "Jean Baptiste Point de Sable," 388–90.

50. According to Thomas Meehan, Point De Sable was believed to be a spy for Major Godfrey de Linctot, who was aiding Major George Rogers Clark during the American Revolution. See Thomas A. Meehan, "Jean Baptiste Point du Sable, the First Chicagoan," *Journal of the Illinois State Historical Society* 56, no. 3 (Autumn 1963): 447.

51. *Report of Pioneer Society*, 393.

52. *Report of Pioneer Society*, 395.

53. Arent Schuyler de Peyster, *Miscellanies by an Officer* (Dumfries, UK: Dumfries and Galloway Courier Office, 1813), 10.

54. Swenson, "Jean Baptiste Point de Sable," 392.

55. A. Keating, *Rising Up from Indian Country*, 27–28.

56. A. Keating, *Rising Up from Indian Country*, 28. For the closeness of the Burnetts' relationship, see Edward S. Kelley, "William Burnett: A Representative Eighteenth Century American Trader, Pioneer, and Home Builder," *Collections and Researches Made by the Michigan Pioneer and Historical Society* 30 (1906): 88–89.

57. Burnett, August 24, 1798, Wilbur Cunningham, ed., *Letter Book of William Burnett: Early Fur Trader in the Land of Four Flags* (St. Joseph, MI: Fort Miami Heritage Society of Michigan, 1967), 107–8.

58. Translation from the French in Milton M. Quaife, ed., "Property of Jean Baptiste Point Sable," *Mississippi Valley Historical Review* 15, no. 1 (June 1928): 91–92. The translation referred to by Quaife was done by Mrs. L. Oughtred Woltz, archivist of the Burton Historical Collection. In a letter dated September

12, 1921, from C. M. Burton to Caroline M. McIlvaine, librarian of the Chicago Historical Society, Burton enclosed the translation of the Point de Sable bill of sale along with some notes by Woltz. Referring to the illegible portion regarding payment, Woltz makes the following comment: "Notice, too, the expression '6000 livres de vignt coppers,' when speaking of the purchase price. This is unusual in a French document but the times were unusual. Everywhere there was complaint about the scarcity of money as currency. . . . Mr. Burnet's extensive trading interests would be sufficient surety for this deal, though there is a definite understanding as to the value of the livre, and Point de Sable takes no chance on local variance. His contract calls for the full value of twenty sous—a copper coin—to the livre, and that the current coinage is mentioned may suggest cash payment. It would seem that his object is to retire from active trading and that the 6000 livre—or about $1200—is to be the 'bird in the hand.'" Letter held in collection of the Chicago History Museum, MSS Alpha DuSable.

59. A. Keating, *Rising Up from Indian Country*, 46.

60. Hugh Heward Journal, Chicago History Museum, MSS Alpha Heward.

61. Quaife, *Checagou*, 40–41.

62. "Point de Sable, Suzanne," in Danckers and Meredith, *Compendium of Early Chicago*, 289.

63. A. Keating, *Rising Up from Indian Country*, 46–47.

64. Frank Grover, *Antoine Ouilmette: A Resident of Chicago A.D. 1790–1826* (Evanston, IL: Evanston Historical Society, 1908), 8.

65. Quaife, *Chicago and the Old Northwest*, 143.

66. Grover, *Antoine Ouilmette*, 8.

67. Grover, *Antoine Ouilmette*, 5–11.

68. William Henry Smith, annotator, *The Life and Public Services of Arthur St. Clair* (Cincinnati: Robert Clarke, 1882), 2:174.

Chapter 5

1. Thomas Jefferson, *Notes on the State of Virginia* (Boston: Wells and Lilly, 1829), 5.

2. Jefferson, *Notes on the State of Virginia*, 7.

3. Quaife, *Chicago and the Old Northwest*, 128.

4. Cunningham, *Letter Book of William Burnett*, 107–8

5. Quaife, *Checagou*, 65–66; quotation from Henry Dearborn in A. Keating, *Rising Up from Indian Country*, 55n13.

6. A. Keating, *Rising Up from Indian Country*, 56n16.

7. A. Keating, *Rising Up from Indian Country*, 56.

8. A. Keating, *Rising Up from Indian Country*, 56–57.

9. For a fuller discussion of Fort Dearborn, see A. Keating, *Rising Up from Indian Country*; Quaife, *Checagou*; and Quaife, *Chicago and the Old Northwest*.

10. I am indebted in the following account to A. Keating, *Rising Up from Indian Country*, 61–64.

11. A. Keating, *Rising Up from Indian Country*, 64–65.

12. Matthew Irwin to William Eustis, December 30, 1809, *The Territory of Illinois, 1809–14*, vol. 16 of *The Territorial Papers of the United States*, ed. Clarence Edwin Carter (Washington, DC: United States Government Printing Office, 1948), 67.

13. Carter, *Territory of Illinois*, 67.
14. A. Keating, *Rising Up from Indian Country*, 88.
15. Irwin to William Eustis, January 19, 1812, Richard Knopf, ed., *Document Transcriptions of the War of 1812*, vol. 6, *Letters to the Secretary of War 1812 Relating to the War of 1812 in the Northwest* (Columbus: Ohio Historical Society, 1959), pt. 1, pp. 18–19.
16. A. Keating, *Rising Up from Indian Country*, 113.
17. Isaac Van Voorhis to William Eustis, May 16, 1812, Knopf, *Document Transcriptions*, 6.1:221.
18. Irwin to Eustis, March 10, 1812, Knopf, *Document Transcriptions*, 6.1:84–85.
19. Carter, *Territory of Illinois*, 212; Irwin to Eustis, April 16, 1812, Knopf, *Document Transcriptions*, 6.1:137.
20. Irwin to Eustis, May 15, 1812, Knopf, *Document Transcriptions*, 6.1:213.
21. Irwin to Eustis, May 15, 1812, Knopf, *Document Transcriptions*, 6.1:214.
22. Van Voorhis to Eustis, May 16, 1812, Knopf, *Document Transcriptions*, 6.1:220.
23. Van Voorhis to Eustis, June 30, 1812, *Document Transcriptions*, 6.1:220.
24. Van Voorhis to Eustis, June 30, 1812, *Document Transcriptions*, 6.1:221.
25. Van Voorhis to Eustis, June 1812, Knopf, *Document Transcriptions*, 6.2:1.
26. Van Voorhis to Eustis, June 30, 1812, Knopf, *Document Transcriptions*, 6.2:67.
27. Van Voorhis to Eustis, June 30, 1812, Knopf, *Document Transcriptions*, 6.2:67.
28. Irwin to Eustis, July 1812, Knopf, *Document Transcriptions*, 6.2:69.
29. Van Voorhis to Eustis, June 30, 1812, *Document Transcriptions*, 6.2:68.
30. Irwin to Eustice, July 1812, *Document Transcriptions*, 6.2:69.
31. To Nathan Heald, April 7, 1812, Richard Knopf, ed., *Document Transcriptions of the War of 1812*, vol. 8, *Letters from the Secretary of War 1812 and 1813 Relating to the War of 1812 in the Northwest* (Columbus: Ohio Historical Society, 1961), 20.
32. Irwin to Eustice, July 1812, 6.2:69.
33. Matthew Irwin to General John Mason, August 6, 1812, in Milo Quaife, "The Fort Dearborn Massacre," *Mississippi Valley Historical Review* 1, no. 4 (1915): 565.
34. For a fascinating account of the murder of Jean Lalime and the subsequent travels made by his remains, see Paul Dailing, "The Long Death of Jean Lalime," *Chicago Reader*, October 18, 2018.
35. Juliette Kinzie, *Narrative of the Massacre at Chicago, August 15, 1812, and of Some Proceeding Events* (Chicago: Fergus Printing Co., 1914), 15 (on Ronan), 30 (on Van Voorhis), 60 (on Lalime).
36. Kinzie, *Narrative of Massacre*, 61–62.
37. Andreas, *History of Chicago*, 1:105.
38. Irwin to Eustice, July 1812, 6.2:70.
39. Matthew Irwin to General John Mason, October 12, 1812, in Quaife, "Fort Dearborn Massacre," 570.
40. Quaife, "Fort Dearborn Massacre," 562.

41. For a discussion of the nativist movement spawned by Tenkswatawa and others, see A. Keating, *Rising Up from Indian Country*, 78–86.

42. Quaife, *Chicago and the Old Northwest*, 216n583.

43. Kinzie, *Wau-Bun*, 166. Helm used almost identical language, writing that Hull's order said "to Evacuate the Post of Fort Dearborne by the route of Detroit of Fort Wayne if Practicable." Quaife, *Chicago and the Old Northwest*, 216, 416. Linai T. Helm, *The Fort Dearborn Massacre: Written in 1814 by Lieutenant Linai T. Helm One of the Survivors, with Letters and Narratives of Contemporary Interest*, ed. Nellie Kinzie Gordon (Chicago: Rand McNally, 1912), 15.

44. A. Keating, *Rising Up from Indian Country*, 130, 130n17.

45. Kinzie, *Wau-Bun*, 166–67.

46. A. Keating, *Rising Up from Indian Country*, 133–34.

47. Geoffrey Johnson, "The True Story of the Deadly Encounter at Fort Dearborn," *Chicago Magazine*, January 4, 2010, https://www.chicagomag.com/Chicago-Magazine/December-2009/The-True-Story-of-the-Deadly-Encounter-at-Fort-Dearborn/.

48. Johnson, "True Story."

49. Quaife, *Chicago and the Old Northwest*, 230, 419; Helm, *The Fort Dearborn Massacre*, 22.

50. Johnson, "True Story."

51. A. Keating, *Rising Up from Indian Country*, 164.

52. A. Keating, *Rising Up from Indian Country*, 170–71.

53. Quaife, *Checagou*, 149.

54. A. Keating, *Rising Up from Indian Country*, 154–55, 155n7.

55. A. Keating, *Rising Up from Indian Country*, 159–60, 160n7.

Chapter 6

1. Hurlbut, *Chicago Antiquities*, 25. Ouilmette, Le Mai, and Pettell are mentioned by name by Julia Whistler, who arrived in Chicago in 1803 with her husband, Second Lieutenant William Whistler.

2. Danckers and Meredith, *Compendium of Early Chicago*, 286. [Please cite essay title that you are quoting from.]

3. Quaife, *Chicago and the Old Northwest*, 288–89.

4. Quaife, *Chicago and the Old Northwest*, 289.

5. Susan Sleeper-Smith, *Indian Women and French Men: Rethinking Cultural Encounter in the Western Great Lakes* (Amherst: University of Massachusetts Press, 2001), 93.

6. Richard White, *The Middle Ground: Indians, Empires, and Republics in the Great Lakes Region, 1650–1815* (Cambridge: Cambridge University Press, 1991), 53n6; See also discussion in Sleeper-Smith, *Indian Women*, 2–5.

7. I am indebted for the following account of the early Métis settlers in Chicago to A. Keating, *Rising Up from Indian Country*, 66–68; and various name entries in Danckers and Meredith, *Compendium of Early Chicago*.

8. Ann Durkin Keating says Shabbona was either brother or father of Mahnaw-bun-no-quah (*Rising Up from Indian Country*, 67), while Danckers and Meredith say he was her brother (*Compendium of Early Chicago*, s.v. "Shabbona," 314). In either event, Shabbona played a significant role in early Chicago

history. He was friendly to the early settlers in Chicago, and although early on he was anti-American and fought with Tecumseh and the British against the Americans, he later reconciled himself to the coming of the Americans. He opposed the Winnebago uprising of 1827 and the Black Hawk War of 1832 and warned the settlers at Chicago about the imminence of the latter. He helped plan the Illinois and Michigan Canal in 1830 and was an important Potawatomi negotiator at the Treaty of Chicago in 1833 (Danckers and Meredith, *Compendium of Early Chicago*, 314).

9. Danckers and Meredith, *Compendium of Early Chicago*, 301–2.

10. Jacqueline Peterson, "'Wild' Chicago: The Formation and Destruction of a Multiracial Community on the Midwestern Frontier, 1816–1837," in *The Ethnic Frontier: Essays in the History of Group Survival in Chicago and the Midwest*, ed. Melvin G. Holli and Peter Jones (Grand Rapids, MI: William B. Eerdmans, 1977), 36.

11. Richard White, "The Middle Ground," n, *Rethinking the Fur Trade: Cultures of Exchange in an Atlantic World*, Susan Sleeper-Smith, ed. (Lincoln: University of Nebraska Press, 2009), 246.

12. Peterson, "'Wild' Chicago," 30.

13. Peterson, "'Wild' Chicago," 31.

14. Peterson, "'Wild' Chicago," 32.

15. R. David Edmunds, "Chicago in the Middle Ground," in *Encyclopedia of Chicago*, ed. James Grossman, Ann Durkin Keating, and Janice L. Reiff (Chicago: University of Chicago Press, 2004), 138–42.

16. Lewis Cass to A. J. Dallas, Acting Secretary of War, June 20, 1815, in Reuben Gold Thwaites, ed., *Collections of the State Historical Society of Wisconsin* (Madison: Democrat Printing Co., 1910), 19:378.

17. John Kinzie to Lewis Cass, July 15, 1815, in Alvord testimony, *Abstract of Proofs*, 1:100–102.

18. The Kinzie home had been temporarily used by two French traders, François Des Pins and Louis Buisson, but upon their return, the Kinzies moved back in. Keating reports that there is some evidence that the Kinzies did not still own the house at that time. In 1821, John Kinzie wrote to his son that they had to "change houses" while awaiting the arrival of "tenants" (A. Keating, *Rising Up from Indian Country*, 215). The legacy of the so-called Kinzie Mansion remains clouded. In 1829 it became a store owned by Anson Taylor, and two years later it became Chicago's first post office and home of Jonathan Bailey. After Bailey, the property was owned by the Mark Noble family. The house fell into disrepair and was later torn down. This did not end the Kinzie legacy, however, because after the city was platted in 1830, John's son Robert Kinzie on March 7, 1831, purchased 102 acres that included the Kinzie homestead. He paid $1.25 acre. He later subdivided this property along with his brother John H. Kinzie, and in a plat dated February 28, 1833, the subdivision is referred to as "Kinzie's Addition to Chicago." Roy Forrey, ed., *Site of the Du Sable Kinzie House* (Chicago: Commission on Chicago Historical and Architectural Landmarks, March 1977), 7. Document contained in collection of the Chicago Historical Society, MSS Alpha DuSable.

19. A. Keating, *Rising Up from Indian Country*, 214.

20. A. Keating, *Rising Up from Indian Country*, 217.

21. Quaife, *Chicago and the Old Northwest*, 278–79.
22. Gurdon S. Hubbard, *The Autobiography of Gurdon Saltonstall Hubbard* (Chicago: Lakeside Press, 1911), 40–43.
23. A. Keating, *Rising Up from Indian Country*, 219.
24. Danckers and Meredith, *Compendium of Early Chicago*, 122.
25. A. Keating, *Rising Up from Indian Country*, 219.
26. Henry R. Schoolcraft, *Narrative Journal of Travels through the Northwestern Regions of the United States* (Albany, NY: E. & E. Hosford, 1821), 384.
27. Schoolcraft, *Narrative Journal*, 384–85.
28. Ebenezer Childs, "Recollections of Wisconsin since 1820," *Collections of the State Historical Society of Wisconsin for the Years 1857 and 1858* (Madison, WI: James Ross, State Printer, 1858), 4:163.
29. William Keating, *Narrative of an Expedition to the Source of St. Peter's River*, 2 vols. in 1 (Philadelphia: H. C. Carey & I. Lea, 1824), 1:164.
30. W. Keating, *Narrative of an Expedition*, 164.
31. John H. Fonda, "Early Reminiscences of Wisconsin," *Collections of the State Historical Society of Wisconsin for the Years 1867, 1868, and 1869* (Madison: Atwood and Rublee, State Printer, 1868), 5: 216–17.
32. A. Keating, *Rising Up from Indian Country*, 198.
33. A. Keating, *Rising Up from Indian Country*, 220.

Chapter 7

1. Rufus Blanchard, *Discovery and Conquests of the Northwest with the History of Chicago* (Chicago: R. Blanchard, 1898), 1:491.
2. Charles G. Davis, "The Indian Boundary Line under the Treaty of August 24, 1816," *Journal of the Illinois State Historical Society* 28, no. 1 (1935): 30.
3. Davis, "Indian Boundary Line," 32. See also *American State Papers, Documents, Legislative and Executive, of the Congress of the United States, From the First Session of the Fourteenth to the Second Session of the Nineteenth Congress, inclusive: Commencing December 4, 1815, and Ending March 3, 1827: Indian Affairs* (Washington, DC: Gales and Seaton, 1834), 2:95–96.
4. Davis, "Indian Boundary Line," 35–36.
5. Davis, "Indian Boundary Line," 37.
6. Davis, "Indian Boundary Line," 27.
7. David W. Scott, "Setting the Northern Border of Illinois," *Journal of the Illinois State Historical Society* 111, no. 3 (2018): 12.
8. Scott, "Setting the Northern Border," 14.
9. Solon Justus Buck, *Illinois in 1818* (Chicago: A. C. McClurg, 1918), 196.
10. James A. Edstrom, "With . . . Candor and Good Faith: Nathaniel Pope and the Enabling Act of 1818," *Illinois Historical Journal* 88, no. 4 (Winter 1995): 242.
11. Buck, *Illinois in 1818*, 203.
12. Buck, *Illinois in 1818*, 209.
13. Edstrom, "With . . . Candor and Good Faith," 242.
14. E. B. Washburne, ed., *The Edwards Papers*, Chicago Historical Society's Collection (Chicago: Fergus Printing Co., 1884), 3:140.
15. Buck, *Illinois in 1818*, 210.
16. Edstrom, "With . . . Candor and Good Faith," 243.

17. Buck, *Illinois in 1818*, 212.
18. Buck, *Illinois in 1818*, 212.
19. Buck, *Illinois in 1818*, 215.
20. Buck, *Illinois in 1818*, 212–13.
21. Buck, *Illinois in 1818*, 219–20.
22. Buck, *Illinois in 1818*, 213.
23. Buck, *Illinois in 1818*, 214.
24. Edstrom, "With . . . Candor and Good Faith," 245.
25. Buck, *Illinois in 1818*, 221.
26. Buck, *Illinois in 1818*, 221.
27. *Western Intelligencer*, March 11, 1818, p. 2, col. 4, quoted in Edstrom, "With . . . Candor and Good Faith," 246.
28. *Annals of the Congress of the United States*, 15th Cong., 1st Sess. (Washington, DC: Gales and Seaton, 1854), 1677.
29. *Annals of Cong.* (1854), 1677.
30. Buck, *Illinois in 1818*, 225–26.
31. Buck, *Illinois in 1818*, 227.
32. Edstrom, "With . . . Candor and Good Faith," 257.
33. *Western Intelligencer*, May 6, 1818, quoted in Buck, *Illinois in 1818*, 229.
34. *Western Intelligencer*, May 6, 1818, p. 3, col. 3, quoted in Edstrom, "With . . . Candor and Faith," 261.
35. *Western Intelligencer*, May 6, 1818, p. 3, cols. 3–34, quoted in Edstrom, "With . . . Candor and Good Faith," 261–62.
36. *Annals of Cong.* (1854), 1677.
37. Thomas Ford, *A History of Illinois from its Commencement as a State in 1818 to 1847* (Chicago: S. C. Griggs, 1854), 22–23.
38. Scott, "Setting Northern Border," 29–30.
39. John Moses, *Illinois, Historical and Statistical, Comprising the Essential Facts of its Planting and Growth as a Province, County, Territory, and State* (Chicago: Fergus Printing Co., 1889), 277.
40. William A. Meese, "Nathaniel Pope," *Journal of the Illinois State Historical Society* 3, no. 4 (January 1911): 16.

Chapter 8

1. W. L. G. Smith, *The Life and Times of Lewis Cass* (New York: Derby & Jackson, 1856), 188.
2. Quaife, *Checagou*, 171–72.
3. The following account of the 1832 epidemic is taken from John Hamilton, "The Epidemics of Chicago," *Bulletin of the Society of Medical History of Chicago* 1, no. 1 (October 1911): 75–79; G. F. Pyle, "The Diffusion of Cholera in the United States in the Nineteenth Century," *Geographical Analysis* 1 (January 1969): 60–65.
4. For the story of Chicago's quest for fresh drinking water, see Benjamin Sells, *The Tunnel under the Lake: The Engineering Marvel That Saved Chicago* (Evanston, IL: Northwestern University Press, 2017). The above account of the first cholera outbreak in Chicago is taken from that book. Sells, *The Tunnel under the Lake*, 11–12.

5. Roger Biles, *Illinois: A History of the Land and its People* (DeKalb: Northern Illinois University Press, 2005), 59.
6. Herbert J. Bassman, ed., *Riverside Then and Now: A History of Riverside, Illinois* (Riverside, IL: Riverside Historical Commission, 1995), 19.
7. Bassman, *Riverside Then and Now*, 23–25.
8. Transcription by the author.
9. Knight and Zeuch, *Location of Chicago Portage*, 51.
10. Knight and Zeuch, *Location of Chicago Portage*, 51.
11. Knight and Zeuch, *Location of Chicago Portage*, 51–52.
12. Bassman, *Riverside Then and Now*, 17.
13. Knight and Zeuch, *Location of Chicago Portage*, 53.
14. Knight and Zeuch, *Location of Chicago Portage*, 66–70.
15. Knight and Zeuch, *Location of Chicago Portage*, 70–71.
16. Philip Vierling, *Chicago Portage Ledger* 4, no. 2 (May–August 2003): 4. Issues of Vierling's self-published *Chicago Portage Ledger*, a newsletter for Friends of the Chicago Portage National Historic Site, 2000–2016, are available online at https://digitalcollections.library.cmu.edu/knowvation/app/consolidatedSearch/#search/v=thumbnails,c=1,q=qs%3D%5B*%5D%2Cfacet-fields%3D%5Bbrowse1_ss%3A%22Chicago%20Portage%22%3E%3Ebrowse2_ss%3A%22Chicago%20Portage%20Ledger%22%5D%2CqueryType%3D%5B64%5D,sm=s,l=library4_lib,a=t.
17. Kinzie, *Wau-bun*, 142–43.
18. Bassman, *Riverside Then and Now*, 19n2.
19. Kinzie, *Wau-bun*, 237.
20. Andreas, *History of Chicago*, 1:192.
21. Quoted in Bassman, *Riverside Then and Now*, 29.
22. Bassman, *Riverside Then and Now*, 29.

Chapter 9

1. *American State Papers, Indian Affairs*, 1:562.
2. Jefferson, *Notes on the State of Virginia*, 5.
3. *American State Papers, Documents, Legislative and Executive, of the Congress of the United States, From the First Session of the First to the Second Session of the Tenth Congress, inclusive: Commencing March 3, 1789, and Ending March 3, 1809: Miscellaneous* (Washington, DC: Gales and Seaton, 1834), 1:735.
4. *Annals of the Congress of the United States*, 11th Cong., 1st and 2nd Sess. (Washington, DC: Gales and Seaton, 1853), 2:1388.
5. *Annals of Cong.* (1853), 1390.
6. "Resources and improvements," *Niles' Weekly Register* 6, no. 23, supplement (Aug. 6, 1814): 394, italic in the original.
7. "Resources and Improvements: Steam Boat Navigation," *Niles' Weekly Register* 6, no. 25 (Aug. 20, 1814): 417.
8. *American State Papers, Documents, Legislative and Executive, of the Congress of the United States, From the First Session of the Eleventh to the Second Session of the Seventeenth Congress, inclusive: Commencing May 22, 1809, and Ending March 3, 1823: Miscellaneous* (Washington, DC: Gales and Seaton, 1834), 2:556. For an extended excerpt of Long's report, see appendix A. For his

full report, see L. H. Long, "Topography," *National Register* 13, no. 3 (March 29, 1817): 193–98.

9. Walter A. Howe, *Documentary History of the Illinois and Michigan Canal: Legislation, Litigation and Titles* (Springfield: State of Illinois, Department of Public Works and Buildings, Division of Waterways, 1956), 34.

10. *American State Papers, Miscellaneous*, 2:557.

11. *American State Papers, Miscellaneous*, 2:557.

12. *American State Papers, Miscellaneous*, 2:557.

13. *American State Papers, Miscellaneous*, 2:535.

14. Samuel A. Storrow, "The North-West in 1817," *Report and Collections of the State Historical Society of Wisconsin, for the years 1869, 1870, 1871 and 1872*, Wisconsin Historical Collections 6 (Madison, WI: State Historical Society of Wisconsin, 1872), 180.

15. James W. Putnam, *The Illinois and Michigan Canal: A Study in Economic History* (Chicago: University of Chicago Press, 1918), 10–11.

16. Quoted in G. P. Brown, *Drainage Channel and Waterway* (Chicago: R. R. Donnelly and Sons, 1894), 133.

17. Excerpt quoted in Lyman E. Cooley, *Diversion of the Waters of the Great Lakes by Way of the Sanitary and Ship Canal of Chicago* (Chicago: Clohesey, 1913), 100. For the full newspaper article, see *Abstract of Proofs*, 1:106–8.

18. Putnam, *Illinois and Michigan Canal*, 12.

19. *Annals of Cong.* (1854), 526.

20. *Annals of Cong.* (1854), 526.

21. *Abstract of Proofs*, 2:2427.

22. *Abstract of Proofs*, 2:2441.

23. Putnam, *Illinois and Michigan Canal*, 24–25.

24. Putnam, *Illinois and Michigan Canal*, 28.

25. Sells, *The Tunnel under the Lake*, 145.

26. For a detailed history of the Illinois and Michigan Canal, see Putnam, *Illinois and Michigan Canal*; G. Brown, *Drainage Channel and Waterway*; Michael P. Conzen and Kay J. Carr, eds., *The Illinois & Michigan Canal National Heritage Corridor: A Guide to Its History and Sources* (DeKalb: Northern Illinois University Press, 1988); A. Berle Clemenson, *Illinois and Michigan Canal, National Heritage Corridor: Historical Inventory, History, and Significance* (Denver: National Park Service, 1985); Howe, *Documentary History of Illinois and Michigan Canal.*

27. National Park Service, "National Historic Areas," last updated March 15, 2019, https://www.nps.gov/subjects/heritageareas/index.htm.

Chapter 10

1. Quaife, *Chicago and the Old Northwest*, 3.

2. *Abstract of Proofs*, 1597–602.

3. Knight and Zeuch, *Location of Chicago Portage*, x.

4. Knight and Zeuch, *Location of Chicago Portage*, 31.

5. Knight and Zeuch, *Location of Chicago Portage*, 20, 34.

6. *Abstract of Proofs*, 1:580.

7. Knight and Zeuch, *Location of Chicago Portage*, 21.

8. Knight and Zeuch, *Location of Chicago Portage*, 38–40. The last number given by Knight and Zeuch was 150 days, which would exceed 365. It has been changed here to 140 days.
9. Andreas, *History of Chicago*, 3:135; Knight and Zeuch, *Location of Chicago Portage*, 37.
10. Knight and Zeuch, *Location of Chicago Portage*, 37.
11. Andreas, *History of Chicago*, 3:135–36.
12. Libby Hill, *The Chicago River: A Natural and Unnatural History* (Chicago: Lake Claremont Press, 2000), 122.
13. Knight and Zeuch, *Location of Chicago Portage*, 33.
14. Knight and Zeuch, *Location of Chicago Portage*, 62, 62n41.
15. Knight and Zeuch, *Location of Chicago Portage*, 62.
16. Knight and Zeuch, *Location of Chicago Portage*, 45–46nn33–35.
17. Knight and Zeuch, *Location of Chicago Portage*, 72.
18. Knight and Zeuch, *Location of Chicago Portage*, 44–46.
19. *Abstract of Proofs*, 1:633–34.
20. Hill, *Chicago River*, 214–15.

Chapter 11

1. *Transcript of Record, Supreme Court of the United States, October Term, 1913, No. 179, The People of the State of Illinois on the Relation of Charles S. Deneen, Governor, and William H. Stead, Attorney General, Plaintiffs in Error vs. The Economy Light and Power Company*, 3 vols. (Washington, DC: Judd & Detweiler, Printers, June 30, 1913), 1:17.
2. "Outlook Is Dark for Canal Board," *Chicago Daily Tribune*, November 23, 1907, 3. The Illinois House of Representatives appointed a committee to investigate the actions of Snively and Sackett regarding their transactions with Griswold and Munroe.
3. "Drainage Board Foe of Monopoly," *Chicago Daily Tribune*, January 16, 1908, 2.
4. Abstract of Proofs, *United States of America vs. Economy Light and Power Company*, United States District Court for the Northern District of Illinois, Eastern Division, In Chancery, no. 29776, 4 vols. (Chicago: Gunthorp-Warren Printing Co., 1912), 3:3183.
5. *Abstract of Proofs*, 3:2475–76.
6. *Transcript of Record, No. 179*, 2:1003–6.
7. "See State Gain; Win Back Rivers?" *Chicago Daily Tribune*, November 21, 1907, 4.
8. "Sanitary District Fights for Land Worth Millions," *Chicago Daily Tribune*, January 25, 1907, 5.
9. "Will Ask State to Remove Dam," *Chicago Daily Tribune*, March 12, 1907, 2.
10. "To Make Chicago Best Lighted City," *Chicago Daily Tribune*, March 13, 1907, 20.
11. "Moving to Indict Officials," *Chicago Daily Tribune*, March 16, 1907, 3.
12. "Deep Waterway Project Boosted," *Chicago Daily Tribune*, April 5, 1907, 4.
13. "Drainage Forces Move on Capital," *Chicago Daily Tribune*, October 22, 1907, 9.

14. "Power Concerns Seek Cooley Aid?" *Chicago Daily Tribune*, March 2, 1911, 13.

15. *Laws of the State of Illinois enacted by the Forty-Fifth General Assembly at the Adjourned Session* (Springfield: Phillips Bros., State Printers, 1908), 32–33.

16. "Senate Paves Way for State Holdup," *Chicago Daily Tribune*, November 2, 1907, 6.

17. "Inspect Canal in Comfort," *Chicago Daily Tribune*, November 13, 1907, 3.

18. "Effort to Check Dresden Inquiry," *Chicago Daily Tribune*, November 24, 1907, 3.

19. "Speaks Up for Economy Co.," *Chicago Daily Tribune*, November 5, 1907, 4, in which Insull says there had been no lobbying; "Block Waterway? No, Says Insull," *Chicago Daily Tribune*, December 28, 1907, 4, in which Insull admits to having lobbyists in Springfield.

20. "Committee Ends Canal Hearings," *Chicago Daily Tribune*, January 1, 1908, 14.

21. "Three Views of the Canal Deal," *Chicago Daily Tribune*, January 16, 1908, 2.

22. "Canal Report Stands Approved," *Chicago Daily Tribune*, January 17, 1908, 6.

23. "Snively Resigns; Sackett to Quit?" *Chicago Daily Tribune*, February 22, 1910, 2.

24. "Precinct Hero Wins Tax Job from Sanborn," *Chicago Daily Tribune*, August 9, 1921.

25. "Editor Snively of Canton, Ill., Dead at 84 Years," *Chicago Daily Tribune*, September 22, 1937.

26. "Dunne to Oust Jobholders," *Chicago Daily Tribune*, July 12, 1913, 4.

27. "Governor Gives Appointments for Many Jobs," *Chicago Daily Tribune*, May 29, 1917, 5; "Wm. L. Sackett, Head of State Waterways, Dies," *Chicago Daily Tribune*, December 16, 1924.

28. *Journal of the House of Representatives of the Forty-Fifth General Assembly of the State of Illinois* (Springfield: Illinois State Journal Co, State Printers, 1908), 1520.

29. *Journal of the House*, 1521.

30. *Journal of the House*, 1522.

31. William H. Stead, *Biennial Report of the Attorney General of the State of Illinois* (Springfield: Illinois State Journal Co., State Printers, December 1908), 90.

32. *Transcript of Record, No. 179*, 1:6–8.

33. *Transcript of Record, No. 179*, 1:9.

34. *Transcript of Record, No. 179*, 1:21.

35. *Transcript of Record, No. 179*, 1:53.

36. *Transcript of Record, No. 179*, 1:681–764.

37. *Transcript of Record, No. 179*, 1:155–62.

38. *Statement of the Case, Brief of Points and Authorities, Argument for the Appellant, In the Supreme Court of Illinois, February Term, A. D. 1909, People of the State of Illinois, ex rel. Charles S. Deneen, Governor, and William H. Stead, Attorney General vs. Economy Light & Power Company* (Chicago: Gunthorp-Warren Printing Co., 1909), appendix 1, 3.

39. *Statement of Case*, 201–28.

40. *Transcript of Record, No. 179*, 3:2577. The court's opinion can also be found at 241 Ill. 290, 89 N.E. 760 (1908). The abstract of record totaled 1,958 pages. *Abstract of Record, In the Supreme Court of Illinois, Original Record returned to October Term, A. D. 1908, and Cause continued to February Term, A. D. 1909, People of the State of Illinois, ex rel. Charles S. Deneen, Governor, and William H. Stead, Attorney General vs. Economy Light & Power Company* (Chicago: Gunthorp-Warren Printing Co., 1908).

41. *Transcript of Record, No. 179*, 3:2585.

42. *Transcript of Record, No. 179*, 3:2587.

43. *Transcript of Record, No. 179*, 3:2589.

44. People of State of Illinois ex rel. Dunne v. Economy Light & Power Company, 234 US 497, 523–24 (1914).

45. *Abstract of Proofs*,4:3200–3201.

46. *Abstract of Proofs*, 4:3205.

47. For Alvord testimony, see *Abstract of Proofs*, 1:1. For McLaughlin, see *Abstract of Proofs*, 1:312. For Thwaites, see *Abstract of Proofs*, 1:363.

48. *Abstract of Proofs*, 1:170.

49. For Lee testimony, see *Abstract of Proofs*, 2:1089. For Quaife, see *Abstract of Proofs*, 2:1399.

50. *Abstract of Proofs*, 4:3237.

51. *Abstract of Proofs*, 4:3237.

52. *Abstract of Proofs*, 4:3237–38.

53. Economy Power & Light Company v. United States, 256 F. 792 (1919) at 793.

54. *Economy Power & Light*, 256 F. 797.

55. *Economy Power & Light*, 256 F. 797. The court, relying on the testimony of Clarence Alvord, cited fourteen specific instances of the use of the Des Plaines River down to the year 1830: Marquette and Joliet, 1673; Perrault, 1783; Marquette, 1674; Joutel, 1688; Heward, 1790; Hubbard, 1819; Furman, 1830; Ebenezer Childs, 1821; Fonda, 1825; Tonty, 1680; La Salle, 1681; Membre, 1682; St.-Cosme, 1698; and Hubbard, 1818. See Alvord testimony, *Abstract of Proofs*, 1:209. Perrault and Furman's accounts of the Chicago Portage route are fleeting. Jean Baptiste Perrault accompanied a trading adventure in 1783 and made passing mention of the Chicago Portage route: "We left Cahokia on the 4th of May, for Mackinac directions were to pass by Chicago, having one barge and one canoe." Perrault's account is found in Henry Schoolcraft, *Archives of Aboriginal Knowledge* (Philadelphia: J. B. Lippincott, 1860), 3:355. Lieutenant John G. Furman, in a letter written from Fort Dearborn in 1830, noted that while pursuing several deserters, "We passed up the left branch of the Chicago to its source, and thence . . . through 'Lac Marias' [Mud Lake] into the river Aux Pleins (Soft Maple River) [Des Plaines River]." Letter quoted in Hurlbut, *Chicago Antiquities*, 88. The remaining accounts are found within the current work.

56. *Economy Power & Light*, 256 F. 799.

57. *Economy Power & Light*, 256 F. 804.

58. Economy Power & Light Company v. United States, 256 U.S. 113 (1921) at 121.

59. *Economy Power & Light*, 256 U.S. at 122.

60. *Economy Power & Light*, 256 U.S. at 123.
61. *Economy Power & Light*, 256 U.S. at 124.
62. *Economy Power & Light*, 256 U.S. at 124.
63. "Way Cleared for State to Build Waterway Link," *Chicago Daily Tribune*, September 9, 1927, 6.
64. "Money Only Bar to Opening Seaway in 1931," *Chicago Daily Tribune*, November 24, 1928, 4.
65. "Midwest Starts Drive to Finish Waterway Job," *Chicago Daily Tribune*, January 19, 1929, 4.
66. "A History of Chicanery," *Chicago Daily Tribune*, May 16, 1911, 8.
67. For the full record of evidence accumulated in the federal case, see *Transcript of Record, Supreme Court of the United States, October Term 1920, No. 104, Economy Power & Light Company vs. The United States of America* (n.p., 1920).

Chapter 12

1. The land that is now the Chicago Portage National Historic Site was owned by various private individuals starting in 1835 and was owned by William B. Ogden in 1856. On August 23, 1893, the property was sold to the Sanitary District of Chicago by Marianne A. Ogden, William O. Wheeler, and Andrew H. Green, the surviving executors and trustees of the last will and testament of William B. Ogden, for $31,485. Philip Vierling, *Chicago Portage Ledger* 1, no. 1 (January/June 2000): 5. For details about this publication and online access to its issues, refer back to note 15 to chapter 8.
2. Forest Preserve District of Cook County, *Official Record of the Proceedings of the Board of Forest Preserve Commissioners for the Forest Preserve District of Cook County, in the State of Illinois* (Chicago: Calumet Publishing, 1929), 289. The Sanitary District had authorized the land grant at its meeting on September 12, 1929. Sanitary District of Chicago, *Proceedings of the Board of Trustees of the Sanitary District of Chicago* (Chicago: Fred. Klein, 1929), 493. The Forest Preserve subsequently approved a resolution accepting an additional parcel from the Sanitary District on March 16, 1931. Forest Preserve District of Cook County, *Official Record of the Proceedings of the Board of Forest Preserve Commissioners for the Forest Preserve District of Cook County, in the State of Illinois* (Chicago: Calumet Publishing, 1931), 88–89.
3. "Portage Will Be Restored as Trading Post in Days of 1673," *Chicago Daily Tribune*, September 21, 1929.
4. "Approve Plans to Restore Ole Chicago Portage: Forest Preserve Board to Start Work in May," *Chicago Daily Tribune*, March 6, 1930.
5. Olaf T. Hagen, *A Study of the Chicago Portage (Proposed National Historic Site)*, (Omaha, NE: National Park Service, 1949), 8.
6. Hagen, *A Study of the Chicago Portage*, 20.
7. Hagen, *A Study of the Chicago Portage*, 20–21.
8. Forest Preserve District of Cook County, *Official Record of the Proceedings of the Board of Forest Preserve Commissioners for the Forest Preserve District of Cook County, in the State of Illinois* (Chicago: Calumet Publishing Co., 1950), 26.
9. "Chicago Portage National Historic Site Designation as a National Historic Site," 17 Fed. Reg. 236 (January 9, 1952). The order is also available in National

Park Service, Department of the Interior, *Proclamations and Orders Relating to the National Park Service: January 1, 1945 to January 20, 2001* (Washington, DC: National Park Service, 2004), 2:16–17. In earlier citations, the order was referred to as "Order of January 3, 1952, designating the Chicago Portage National Historic Site, Illinois," *Cooperative Agreements and Historic Site Designation Orders, Historic Site Designation Orders, General*, pt. 170, chap. 14, sect. 1.23. According to the United States Department of the Interior, "The Interior Department's *Cooperative Agreement and Historic Site Designation Orders* was a compilation of orders, directives, and memorandums mainly approved at the Secretarial level and reorganized by subject matter by the Department of the Interior into volumes under that title. The subject areas were also assigned specific classification numbers." George Franchois, director, United States Department of the Interior Library, email message to author, July 25, 2019. This compilation ceased around the late 1950s or early 1960s. A copy of the cooperative agreement is reprinted in William E. Rose and Associates, *Design Study: The Chicago Portage and Laughton Trading Post Area, "The Waterway West"* (Hinsdale, IL: Wm. E. Rose and Associates, 1975), 55–56. For the full text of the order, see appendix C.

10. Philip E. Vierling, *Chicago Portage Ledger* 3, no. 2 (May/August 2002): 8–9.

11. A copy of the resolution can be found in Roland F. Eisenbeis, *Background, Purpose, and Objectives for the Archeological Exploration of the Chicago Portage and Laughton's Trading Post in the Forest Preserve District of Cook County* (River Forest, IL: Forest Preserve District of Cook County, 1974), 14. Document located in the collection of the Chicago History Museum, qF38HS:C66.

12. Eisenbeis, *Background, Purpose, and Objectives*, 8.

13. Eisenbeis, *Background, Purpose, and Objectives*, 18.

14. Margaret Kimball Brown, "The Laughton Trading Post," in Rose, *Design Study*, 67.

15. Prairie Research Institute, *Natural and Cultural Resources Master Plan* (Champaign: University of Illinois, 2014), 48.

16. Paula Bryant, email message to author, May 6, 2019.

17. Bryant email, May 6, 2019.

18. Paula Bryant, email message to author, May 7, 2019.

19. Rose, *Design Study*, 35–36.

20. Rose, *Design Study*, 36.

21. Rose, *Design Study*, 38–41.

22. Rose, *Design Study*, 42.

23. Rose, *Design Study*, 47.

24. "National Registry of Historic Places Inventory—Nomination Form—Chicago Portage National Historic Site," United States Department of the Interior, received Feb. 22, 1978, approved Nov. 11, 1978, Asset ID 35a222f6-7913-4c4b-9627-d34dd0864e10, NPGallery Digital Asset Management System, National Park Service, https://npgallery.nps.gov/AssetDetail/NRIS/66000108.

25. John D. Peine, Debora A. Neurohr, *Illinois and Michigan Canal Corridor: A Concept Plan* (Ann Arbor, MI: National Park Service, 1981).

26. Peine and Neurohr, *Illinois and Michigan Canal Corridor*, iii, 17.

27. Peine and Neurohr, *Illinois and Michigan Canal Corridor*, 46.

28. For a full discussion of the establishing of the heritage corridor, see Canal Corridor Association, *A Roadmap for the Future* (LaSalle, IL: Canal Corridor Association, 2011), https://iandmcanal.org/road-map/. See also National Park Service, "National Historic Areas."

29. Illinois and Michigan Canal National Heritage Corridor Civic Center Authority, *Application for State Financial Support for the Chicago Portage Historical Site Interpretive Center* (Willow Springs, IL: Illinois and Michigan Canal National Heritage Corridor Civic Center Authority, 1990).

30. *Chicago Tribune*, July 15, 1983.

31. The above account of the design, fabrication, installation, and construction details are from Glenn Rebechini, Ferdinand G. Rebechini's son, in a telephone conversation with the author, January 4, 2021.

32. Illinois and Michigan Canal National Heritage Corridor Civic Center Authority, *Application*, 320.

33. Illinois and Michigan Canal National Heritage Corridor Civic Center Authority, *Application*, 31.

34. July 24, 1989, letter in Illinois and Michigan Canal National Heritage Corridor Civic Center Authority, *Application*," 33.

35. Illinois and Michigan Canal National Heritage Corridor Civic Center Authority, *Application*, 324.

36. Illinois and Michigan Canal National Heritage Corridor Civic Center Authority, *Application*, 364–83.

37. Illinois and Michigan Canal National Heritage Corridor Civic Center Authority, *Application*, 322.

38. Illinois and Michigan Canal National Heritage Corridor Civic Center Authority, *Application*, 325.

39. General Superintendent Joseph N. Nevius to President and Members of the Board of Forest Preserve Commissioners, January 14, 1999. Forest Preserve District of Cook County.

40. Nevius to Commissioners.

41. Archaeological Research, *Chicago Portage Literature Overview and Assessment* (Chicago: Archaeological Research, 1999), i.

42. Archaeological Research, *Chicago Portage Literature*, 3.

43. See Chicago Portage website, http://drupal.library.cmu.edu/chicago/.

44. Gary Mechanic, telephone conversation with the author, June 24, 2019. Mechanic provided much of the foregoing history regarding the founding of the Friends of the Chicago Portage.

45. The Swamp to City curriculum is available online at http://drupal.library.cmu.edu/chicago/node/133.

46. Philip E. Vierling, *A Self Guided Loop Hiking Trail to the Chicago Portage National Historic Site* (Chicago: Illinois Country Hiking Guide, 1973).

47. Chicago Portage, "Friends Forever," accessed June 24, 2019, http://drupal.library.cmu.edu/chicago/node/142.

48. Canal Corridor Association, *I&M Canal National Heritage Corridor Interpretive Plan 2005* (La Salle, IL: Canal Corridor Association, 2005), 43.

49. Canal Corridor Association, *I&M Interpretive Plan*, 43.

50. Canal Corridor Association, *I&M Interpretive Plan*, 50.

51. Kindy Kruller, in-person conversation with the author, July 12, 2019.

52. Design Workshop, *Chicago Portage National Historic Site Master Plan* (Chicago: Design Workshop, 2018), 1.
53. Design Workshop, *Master Plan*, 23–27.
54. Design Workshop, *Master Plan*, 30–33.
55. Design Workshop, *Master Plan*, 36.
56. Design Workshop, *Master Plan*, 36.
57. Design Workshop, *Master Plan*, 37.

BIBLIOGRAPHY

Abstract of Proofs, United States of America vs. Economy Light and Power Company, United States District Court for the Northern District of Illinois, Eastern Division, In Chancery, No. 29776, 4 vols. Chicago: Gunthorp-Warren Printing Co., 1912.

Abstract of Record, In the Supreme Court of Illinois, Original Record returned to October Term, A. D. 1908, and Cause continued to February Term, A. D. 1909, People of the State of Illinois, ex rel. Charles S. Deneen, Governor, and William H. Stead, Attorney General vs. Economy Light & Power Company. Chicago: Gunthorp-Warren Printing Co., 1908.

Alden, William C. "Description of the Chicago District." In *Geologic Atlas of the United States*, folio 81. Reston, Va.: US Geological Survey, 1902.

American State Papers, Documents, Legislative and Executive, of the Congress of the United States, From the First Session of the Eleventh to the Second Session of the Seventeenth Congress, inclusive: Commencing May 22, 1809, and Ending March 3, 1823: Miscellaneous. Vol. 2. Washington, DC: Gales and Seaton, 1834.

American State Papers, Documents, Legislative and Executive, of the Congress of the United States, From the First Session of the First to the Second Session of the Tenth Congress, inclusive: Commencing March 3, 1789, and Ending March 3, 1809: Miscellaneous. Vol. 1. Washington, DC: Gales and Seaton, 1834.

American State Papers, Documents, Legislative and Executive, of the Congress of the United States, From the First Session of the First to the Third Session of the Thirteenth Congress, inclusive: Commencing March 3, 1789, and Ending March 3, 1815: Indian Affairs. Vol. 1. Washington, DC: Gales and Seaton, 1832.

American State Papers, Documents, Legislative and Executive, of the Congress of the United States, From the First Session of the Fourteenth to the Second Session of the Nineteenth Congress, inclusive: Commencing December 4, 1815, and Ending March 3, 1827: Indian Affairs. Vol. 2. Washington, DC: Gales and Seaton, 1834.

Andreas, Alfred T. *History of Chicago from the Earliest Period to the Present Time*. 3 vols. Chicago: Alfred T. Andreas, 1884–86.

Archaeological Research. *Chicago Portage Literature Overview and Assessment* Chicago: Archaeological Research, 1999.

Bassman, Herbert, ed. *Riverside Then and Now: A History of Riverside, Illinois*. Riverside, IL: Riverside Historical Commission, 1995.

Baumann, Timothy. "The Du Sable Grave Project in St. Charles, Missouri." *Missouri Archaeologist* 66 (December 2005): 59–66.

Beckwith, Hiram. *The Illinois and Indiana Indians*. Chicago: Fergus Printing Company, 1884.

———, ed. *Collections of the Illinois State Historical Library*. Vol. 1. Springfield, IL: H. W. Rokker, 1903.

Biles, Roger. *Illinois: A History of the Land and Its People*. DeKalb: Northern Illinois University Press, 2005.

Perrot, Nicholas. "Memoir of the Manners, Customs, and Religions of the Savages of North America." In *The Indian Tribes of the Upper Mississippi Valley and Region of the Great Lakes.*, edited by Emma Helen Blair. Cleveland: Arthur H. Clarke, 1911.

Blanchard, Rufus. *Discovery and Conquests of the North-West, with the History of Chicago*. Wheaton, IL: R. Blanchard, 1881.

———. *Discovery and Conquests of the Northwest with the History of Chicago*. Vol. 1. Chicago: R. Blanchard, 1898.

Blasingham, Emily. "Indians of the Chicago Area." In *Chicago Area Archaeology*, Illinois Archaeological Survey Bulletin 3, rev. ed., edited by Elaine A. Bluhm, 163–73. Urbana: University of Illinois, 1983. First published 1961 by Southern Illinois University.

Bretz, J. Harlan. "The Double Calumet Stage of Lake Chicago." *Journal of Geology* 67, no. 1 (November 1959): 675–84.

———. *Geology of the Chicago Region: Part II–The Pleistocene*. Illinois State Geological Survey Bulletin 65, pt. 2. Urbana: State of Illinois Department of Registration and Education, 1955.

Brown, G. P. *Drainage Channel and Waterway: A History of the Effort to Secure an Effective and Harmless Method for the Disposal of the Sewage in the City of Chicago and to Create a Navigable Channel between Lake Michigan and the Mississippi River*. Chicago: R. R. Donnelly and Sons, 1894.

Brown, James A. "The Northeastern Extension of the Havana Tradition." In *Hopewellian Studies*, edited by Joseph Caldwell and Robert Hall, 107–22. Illinois State Museum Scientific Papers 12.4. Springfield: Illinois State Museum, 1964.

———. "The Prairie Peninsula: An Interaction Area in the Eastern United States." PhD diss., University of Chicago, 1965.

Buck, Solon Justus. *Illinois in 1818*. Chicago: A. C. McClurg, 1918.

Burton, M. Agnes, ed. *Collections and Researches Made by the Michigan Pioneer and Historical Society*, reprint 19. Lansing, MI: Wynkoop Hallenbeck Crawford, 1911.

———. *Collections and Researches Made by the Michigan Pioneer and Historical Society*, reprint 20. Lansing, MI: Wynkoop Hallenbeck Crawford, 1912.

Canal Corridor Association. *I&M Canal National Heritage Corridor Interpretive Plan 2005*. La Salle, IL: Canal Corridor Association, 2005.

———. *Illinois and Michigan Canal National Heritage Corridor: A Roadmap for the Future, 2011–2021*. La Salle, IL: Canal Corridor Association, 2011. https://iandmcanal.org/road-map/.

Carter, Clarence Edwin, ed. *The Territory of Illinois, 1809–14*. Vol. 16 of *The Territorial Papers of the United States*. Washington, DC: United States Government Printing Office, 1948.

Chardon, Roland. "The Linear League in North America." *Annals of the Association of American Geographers* 70, no. 2 (June 1980): 129–53.

Chicago Historical Society. *Chicago Historical Society Annual Report: 1905.* Chicago: Chicago Historical Society, 1905.

Childs, Ebenezer. "Recollections of Wisconsin since 1820." In *Collections of the State Historical Society of Wisconsin for the Years 1857 and 1858*, 4:163–95. Madison: James Ross, State Printer, 1858.

Chrzastowski, Michael J. *The Chicago River—a Legacy of Glacial and Coastal Processes: Guidebook for the 2009 Meeting of the North-Central Section of the Geological Society of America.* Champaign: Illinois Geological Survey, 2009.

Chrzastowski, Michael J., and Todd A. Thompson. "Late Wisconsinan and Holocene Geologic History of the Illinois-Indiana Coast of Lake Michigan." *Journal of Great Lakes Research* 20, no. 1 (January 1994): 9–26.

Clemenson, A. Berle. *Illinois and Michigan Canal, National Heritage Corridor: Historical Inventory, History, and Significance.* Denver: National Park Service, 1985.

Conzen, Michael P., and Kay J. Carr, eds. *The Illinois & Michigan Canal National Heritage Corridor: A Guide to Its History and Sources.* DeKalb: Northern Illinois University Press, 1988.

Cooley, Lyman E. *Diversion of the Waters of the Great Lakes by Way of the Sanitary and Ship Canal of Chicago: A Brief of the Facts and Issues.* Chicago: Clohesey, 1913.

Cunningham, Wilbur, ed. *Letter Book of William Burnett: Early Fur Trader in the Land of Four Flags.* St. Joseph, MI: Fort Miami Heritage Society of Michigan, 1967.

Dailing, Paul. "The Long Death of Jean Lalime." *Chicago Reader*, October 18, 2018.

Danckers, Ulrich. "French Chicago during the 18th Century." In Danckers and Meredith, *Compendium of Early History of Chicago*, 383–87.

Danckers, Ulrich, and Jane Meredith, eds. *A Compendium of the Early History of Chicago to the Year 1835 when the Indians Left.* River Forest, IL: Early Chicago, 2000.

Davis, Charles G. "The Indian Boundary Line under the Treaty of August 24, 1816." *Journal of the Illinois State Historical Society* 28, no. 1 (April 1935): 26–64.

Delanglez, Jean. "The Jolliet Lost Map of the Mississippi." *Mid-America: An Historical Review*, n.s., 17, no. 2 (April 1946): 67–144.

———. *Life and Voyages of Louis Jolliet (1645–1700).* Chicago: Institute of Jesuit History, 1948.

———. "The 'Recit des voyages et des decouvertes du Pere Jacques Marquette' Part 1." *Mid-America: An Historical Review*, n.s., 17, no. 3 (July 1946): 173–94.

Design Workshop. *Chicago Portage National Historic Site Master Plan.* Chicago: Design Workshop, 2018.

Dolin, Eric Jay. *Fur, Fortune, and Empire: The Epic History of the Fur Trade in America.* New York: W. W. Norton, 2010.

Edmunds, R. David. "Chicago in the Middle Ground," in Grossman, Keating, and Reiff, *Encyclopedia of Chicago*, 138–42.

Edstrom, James A. "With . . . Candor and Good Faith: Nathaniel Pope and the Enabling Act of 1818." *Illinois Historical Journal* 88, no. 4 (Winter 1995): 241–62.

Eisenbeis, Roland F. *Background, Purpose, and Objectives for the Archeological Exploration of the Chicago Portage and Laughton's Trading Post in the Forest Preserve District of Cook County*. River Forest, IL: Forest Preserve District of Cook County, 1974. Chicago History Museum, qF38HS:C66.

Emerson, Thomas. "Some Perspectives on Cahokia and the Northern Mississippian Expansion." In Emerson and Lewis, *Cahokia and the Hinterlands*, 221–36.

Emerson, Thomas, and Barry Lewis, eds. *Cahokia and the Hinterlands: Middle Mississippian Cultures of the Midwest*. Urbana: University of Illinois Press, 1991.

Fonda, John H. "Early Reminiscences of Wisconsin." *Collections of the State Historical Society of Wisconsin for the Years 1867, 1868, and 1869*. Vol. 5, 205–84. Madison: Atwood and Rublee, State Printer, 1868.

Ford, Thomas. *A History of Illinois from its Commencement as a State in 1818 to 1847*. Chicago: S. C. Griggs, 1854.

Forest Preserve District of Cook County. *Official Record of the Proceedings of the Board of Forest Preserve Commissioners for the Forest Preserve District of Cook County, in the State of Illinois*. Chicago: Calumet Publishing, 1929.

———. *Official Record of the Proceedings of the Board of Forest Preserve Commissioners for the Forest Preserve District of Cook County, in the State of Illinois*. Chicago: Calumet Publishing, 1931.

———. *Official Record of the Proceedings of the Board of Forest Preserve Commissioners for the Forest Preserve District of Cook County, in the State of Illinois*. Chicago: Calumet Publishing, 1950.

Forrey, Roy, ed. *Site of the Du Sable Kinzie House*. Chicago: Commission on Chicago Historical and Architectural Landmarks, 1977. Chicago History Museum, MSS Alpha DuSable.

Goldthwait, James Walter. *Physical Features of the Des Plaines Valley*. Illinois State Geological Survey Bulletin 11. Urbana: University of Illinois, 1909.

Greenberg, Joel. *A Natural History of the Chicago Area*. Chicago: University of Chicago Press, 2002.

Grossman, James, Ann Durkin Keating, and Janice L. Reiff, eds. *Encyclopedia of Chicago*. Chicago: University of Chicago Press, 2004.

Grover, Frank. *Antoine Ouilmette: A Resident of Chicago A.D. 1790–1826; The First Settler of Evanston and Wilmette (1826–1838) with a Brief History of his Family and the Ouilmette Reservation*. Evanston, IL: Evanston Historical Society, 1908.

———. *Our Indian Predecessors: The First Evanstonians*. Evanston, IL: Evanston Historical Society, 1901.

Hagen, Olaf T. *A Study of the Chicago Portage (Proposed National Historic Site)*. Omaha, NE: National Park Service, 1949.

Hall, Robert. "Relating the Big Fish and the Big Stone: Reconsidering the Archaeological Identity and Habitat of the Winnebago in 1634." In *Oneota*

Archaeology, Past, Present, and Future, edited by William Green, 19–32. Iowa City: University of Iowa Press, 1995.

———. "Rethinking Jean Nicolet's Route to the Ho-Chunks in 1634." In *Theory, Method, and Practice in Modern Archaeology*, edited by Robert Jeske and Douglas Charles, 238–51. Westport, CT: Praeger, 2003.

Hamilton, John. "The Epidemics of Chicago." *Bulletin of the Society of Medical History of Chicago* 1, no. 1 (October 1911): 73–86.

Helm, Linai T. *The Fort Dearborn Massacre: Written in 1814 by Lieutenant Linai T. Helm One of the Survivors, with Letters and Narratives of Contemporary Interest*. Edited by Nellie Kinzie Gordon. Chicago: Rand McNally, 1912.

Heward, Hugh. Hugh Heward Journal. Copy. Chicago History Museum, MSS Alpha Heward. 1790.

Hill, Libby. *The Chicago River: A Natural and Unnatural History*. Chicago: Lake Claremont Press, 2000.

Hopkins, Timothy. *The Kelloggs in the Old World and the New*. Vol. 1. San Francisco: Sunset Press, 1903.

Howe, Walter A. *Documentary History of the Illinois and Michigan Canal: Legislation, Litigation and Titles*. Springfield: State of Illinois, Department of Public Works and Buildings, Division of Waterways, 1956.

Hubbard, Gurdon S. *The Autobiography of Gurdon Saltonstall Hubbard*. Chicago: Lakeside Press, 1911.

Hulbert, Archer Butler. *Portage Paths: The Keys to the Continent*. Cleveland: Arthur H. Clark, 1903.

Hurlbut, Henry. *Chicago Antiquities: Comprising Original Items and Relations, Letters, Extracts, and Notes, Pertaining to Early Chicago; Embellished with Views, Portraits, Autographs, Etc.* Chicago: Fergus Printing Co., 1881.

Illinois and Michigan Canal National Heritage Corridor Civic Center Authority. *Application for State Financial Support for the Chicago Portage Historical Site Interpretive Center*. Willow Springs, IL: Illinois and Michigan Canal National Heritage Corridor Civic Center Authority, 1990.

Innis, Harold. *The Fur Trade in Canada: An Introduction to Canadian Economic History*. New Haven, CT: Yale University Press, 1930.

James, James Alton. "The Significance of the Attack on St. Louis, 1780." In *Proceedings of the Mississippi Valley Historical Association for the Year 1908–09*, 2:199–217. Cedar Rapids, IA: Torch Press, 1910.

Jefferson, Thomas. *Notes on the State of Virginia*. Boston: Wells and Lilly, 1829.

Johnson, Geoffrey. "The True Story of the Deadly Encounter at Fort Dearborn." *Chicago Magazine*, January 4, 2010. https://www.chicagomag.com/Chicago-Magazine/December-2009/The-True-Story-of-the-Deadly-Encounter-at-Fort-Dearborn/.

Journal of the House of Representatives of the Forty-Fifth General Assembly of the State of Illinois. Springfield: Illinois State Journal Co., State Printers, 1908.

Jung, Patrick J. *The Misunderstood Mission of Jean Nicolet: Uncovering the Story of the 1634 Journey*. Madison: Wisconsin Historical Society Press, 2018.

Keating, Ann Durkin. *Rising Up from Indian Country: The Battle of Fort Dearborn and the Birth of Chicago*. Chicago: University of Chicago Press, 2012.

Keating, William. *Narrative of an Expedition to the Source of St. Peter's River, Lake Winnipeek, Lake of the Woods, etc., etc., Performed in the Year 1823, by order of the Hon. John C. Calhoun, Secretary of War, under the command of Stephen R. Long, Major U.S.T.E.* 2 vols. in 1. Philadelphia: H. C. Carey and I. Lea, 1824.

Kelley, Edward S. "William Burnett: A Representative Eighteenth Century American Trader, Pioneer, and Home Builder." *Collections and Researches Made by the Michigan Pioneer and Historical Society* 30 (1906): 85–95.

Kellogg, Louise Phelps. *Early Narratives of the Northwest, 1634–1699*. New York: Charles Scribner's Sons, 1917.

———. *The French Regime in Wisconsin and the Northwest*. Madison: State Historical Society of Wisconsin, 1925.

———, ed. *Journal of a Voyage to North America*. 2 vols. Chicago: Caxton Club, 1928.

Kelly, John E. "Cahokia and Its Role as a Gateway Center in Interregional Trade." In Emerson and Lewis, *Cahokia and the Hinterlands*, 61–80.

Kinzie, Juliette. *Narrative of the Massacre at Chicago, August 15, 1812, and of Some Proceeding Events*. Chicago: Fergus Printing Co., 1914.

———. *Wau-Bun: The Early Day in the Northwest*. Philadelphia: J. B. Lippincott, 1873.

Kirkland, Joseph. *The Story of Chicago*. Chicago: Dibble Publishing, 1892.

Knight, Robert, and Lucius H. Zeuch. *The Location of the Chicago Portage Route of the Seventeenth Century*. Chicago: Chicago Historical Society, 1928.

Knopf, Richard, ed. *Document Transcriptions of the War of 1812*. Vol. 6, *Letters to the Secretary of War 1812 Relating to the War of 1812 in the Northwest*. Columbus: Ohio Historical Society, 1959.

———. *Document Transcriptions of the War of 1812*. Vol. 8, *Letters from the Secretary of War 1812 and 1813 Relating to the War of 1812 in the Northwest*. Columbus: Ohio Historical Society, 1961.

Koldehoff, Brad. *Paleoindian and Archaic Settlement and Lithic Procurement in the Illinois Uplands*. Illinois State Archaeological Survey Technical Report 148. Urbana: University of Illinois, 2013.

Laws of the State of Illinois enacted by the Forty-Fifth General Assembly at the Adjourned Session. Springfield, IL: Phillips Bros., State Printers, 1908.

Long, L. H. "Topography," *National Register* 13, no. 3 (March 29, 1817): 193–98.

Lurie, Nancy O., and Patrick J. Jung. *The Nicolet Corrigenda: New France Revisited*. Arlington Heights, IL: Waveland Press, 2009.

Margry, Pierre. *Découvertes et établissements des français dans l'ouest et dans le sud de l'Amérique septentrionale (1614–1754): Mémoires et documents originaux*. 3 vols. Paris: Imprimerie D. Jouaust, 1877–78.

Markman, Charles. *Chicago before History: The Prehistoric Archaeology of a Modern Metropolitan Area*. Springfield: Illinois Historic Preservation Agency, 1991.

Mason, Edward G. *Chapters from Illinois History*. Chicago: Herbert S. Stone, 1901.

Matson, Nehemiah. *French and Indians of Illinois River*. Princeton, IL: Republican Job Printing Establishment, 1874.

McCafferty, Michael. "A Fresh Look at the Place Name Chicago," *Journal of the Illinois State Historical Society (1998–)* 96, no. 2 (Summer 2003): 116–29.

Meehan, Thomas A. "Jean Baptiste Point du Sable, the First Chicagoan." *Journal of the Illinois State Historical Society* 56, no. 3 (Autumn 1963): 439–53.

Meese, William A. "Nathaniel Pope." *Journal of the Illinois State Historical Society* 3, no. 4 (January 1911): 7–21.

Monet, Jacques. "Marquette, Jacques." In *Dictionary of Canadian Biography*. Vol. 1, *1000–1700*. Toronto: University of Toronto/Université Laval, 2003. http://www.biographi.ca/en/bio/marquette_jacques_1E.html.

Moses, John. *Illinois, Historical and Statistical, Comprising the Essential Facts of its Planting and Growth as a Province, County, Territory, and State*. Chicago: Fergus Printing Co., 1889.

National Registry of Historic Places Inventory—Nomination Form: Chicago Portage National Historic Site. United States Department of the Interior, received February 22, 1978, approved November 11, 1978. Asset ID 35a222f6-7913-4c4b-9627-d34dd0864e10, NPGallery Digital Asset Management System, National Park Service. https://npgallery.nps.gov/AssetDetail/NRIS/66000108.

National Park Service. "National Historic Areas." Last updated March 15, 2019. https://www.nps.gov/subjects/heritageareas/index.htm.

National Park Service, U.S. Department of the Interior. *Proclamations and Orders Relating to the National Park Service*. Vol 2, *January 1, 1945 to January 20, 2001*. Washington, DC: National Park Service, 2004. https://www.nps.gov/subjects/legal/proclamations-and-orders-volume-2.htm.

Neill, Edward. "Discovery along the Great Lakes." In Winsor, *Narrative and Critical History of America*, 4:163–96.

O'Callaghan, E. B., ed. *Documents Relative to the Colonial History of the State of New-York: Procured in Holland, England, and France by John Romeyn Brodhead, Esq*. Vol. 5. Albany: Weed, Parsons, 1855.

Parkman, Francis. *La Salle and the Discovery of the Great West*. Boston: Little, Brown, 1902.

Pauketat, Timothy. *Ancient Cahokia and the Mississippians*. Cambridge: Cambridge University Press, 2004.

———. *A Tour Guide to the Prehistory and Native Cultures of Southwestern Illinois and the Greater St. Louis Area*. Springfield: Illinois Historic Preservation Agency, 1993.

Peine, John D., and Debora A. Neurohr. *Illinois and Michigan Canal Corridor: A Concept Plan*. Ann Arbor, MI: National Park Service, 1981.

Peterson, Jacqueline. "'Wild' Chicago: The Formation and Destruction of a Multiracial Community on the Midwestern Frontier, 1816–1837." In *The Ethnic Frontier: Essays in the History of Group Survival in Chicago and the Midwest*, edited by Melvin G. Holli and Peter Jones, 25–27. Grand Rapids, MI: William B. Eerdmans, 1977.

Peyster, Arent Schuyler de. *Miscellanies by an Officer*. Dumfries, UK: Dumfries and Galloway Courier Office, 1813.

Pierce, Bessie Louise. *A History of Chicago: The Beginning of a City, 1673–1848*. Chicago: University of Chicago Press, 1937.

Prairie Research Institute. *Natural and Cultural Resources Master Plan*. Champaign: University of Illinois, 2014.

Putnam, James W. *The Illinois and Michigan Canal: A Study in Economic History*. Chicago: University of Chicago Press, 1918.

Pyle, G. F. "The Diffusion of Cholera in the United States in the Nineteenth Century." *Geographical Analysis* 1 (January 1969): 59–75.

Quaife, Milo Milton. *Chegagou: From Indian Wigwam to Modern City, 1673–1835*. Chicago: University of Chicago Press, 1933.

———. *Chicago and the Old Northwest, 1673–1835*. Chicago: University of Chicago Press, 1913.

———. "The Fort Dearborn Massacre." *Mississippi Valley Historical Review* 1, no. 4 (1915): 561–78.

———. "Property of Jean Baptiste Point Sable." *Mississippi Valley Historical Review* 15, no. 1 (June 1928): 89–92.

———. "Was There a French Fort in Chicago?" *Publications of the Illinois State Historical Library, Illinois State Historical Society*, no. 17 (1912): 115–21.

———, ed. *The Western Country in the Seventeenth Century: The Memoirs of Lamothe Cadillac and Pierre Liette*. Chicago: Lakeside Press, 1947.

Report concerning Canadian Archives for the Year 1905. Vol. 1. Ottawa: S. E. Dawson, Printer to the King's Most Excellent Majesty, 1906.

Reynolds, John. *The Pioneer History of Illinois: Containing the Discovery, in 1673, and the History of the Country to the Year 1818, when the State Government was Organized*. Chicago: Fergus Printing Co., 1887.

Sanitary District of Chicago. *Proceedings of the Board of Trustees of the Sanitary District of Chicago*. Chicago: Fred. Klein, 1929.

Sarich, Steven. "Deconstructing the Hopewell Interaction Sphere." *Nebraska Anthropologist* 25 (2010): 42–50. http://digitalcommons.unl.edu/nebanthro/59.

Schneider, Allan, and Gordon Fraser, eds. *Late Quaternary History of the Lake Michigan Basin*. Boulder, CO: Geological Society of America, 1990.

Schneider, Allan, and Ardith Hansel. "Evidence for Post-Two Creeks Age of the Type Calumet Shoreline of Glacial Lake Chicago." In Schneider and Fraser, *Late Quaternary History of the Lake Michigan Basin*, 1–8.

Schoolcraft, Henry R. *Archives of Aboriginal Knowledge. Containing all the Original Papers laid before Congress, respecting the History, Antiquities, Language, 181 Ethnology, Pictography, Rites, Superstitions, and Mythology of the Indian Tribes of the United States*. Vol. 3. Philadelphia: J. B. Lippincott, 1860.

———. *Ethnological Researches, Respecting the Red Man of America: Information Respecting the History, Conditions, and Prospects of the Indian Tribes of the United States*, part. 4. Philadelphia: Lippincott, Grambo, 1854.

———. *Narrative Journal of Travels through the Northwestern Regions of the United States Extending from Detroit through the Great Chain of American Lakes to the Sources of the Mississippi River*. Albany, NY: E. & E. Hosford, 1821.

Scott, David W. "Setting the Northern Border of Illinois." *Journal of the Illinois State Historical Society* 111, no. 3 (Fall 2018): 9–33.

Sells, Benjamin. *The Tunnel under the Lake: The Engineering Marvel That Saved Chicago*. Evanston, IL: Northwestern University Press, 2017.

Shea, John Gilmary. *Discovery and Exploration of the Mississippi Valley: with the original narratives of Marquette, Allouez, Membré, Hennepin, and Anastase Douay*. Clinton Hall, NY: Redfield, 1852.

Sleeper-Smith, Susan. *Indian Women and French Men: Rethinking Cultural Encounter in the Western Great Lakes*. Amherst: University of Massachusetts Press, 2001.

Smith, William Henry, annotator. *The Life and Public Services of Arthur St. Clair. Soldier of the Revolutionary War; President of the Continental Congress; and Governor of the Northwestern Territory, with his Correspondence and other Papers*. Vol. 2. Cincinnati: Robert Clarke, 1882.

Smith, W. L. G. *The Life and Times of Lewis Cass*. New York: Derby & Jackson, 1856.

Statement of the Case, Brief of Points and Authorities, Argument for the Appellant, In the Supreme Court of Illinois, February Term, A. D. 1909, People of the State of Illinois, ex rel. Charles S. Deneen, Governor, and William H. Stead, Attorney General vs. Economy Light & Power Company. Chicago: Gunthorp-Warren Printing Co., 1909.

Stead, William H. *Biennial Report of the Attorney General of the State of Illinois*. Springfield: Illinois State Journal Co., State Printers, December 1908.

Steck, Francis Borgia. *The Jolliet-Marquette Expedition, 1673*. Glendale, CA: Arthur H. Clarke, 1928.

———. "What Became of Jolliet's Journal." *Americas* 5, no. 2 (1948): 172–99.

Steward, John F. "Chicago—Origin of the Name of the City and the Old Portages." In *Transactions of the Illinois State Historical Society for the Year 1904*, 460–66. Springfield, IL: Philips Bros., State Printers, 1904. https://archive.org/details/transactionsofil1904illi/page/460/mode/2up.

Storrow, Samuel A. "The North-West in 1817." In *Report and Collections of the State Historical Society of Wisconsin, for the years 1869, 1870, 1871 and 1872*, 6:154–87. Madison, WI: Atwood and Culver, State Printers, 1872.

Strong, William. *The Indian Tribes of the Chicago Region with Special Reference to the Illinois and the Potowatomi*. Chicago: Field Museum of Natural History, 1938.

Sullivan, Jerry. *Chicago Wilderness: An Atlas of Biodiversity*. Chicago: Chicago Region Biodiversity Council, 1999.

Swenson, John F. "Jean Baptiste Point de Sable—The Founder of Modern Chicago." In Danckers and Meredith, *Compendium of the Early History of Chicago*, 388–94.

[Swenson, John F.] "La Compt, Madam." In Danckers and Meredith, *Compendium of the Early History of Chicago*, 227–28.

Temple, Wayne C. *Indian Villages of the Illinois Country: Historic Tribes*. Scientific Papers 2.2. Rev ed. 1966; reprint, Springfield: Illinois State Museum, 1987.

Thevenot, Melchisédech. *Recueil de voyages de Mr. Thevenot*. Paris: Étienne Michallet, 1681.

Thompson, Joseph J. "The Time and a Place for a Monument to Marquette." *Illinois Catholic Historical Review* 4, no. 2 (October 1921), 115–34.

Thwaites, Reuben, ed. *Collections of the State Historical Society of Wisconsin*. Vol. 19. Madison, WI: Democrat Printing Co., 1910.

———, ed. *The Jesuit Relations and Allied Documents*. Vol. 58, *Travels and Explorations of the Jesuit Missionaries in New France, 1610–1791: Ottawas, Lower Canada, Iroqouois, 1672–1674*. Cleveland: Burrows Brothers, 1899.

———, ed. *The Jesuit Relations and Allied Documents*. Vol. 59, *Travels and Explorations of the Jesuit Missionaries in New France, 1610–1791: Lower Canada, Illinois, Ottawas, 1673–1677*. Cleveland: Burrows Brothers, 1900.

———, ed. *The Jesuit Relations and Allied Documents*. Vol. 65, *Travels and Explorations of the Jesuit Missionaries in New France, 1610–1791: Lower Canada, Mississippi Valley, 1696–1702*. Cleveland: Burrows Brothers, 1900.

Transcript of Record, Supreme Court of the United States, October Term, 1913, No. 179, The People of the State of Illinois on the Relation of Charles S. Deneen, Governor, and William H. Stead, Attorney General, Plaintiffs in Error vs. The Economy Light and Power Company. 3 vols. Washington, DC: Judd & Detweiler, Printers, 1913.

Transcript of Record, Supreme Court of the United States, October Term 1920, No. 104, Economy Power & Light Company vs. The United States of America. N.p., 1920.

Vierling, Philip E. *A Self Guided Loop Hiking Trail to the Chicago Portage National Historic Site*. Chicago: Illinois Country Hiking Guide, 1973.

Washburne, E. B., ed. *The Edwards Papers*. Chicago Historical Society's Collection. Vol. 3. Chicago: Fergus Printing Co., 1884.

White, A. J, Samuel E. Munoz, Sissle Schroeder, and Lora R. Stevens. "After Cahokia: Indigenous Repopulation and Depopulation of the Horseshoe Lake Watershed, AD 1400–1900." *American Antiquity* 85, no. 2 (2020): 263–78. doi:10.1017/aaq.2019.103.

White, Richard. *The Middle Ground: Indians, Empires, and Republics in the Great Lakes Region, 1650–1815*. Cambridge: Cambridge University Press, 1991.

———. "The Middle Ground." In *Rethinking the Fur Trade: Cultures of Exchange in an Atlantic World*. Sleeper-Smith, Susan, ed. Lincoln: University of Nebraska Press, 2009.

Wm. E. Rose and Associates. "*The Waterway West*." Hinsdale, IL: Wm. E. Rose and Associates, 1975.

Willman, H. B. *Summary of the Geology of the Chicago Area*. Illinois Geological Survey Circular 460. Urbana: State of Illinois Department of Registration and Education, 1971.

Winsor, Justin, ed. *Narrative and Critical History of America*. Vol. 4, *French Explorations and Settlements in North America and Those of the Portuguese, Dutch, and Swedes, 1500–1700*. New York: Houghton, Mifflin, 1884.

INDEX

Numbers in italics refer to illustrations.

Second to None: Chicago Stories celebrates the authenticity of a city brimming with rich narratives and untold histories. Spotlighting original, unique, and rarely explored stories, Second to None unveils a new and significant layer to Chicago's big-shouldered literary landscape.

Harvey Young, series editor